Mark Twain's
Travel Literature

Mark Twain's Travel Literature
The Odyssey of a Mind

HAROLD H. HELLWIG

McFarland & Company, Inc., Publishers
Jefferson, North Carolina, and London

Frontispiece: "The Author's Memories" in *A Tramp Abroad*. Illustration by True Williams.

LIBRARY OF CONGRESS CATALOGUING-IN-PUBLICATION DATA

Hellwig, Harold H., 1950–
　　Mark Twain's travel literature: The odyssey of a mind / Harold H. Hellwig.
　　　　p.　　cm.
　　Includes bibliographical references and index.

　　ISBN 978-0-7864-3651-4
　　softcover : 50# alkaline paper ∞

　　1. Twain, Mark, 1835–1910—Criticism and interpretation. 2. Twain, Mark, 1835–1910—Travel.　3. Travelers' writings, American—History and criticism.　4. Travel in literature. 5. Time in literature.　6. Place (Philosophy) in literature. 7. Identity (Psychology) in literature.　I. Title.
　　PS1342.T73H46　　2008
　　818'.409—dc22　　　　　　　　　　　　　　　2008000644

British Library cataloguing data are available

©2008 Harold H. Hellwig. All rights reserved

No part of this book may be reproduced or transmitted in any form or by any means, electronic or mechanical, including photocopying or recording, or by any information storage and retrieval system, without permission in writing from the publisher.

On the cover: "Sunny South," Calvert Lithograph & Engraving Company, color lithograph, 1883 (Library of Congress). Front cover by TG Design

Manufactured in the United States of America.

McFarland & Company, Inc., Publishers
　Box 611, Jefferson, North Carolina 28640
　　www.mcfarlandpub.com

Mark Twain's Travel Literature

The Odyssey of a Mind

Harold H. Hellwig

McFarland & Company, Inc., Publishers
Jefferson, North Carolina, and London

Frontispiece: "The Author's Memories" in *A Tramp Abroad*.
Illustration by True Williams.

LIBRARY OF CONGRESS CATALOGUING-IN-PUBLICATION DATA

Hellwig, Harold H., 1950–
  Mark Twain's travel literature: The odyssey of a mind / Harold H. Hellwig.
    p.   cm.
  Includes bibliographical references and index.

  ISBN 978-0-7864-3651-4
  softcover : 50# alkaline paper ∞

  1. Twain, Mark, 1835–1910—Criticism and interpretation. 2. Twain, Mark, 1835–1910—Travel. 3. Travelers' writings, American—History and criticism. 4. Travel in literature. 5. Time in literature. 6. Place (Philosophy) in literature. 7. Identity (Psychology) in literature. I. Title.
  PS1342.T73H46   2008
  818'.409—dc22   2008000644

British Library cataloguing data are available

©2008 Harold H. Hellwig. All rights reserved

No part of this book may be reproduced or transmitted in any form or by any means, electronic or mechanical, including photocopying or recording, or by any information storage and retrieval system, without permission in writing from the publisher.

On the cover: "Sunny South," Calvert Lithograph & Engraving Company, color lithograph, 1883 (Library of Congress). Front cover by TG Design

Manufactured in the United States of America.

McFarland & Company, Inc., Publishers
  Box 611, Jefferson, North Carolina 28640
    www.mcfarlandpub.com

Acknowledgments

I first began thinking of this project in a class on Mark Twain I taught in the spring semester of 1995 at Idaho State University. I had assigned the usual "great works" of Twain, but included *Roughing It* and *Following the Equator* because these works seemed neglected by critics at the time. Carlen Heisler (now Donovan), Dan Welch, and Pat Billman, among others, were curious why I made them read these travel works, particularly *Following the Equator*. I had emphasized Twain's social criticism in *A Connecticut Yankee in King Arthur's Court*, and his questions about identity in *The Prince and the Pauper* and in *Adventures of Huckleberry Finn*, and students were finding patterns in the travel works and in the fiction that seemed parallel. One night, while discussing *The Prince and the Pauper* and trying to relate that work to themes of colonialism in *Following the Equator*, I realized that I had undervalued travel writings. In fact, I had myself neglected the virtues of *The Prince and the Pauper*. It was a night the students taught the teacher.

In other Twain courses (2003 and 2007) my students have challenged me to connect the travel works with the "great works" of Sam Clemens. *Life on the Mississippi*, in particular, has been useful in following the journey of Huck toward a higher purpose and moral compass. Teaching the one travel experience, full of cemetery thoughts and death (as some of my students have phrased it), makes the masterpiece of *Huckleberry Finn* seem more the hope of life, framing the novel with the piano practice that the journey in *Life on the Mississippi* must have been for Twain. Knowledge, the kind of book learning that the travel work demonstrates, becomes an instinctual effort for Huck, transcending the kinds of knowledge that the reader finds in the travel text. It is my hope for my students that they, too, will find the levels of knowledge found in Twain's works, and that they, too, discover the intuitive knowledge that Huck demonstrates. I am indebted to these students, some long gone to my history, others to distinguished travels and paths of their own, and others on their own journeys yet to begin.

Using a travel-to-collection grant from Idaho State's Graduate Studies and Research and the Department of English and Philosophy, I journeyed in the fall of 1995 to the University of California at Berkeley, the location of the Mark Twain Project, where I had access to manuscripts, letters, articles, books, and, most importantly, the editors of the Mark Twain Project for a few precious days. An acknowledged center for research on Twain's work, this place allowed me to review my assumptions, test them, and discuss with key individuals the possibilities of this study of travel literature. I am indebted to Victor Fischer, in particular, for allowing me hours of his time so that I could understand the nature of my project.

While on sabbatical from Idaho State University in 1997, and with the benefit of a travel grant provided by ISU, I traveled to Berkeley for a two-week stay, collecting as much material relating to travel as I could. The editors at the Mark Twain Project were again quite helpful. They may not remember me well, but I thank Robert Hirst, Victor Fischer, Michael Frank, Harriet Elinor Smith, Lin Salamo, Robert Pack Browning, and Kenneth Sanderson for their time. I also thank David Briggs, Anh Bui, and Louis Suarez-Potts for locating materials I needed.

Much later I presented some material on *Following the Equator* at an American Literature Association conference in the year 2000. I thank Joseph McCullough for his encouragement and advice. I also recall fondly a dinner at the ALA conference that Bruce Michelson encouraged me to attend; I met Kent Rasmussen, Alan Gribben, and Laura Skandera-Trombley, among others, and enjoyed the evening immensely. I also felt a bit intimidated by the company of scholars, and embarrassed (even then) that this project seemed endless in its completion.

I am indebted to John Kijinski, a colleague at ISU, for having read a very early version of this book, and for having continued to encourage me to finish it. I am also grateful to a former dean of the College of Arts and Sciences, Butch Hjelm, for having been so patient on my working on this. All of my colleagues at Idaho State University were models of good teaching, service, and scholarship. I received a sabbatical for the spring semester of 2004 from ISU so that I could finish the project that I had nibbled away at for a number of years.

I helped raise two sons, Benjamin and David, during this project, and I am grateful that they understood why Dad had to work on occasion in the basement study. I spent a lot of time with them, too, even as a soccer coach for awhile, though I found using a laptop convenient when I became just a soccer parent. I have been to many soccer games, including all tournament games out of town. Coach Dave Nichalson and Coach Jeff Van Sickle have been a part of that experience, and I owe them for the enjoyment of the game. My deepest gratitude is for my wife, Ann Hackert, who supported my work, and who patiently waited for it to be done.

Table of Contents

Acknowledgments	v
Preface	1
1. Travel as a Quest for Knowledge	7
2. Travel as a Method of Piloting the River of Life	29
3. *Innocents Abroad*: A Parody of Tourist Books	45
4. *Roughing It*: Travel as a Way to Find an Identity	61
5. *A Tramp Abroad*: Travel Experiment and Narrative Lapse	80
6. *Life on the Mississippi*: Travel as a Form of Knowledge	98
7. *Following the Equator*: Travel as Nostalgia, Loss and Recovery	116
8. Mark Twain's Travel: Looking for an Identity in Fiction	144
9. Mark Twain's Travel: Looking for Stable Time in His Fiction	163
Appendix: Travel Works Probably Read and Owned by Samuel L. Clemens (Mark Twain)	181
Notes	201
Bibliography	207
Index	213

Preface

> October 12, the Discovery. It was wonderful to find America,
> but it would have been more wonderful to miss it.
> — Pudd'nhead Wilson's Calendar.

Mark Twain's travel literature, *Roughing It, A Tramp Abroad, The Innocents Abroad, Life on the Mississippi, Following the Equator*, and his other works of journalism, demonstrate the clash of cultures and civilizations and the importance of nature, time, identity, place and home. These are themes found in his canonized literature as well. Travel is a theme throughout Twain's existence as a writer, a lecturer, and humorist. *A Connecticut Yankee in King Arthur's Court, The Adventures of Huckleberry Finn, The Adventures of Tom Sawyer, The Prince and the Pauper, Pudd'nhead Wilson, The Mysterious Stranger*: all of Twain's more familiar novels contain travelers who observe another time, another place, often from the context of ironic detachment, exotic danger, and incomplete quest for one's identity. Nearly all of Twain's works (including novels) contain the theme of travel as part of the backdrop or sometimes the central core. The Yankee travels in time and in space and attempts to recreate his civilization in ancient England; Huck travels along the river to come to terms with his evolving conscience; the Italian twins travel to Dawson's Landing to offer some comic relief to the tragedy of identities being switched.

Opposite: "The Miner's Dream" in *Roughing It* (frontispiece). Illustration by Roswell Morse Shurtleff.

Twain's travel works allow an examination of his sense of nostalgia from his perspective of an engaged traveler in an evolving American landscape (a study now incomplete in the criticism of Twain's work), a nostalgia about a disappearing frontier perspective, a growing concern about the assimilation of native cultures by Christian or Western ones, a continual questioning of identity, both personal and national, and a search for stable moral beliefs which would guide not only himself but the American reader. Twain's nostalgia takes place in a realm of timelessness, which Twain often attempts to create yet fails to maintain. It becomes an attempt to defeat time. As a traveler in historical time, Twain tries to locate himself within an imaginative recovery of the past, while realizing that the present intrudes, and that the future brings inevitable death. Travel for Twain represents challenge, loss, and remembrance. These works about his travels become a map of his mind; these works reflect themes found in his work as a whole. It does seem odd at first that these works should contain serious concerns about life and ultimate realities of the world; part of the genius of Twain is the sense of contradiction and effacement of his own role in the expression of a philosophy of thinking, something, given the desultory nature of Twain's own reading of philosophers, which makes sense until one realizes how even this proves to be an attempt to fathom the mysteries of human existence. One of the mythic structures the traveler should possess, according to Twain, is the ability to doubt one's own thinking, lest one slip into a blind acceptance of reality.

I am using structuralist principles to follow the phenomenology of Twain's travels. That is, what are the codes (developed by Twain into personal archetypes) that appear consistently in this body of work? What appears to control the relationship of Twain to his environment as he travels? What racial stereotyping occurs? Which personal asides develop into dominant criticism of his era? What is the pattern to his travels? What are the codes that he uses to express notions of civilization, nature, and an American identity? What does he attempt to do in terms of time and space?

Phenomenology, loosely defined, is the study of experiences from the first-person point of view, particularly the structures of consciousness; I am using the term "phenomenology" to discuss the structures or concepts that Twain used in order to frame his travel experiences. Tourism, for example, consists of the traveler, the sites visited, the mode of transportation, methods of payment for services, lodging, and food; how these interplay affects the tourist's experiences and the mental constructs used to express these experiences. A hobo riding the rails from California to Pennsylvania in order to visit Civil War battlefields has a different perception of time, risk, and place from someone who makes the trip aboard any of the current airlines. The hobo may feel personally the class differences in America; the terror of the train itself; the insecurity of sleep, food, and self-worth; and the elapse of time itself, and the battlefields may then acquire a visceral meaning that the airline traveler will not understand. The airline traveler, one might assume, is distanced from the earthy experience of the unwashed hobo.

Twain perceptively illustrates the differences between train travel and stagecoach travel, focusing in part on the changed perception of time, the amount of time it takes to go across the continent, when he refers to a *New York Times* sketch he excerpts at the end of Chapter 4 of *Roughing It*. This excerpt demonstrates how wealth can buy the best food on a train — "a repast at which Delmonico himself could have had no occasion to blush"— and buy the ease of transportation with a comfort unequalled by the lowly stagecoach. However, *Roughing It* glorifies the stagecoach and the trip that Twain took, along with the inconveniences that he experienced. The more modern train experience was truly still alien to Twain, still emphasizing the difference in social classes between himself and the cultured train travelers who can sip champagne and sing the "grand old hymns" as "our train, with its great, glaring Polyphemus eye, lighting up long vistas of prairie, rushed into the night and the Wild." (Polyphemus is the Greek mythical Cyclops who is not particularly hospitable to travelers, notably Odysseus and his men. Even though Twain is quoting from this *New York Times* sketch, the mythical connection is striking, as the modern train is less hospitable to Twain than is the stagecoach.)

This book competes directly with Jeffrey Alan Melton's *Mark Twain, Travel Books, and Tourism: The Tide of a Great Popular Movement* (Tuscaloosa: The University of Alabama Press, 2002). While Melton describes quite appropriately the conventions of tourism as they apply to Twain's works, Melton does not discuss the phenomenological structures that I have explored, nor does Melton apply his observations to Twain's fiction. I also append a bibliography of Twain's library, a set of works relating to travel, something that Melton alludes to but does not describe at length. Melton's observations about travel conventions are straightforward but tend to ignore implications that some travel theorists have discussed.

Twain on the Hannibal railway platform May 1902 during his last visit to Hannibal (courtesy of the Mark Twain Project, Bancroft Library, University of California, Berkeley).

This book also competes indirectly with Richard Bridgman's *Traveling in Mark Twain* (Berkeley: University of California Press, 1987). Bridgman's work found little unity in Twain's works; his analysis tends to be as desultory as his assumption about Twain's travels. However, his close reading of particular passages does make sense. Melton transcends this text, which, until 2002, had been the standard critical review of Twain's travel writings.

Robert M. Rodney's *Mark Twain Overseas: A Biographical Account of His Voyages, Travels, and Reception in Foreign Lands, 1866–1910* (Washington,

D.C.: Three Continents Press, 1993) is a solid historical review of Twain's travels, but is just that, and not much more. It's a good biographical sketch. There is some discussion of the travel works as Twain wrote them, but the major themes of travel are not analyzed.

My major claim is that Twain's work is unified, that the same phenomenological structures run through his fiction as well as his travel writings. While I have used some of the historical information that Rodney presents, I do not attempt to outline the geographical map of Twain's travels. Bridgman found the travel writings unrelated to Twain's fiction or to his philosophy of life. I believe I contradict that approach. Melton is rather appealing, because he does find some focus to Twain's travel works, but he doesn't show how the evolution of Twain's thinking toward travel fits within the context of Twain's mental landscape with all of the travel works and with much of his other writing as well. My approach allows for an interplay among the travel works, Twain's philosophy of life (and travel), and his fiction. This study reflects on the importance of travel as a major theme throughout all of Twain's works, including the major novels.

Most travel works revolve around a hero's quest for truth, a truth that can be presented to the community upon the hero's return. Twain knew the outlines of travel writing; he took the genre into parody and transcended the common themes of travelogues. He wished to be a writer in order to make money, of course, because he knew at the beginning of his career he could not claim that he was a writer of literature, but his travel writing became an integral part of his canon, incorporating phenomenological threads into both his fiction at large and his travel works. His truths about the human experience—for he is often treated as a great American philosopher, even if his philosophy of life is suspect from a number of perspectives—stem from his method of traveling. His heroes do travel, and generally they do return to a community and share their experiences; Huck floats along the great Mississippi and evolves as an American conscience about slavery; Hank attempts to create a technological and capitalist world without offering a morality equal to it; Satan travels to the new planet, Earth, and sends travel observations about humans without sense back to fellow angels. In the end Twain begins to believe that he must travel in dreams in order to understand himself and the world, as shown by his last travel book, *Following the Equator*, a text that almost finds a harmony with the community that he has left so long ago in his first adventures outside of Hannibal, Missouri.

1

Travel as a Quest for Knowledge

> *Training is everything. The peach was once a bitter almond; cauliflower is nothing but cabbage with a college education.*
> — Pudd'nhead Wilson's Calendar.

    Travel literature often seems relegated to a subgenre of nonfiction writing, sometimes reduced to a variety of journalism ill suited for the themes and structures of literature. One thinks of Boswell and Johnson, for example, who may have written works of literature while traveling, but their efforts are often viewed as forms of biography. Few travel writers achieve prestige by having their works added to a literary canon. One may be amused or informed by a Rick Steves travelogue, but it would be difficult to view it as a work of literature.[1] (However, even Steves seems to recognize the landscape of attitudes that travel encompasses as a set of structures that can guide the novice traveler, structures more complex than one might first realize.) Rarely does a great books course include a work about travel, although *Moby Dick* or *Gulliver's Travels* might suffice in that course. Mark Twain is better known in such a great books course with *Adventures of Huckleberry Finn*. (Of course, it should be there.) However, Mark Twain's travels allowed him the opportunity to explore the themes and structures of literature and to incorporate these into his fiction. Indeed, Twain's fiction, which reflects his own thinking on a great many topics, can be mirrored by his nonfictional travels. While his works of fiction do suggest the phenomenology of Twain's mind, the map of his mind can also be found in these works about travel. The question of genre, posed this way, might then be misleading, for the relative importance (whether literature or not) does not matter. Rather, it is useful to see what Twain made of this genre, to see that travel writing allowed Twain to examine personal themes, and to see that the structure and the phenomenology of travel writing (with an inherent structure of genre characteristics) provides Twain a fertile playground for his ideas. Twain developed a coherent structure of ideas connected to travel, some of which appear in his fiction, and while it can be said that his travel works are a form of fiction, particularly when these travel works violate traditional genre characteristics of the travelogue, becoming pseudo novels or experimental works of nonfiction, his travel works show that his entire canon reveals elements of that structure as well.

Indeed, Percy G. Adams, in *Travel Literature and the Evolution of the Novel*, equates travel works with literature: "Prose fiction and the travel account have evolved together, are heavily indebted to each other, and are often similar in both content and technique" (279). Adams admits that the novel has evolved differently in terms of such things as plot and character, and that the travel work has often a different shape from the novel form. However, in his exhaustive survey of travel writings before 1800, Adams defines well the connections that travel writers have had to the evolving genre of the novel. Similarly, Paul Fussell in *Abroad: British Literary Traveling Between the Wars* argues that the travel writings produced during these years (1918–1939) also merit the attention that literature enjoys: "Yet between the wars writing travel books was not at all considered incompatible with a serious literary career" (213). Adams discusses thoroughly the themes of travel literature in relation to those found in traditional genres: the journey itself as a quest motif, the narrator as a kind of hero, the narrative forms used (mostly autobiographical, but sometimes "pseudoautobiographical" as Adams terms it), the forms of plot and character developed for these "quest" forms of writing, the language and style that demonstrate a wide range of forms and strategies, and, among other things, the character types and motifs appearing in travel works (such as the coach and the inn as ways of structuring symbolic forms of transportation). The hero journeys to a land, encounters new forms of culture, sees exotic landscapes, learns about these new forms and scenery, and returns an invigorated narrator who shares the growth of knowledge with readers, reaffirming the vitality and stability of the culture the hero represents.

Fussell examines an assortment of themes in British literary traveling between the wars: the fascination with traveling, the sensation of being away from one's home, the traveling companion as a useful ideological mirror, the commercial notes of traveling (beggars, odd things to sell and buy), and other mythic structures, such as "the archetypal monomyth of heroic adventure ... first, the setting out, the disjunction from the familiar; second, the trials of initiation and adventure; and third, the return and the hero's reintegration into society" (208). Twain's travel works contain these elements; in *Roughing It*, as one brief example, Twain creates a fictive narrator who sets out for new adventures, encounters a number of interesting characters in a stagecoach ride across America, seems fascinated with the notion of traveling and the idea of being away from home, finds an occasional partner who reflects his concerns (prospecting in Nevada, fellow journalists, his brother Orion), and finds his way back into civilized society after his voyage among the heathens of the West and Hawaii as a journalist and lecturer reporting his journey. Twain much later isolates a pragmatic hero in his time travel novel, *A Connecticut Yankee in King Arthur's Court*, Hank Morgan, who must rebuild his notion of civilization in the savage land of sixth-century England, telling his tale first as someone who has returned to his nineteenth century by way of a long Rip Van Winkle sleep and later letting a reader continue the tale in the context of an ancient manuscript given to a journalist. Both travelers attempt to find a place in society and a secure identity, Hank Morgan creating one for himself and losing it, Twain discovering that he has an identity as a journalist and lecturer.

While Dean MacCannell's *The Tourist: A New Theory of the Leisure Class* seems to apply most immediately to modern travel, this sociological review of travel examines travel experiences before the twentieth century: the semiotics of the travel site (or "tourist districts"), the "staged authenticity" of cultural locations, the difference between truth and fiction in tourist settings, and the notion of the "genuine" experience that a traveler seeks. At one point, on reviewing how a "marker" (representation of the site in words or pictures) is different from "sight involvement" (the lack of "relevant information," or the inability to understand why a site is important or interesting), MacCannell refers to Twain's description of the painting *The Last Supper* as a decrepit ruin in *Innocents Abroad* (190–93); Twain "means to be ironic, but ironic humor does not succeed unless it exposes some truth. The truth is that marker involvement can prevent a tourist's realizing that the sight he sees may not be worth his seeing it. Mark Twain is trying to combat a tendency on the part of some sightseers to transfer the 'beauty' of the calendar version of *The Last Supper* to the original, but his is a losing battle" (112). MacCannell may not quite appreciate Twain's book, however, as a success in having recognized this "tendency" and having neatly analyzed it in terms of the tourist lacking an imagination:

> It was what I thought when I stood before the Last Supper and heard men apostrophizing wonders, and beauties and perfections which had faded out of the picture and gone, a hundred years before they were born. We can imagine the beauty that was once in an aged face; we can imagine the forest if we see the stumps; but we can not absolutely *see* these things when they are not there. I am willing to believe that the eye of the practiced artist can rest upon the Last Supper and renew a luster where only a hint of it is left, supply a tint that has faded away, restore an expression that is gone; patch, and color, and add, to the dull canvas until at last its figures shall stand before him aglow with the life, the feeling, the freshness, yea, with all the noble beauty that was theirs when first they came from the hand of the master. But *I* can not work this miracle. Can those other uninspired visitors do it, or do they only happily imagine they do? [*Innocents Abroad*, 192–93].

Twain works the miracle simply by noting that he can visualize the original beauty, even if he claims that he has not the power. Simply by observing that it is possible, he creates the possibility that one can see the authentic and recognize the "noble beauty" at its origin, even if the painting has faded over time. Tourists, according to MacCannell, do seek the original, the authentic, even when they realize or know that sometimes they see the "site" as a reproduction of some kind, virtually a copy of the "site" rather than the original. One of the running jokes of *Innocents Abroad* is the abundance of nails used during the Crucifixion; Twain finds these authentic nails everywhere, realizing, of course, that many, if not all, are fake. No matter how often Twain rails against the Great Masters, and he does this throughout *Innocents Abroad*, he still presents a pretense of being an authority about art, of being able to tell the difference between bad and good art. Twain's eye is the genuine article, and the perceptive reader knows it. Hardly a "losing battle."

Twain's response to art in *Innocents Abroad* is typical of his early American distaste for art that does not present reality as it is. In this Twain is a proponent of American Realism, even if the movement still needs a voice, such as William Dean Howells. Twain is perfectly at home with the Grand Masters of Europe, and he is rightly, in terms of American literature,

1. Travel as a Quest for Knowledge

"Full-Dressed Tourist" in *Innocents Abroad*. Illustration by True Williams.

in full throes of revolt against what Europe represents. His early journalism and fiction both use vernacular language and reflect the themes of regional literature, attempting to describe the local and the unique. His knowledge of Old Southwest humorists is fairly good, those humorists coming from and reporting on the lives and local scenery of one area, whether it be Georgia or Mississippi. In art, also, Twain prefers the paintings that are American as long as they are real. He is somewhat miffed by his fellow countryman Albert Bierstadt's efforts at painting the Yosemite Valley in a letter dated June 2, 1867, from New York City, while waiting for *Quaker City* tour to begin (*Travels with Mr. Brown*, 251). The sky is quite unrealistic and romanticized. When he later looks at art in *A Tramp Abroad*, his attitudes have modified only slightly, because he senses European art as noble; he prefers what he calls "Bassano's immortal Hair Trunk" (382), actually Bassano's *Pope Alexander III and the Doge Ziani*, because he sees one element of this large painting as quite realistic, claiming that he once saw a customs inspector bring out a piece of chalk in order to mark the Hair Trunk for inspection (385). The Hudson River school of landscape painting in America would not bear up to the same kind of inspection, it appears. These painters, beginning

"Yours Truly, Mark Twain" *in A Tramp Abroad.* Engraving by J.A.J. Wilcox.

with Thomas Cole and Asher B. Durand, were dominant in nineteenth-century American art. Influenced by European Romanticism, for example, Caspar David Friedrich in Germany and John Constable in England, these American painters sought to create a purely American art, separated from Europe. Many paintings from this movement isolated man within a large and majestic natural landscape, emphasizing the greatness of nature and the smallness of mankind, while fostering a sense of optimism for the resources that nature could provide for mankind. Twain's optimism is the reverse of the Hudson River artists, for he wanted the individual to be greater than the sum of the parts of nature.

Other sociologists, such as Jennifer Craik, Carol Crawshaw, John Urry, George Ritzer, and Allan Liska, among others, discuss modern perspectives on travel, perspectives useful to this study of Twain's journeys. This sociological approach analyzes the traveler and the place visited in a variety of contexts, for example, in terms of the Grand Tour, sites, the "McDonaldsization" of post-modernist tourism, photography, and cultural self-improvement.[2] These writers, along with Adams, Fussell, and MacCannell, offer ways to approach Twain's travel works. They form a useful backdrop of sociological structures that help inform us about universal patterns and experiences of common travels. However, my general approach here is to find phenomenological structures that further explain Twain's themes in these travel works, because, while these useful sociological structures help define the nature of tourism, Twain transcends the structures that most travelers expect. He mocks traditional travel accounts; he attacks assumptions of the ordinary traveler; he creates new forms and new concepts to contain his thoughts.[3] As I will argue, Twain develops early on a way to read life in much the same way a cub pilot learns to read the river. He learns a method of dealing with events, locations, companions, landmarks, and vistas that allows him to manage a journey with a measure of comfort and informed competence. In terms of phenomenological structures, Wolfgang Iser's "implied reader" comes to mind here: "In the act of reading, having to think something that we have not yet experienced does not mean only being in a position to conceive or even understand it; it also means that such acts of conception are possible and successful to the degree that they lead to something being formulated in us. For someone else's thoughts can only take a form in our consciousness if, in the process, our unformulated faculty for deciphering those thoughts is brought into play — a faculty which, in the act of deciphering, also formulates itself."[4] Twain develops a set of structures by which to control the travel experience, so that this travel becomes familiar to the reader.

Mark Twain's travel literature, *Roughing It*, *A Tramp Abroad*, *The Innocents Abroad*, *Life on the Mississippi*, *Following the Equator*, and other works of journalism, demonstrates the clash of cultures and civilizations and the importance of nature, identity, place and home. These are themes found in his canonized literature as well. Travel is a theme throughout Twain's existence as a writer, a lecturer, and a humorist. *A Connecticut Yankee in King Arthur's Court*, *The Adventures of Huckleberry Finn*, *The Adventures of Tom Sawyer*, *The Prince and the Pauper*, *Pudd'nhead Wilson*, *The Mysterious Stranger*: all of Twain's more familiar novels contain travelers who observe another time, another place, often from the context of ironic detachment, exotic danger, and incomplete quest for one's identity. Nearly all of Twain's works (including novels) contain the theme of travel as part of the backdrop or sometimes the central core. The Yankee travels in time and in space and attempts to re-create his civilization in ancient England; Huck travels along the river to come to terms with his evolving conscience; the Italian twins travel to Dawson's Landing to offer some comic relief to the tragedy of identities being switched. Twain's travel works allow an examination of his sense of nostalgia from his perspective of an engaged traveler in an evolving American landscape, a study now incomplete in the criticism of Twain's work, a nostalgia about a disappearing frontier perspective, a growing concern about the assimilation of native cultures by Christian or Western ones, a continual questioning of identity, both personal and national, and a search for stable moral beliefs which would guide not only himself but the American reader. The nostalgia that Twain feels takes place in a realm of timelessness, which Twain often attempts to create yet fails to maintain, becoming an attempt to defeat time; as a traveler in historical time, Twain tries to locate himself within an imaginative recovery of the past, while realizing that the present intrudes and the future brings inevitable death. Travel for Twain represents challenge, loss, and remembrance. These works about his travels become a map of his mind; these works reflect themes found in his work as a whole. It does seem odd at first that these works should contain serious concerns about life and ultimate realities of the world; part of the genius of Twain is the sense of contradiction and effacement of his own role in the expression of a philosophy of thinking, something, given the desultory nature of Twain's own reading of philosophers, that makes sense until one realizes how even this proves to be an attempt to fathom the mysteries of human existence. One of the mythic structures the traveler should possess, according to Twain, is the ability to doubt one's own thinking, lest one slip into a blind acceptance of reality.

One should remember that Twain did not attempt to be a serious travel writer.[5] His earlier works on travel were designed to parody travel literature; his last major attempt, *Following the Equator*, reveals a brooding self in conflict with his identity and in conflict with the humor that Twain used in his earlier travel works. *Roughing It*, for example, establishes the ground rules for Twain's early structures about travel: during the trip West, he incorporates elements of the tall tale and creates a myth about the West, rather than reporting factually what may have happened on his journey. His dedication to Calvin Higbie, "when we two were millionaires for ten days," begins the game of creating a set of falsehoods about the West — here, briefly stated, the two were able to claim a rich vein of silver but were unable to maintain rights to it, thus fulfilling one of the myths of the West, that the rugged individual will find fortune. And his preface, which pretends that this book is just a "personal narrative" which will allow the reader some amusement rather "than afflict him with metaphysics," ends on the curious note that the book contains a "good deal of information." Indeed, he cannot "retain my facts," and suggests that he will "leak wisdom" the more he tries to "caulk up the sources" of all this information. When Twain refers later to a camel in Syria eating his works of journalism, he claims that the camel "choked to death on one of the mildest and gentlest statements of fact that I ever laid before a trusting public." This self-effacing sketch reminds us all that facts contained in humor may contain indigestible truths; they also reveal the "personal narrative" which creates the identity of the traveling author, an invented guise, the identity of a journalist who reports truthfully what he encounters in his travels and then undercuts the notion that this journalist can be trusted. After all, many of the "facts" that he reports are fiction. He literally warns us that he ought not to be taken seriously. This also reminds us that truth, being relative, can be conveyed by a falsehood, a kind of tautological truism about the nature of fiction becoming reality.

Following the Equator, on the other hand, while maintaining this pretense of a journalist, becomes a "personal narrative" that dwells on "metaphysics" of Twain's psyche, resulting in less humor and more philosophy. This text, while it certainly contains some of the parodic elements of early travel works, takes itself seriously as a personal reflection on the cultures that Twain examines. Depending on the country he visits, Twain tends to be more of a journalist, reporting what he sees. He then attempts to explain the context of that culture in general principles of life. For example, he relates, without using apparent tools of humor, the story of the doctor in South Africa who is found at death to be a woman rather than a man. Other commentary about South Africa can be termed humorous, but this brief discussion at the end of the book simply ends on a note of conjecture that she might have been escaping some kind of disgrace in her family. Twain uses gender transformation as a darker theme in *Pudd'nhead Wilson*, and elsewhere, as in *Adventures of Huckleberry Finn*, as a theme for humor. In these novels gender roles are problematic, enigmatic, and emblematic: women have less power than men, genders that transform themselves into their opposites (Huck taking on the guise of a girl, Roxy's son pretending to be a woman) demonstrate false identities in conflict with their societies, and crossed genders reveal a classic tension and confusion about power hierarchies. *Following the Equator*, while it is notable in other kinds of transformation, lends itself to the criticism that it seems to be forced labor, a book written to capitalize on the efforts to recover from virtual bankruptcy, as the lecture trip around the globe proved to be. Twain simply doesn't capitalize on the South African doctor's story, perhaps because that train of thought has been used up in other contexts, principally in his fiction. There are other aspects of Twain's thinking or psyche, however, that this last travel book reveals, other sides that are less developed in earlier travel works.

Little suggests that Twain wished to be a travel writer; rather, he needed money to survive, and journalism provided an easy route, which he writes about in *Roughing It* as a theme for his travels through the West. His voyage to Hawaii, and later his trip to Europe and the Holy Land (retold in *Innocents Abroad*), were ways to continue to work in journalism without the tedium of daily reporting. This allowed him to maintain the illusion that he was developing, an illusion that he was a writer compelled to report on Americans traveling abroad, while his real intent seems to have been to use his natural talents with humor as a way of creating a career as a writer. His job, as he had helped to define it with newspaper publishers, was to write about his travels, a definition that allowed him to be a writer outside of the box of journalism while remaining within it.

A number of other travelers chose to write about their experiences from the vantage point of moral instructors, showing the reader how best to cope with foreign cultures. Eliza Lavin and Mrs. Annie P. White, for example, took their charge seriously to advise Americans on how to travel.[6] Twain's apparent nature as an uncouth humorist prevented him from becoming a moralist about manners. It is more than just that, of course. After the publication of *The Innocents Abroad,* he found that he could write about humorous scenes and incidents at length, and could illuminate these moments of humor as a lecturer who had written a book. Early stories and sketches established Twain as a humorist; travel works allowed him to construct book-length excursions of his thoughts and within his new identity as a humorist elaborate on what he found, both in his mind (as a philosopher of America) and in his travels (as a journalist of America). He did not need to be a moralist or a teacher, even though it is a common practice to treat him as one. These early stories, sketches, and travelogues launched Twain into a career as a writer of books and as a lecturer about his travels. Travel works also allowed Twain to redefine his identity as he needed to, even after becoming a novelist and cultural icon. In fact, maintaining a stable identity was both a threat and a promise to him.[7]

Humor is one of the avenues Twain uses to express himself and his insights, of course; his travel works suggest similar structures of thought (humor leading to commentary on the human condition) that are found in his novels and short stories. What seems remarkable about all this is the deliberate tension between the identity he sought and the identity he denied: Twain undercut as a deconstructive act any notion that he was a serious writer or a moralist at the same time he was becoming one. It seems a parallel act to his public role as an uncouth humorist of the California slopes, someone who represented vernacular values, when, in fact, Twain read not just the Old Southwest humorists but also the contemporary serious authors, such as Charles Dickens and Charles Darwin. He wanted both worlds while denying it.

He was not a naive traveler by any stretch of the imagination, particularly after his first few trips abroad. His family lived in Europe for long periods of time, England for three years, France for two, for example; financial hardships in America occasionally made traveling abroad a less expensive proposition than living at home in Elmira or elsewhere. Howard Baetzhold, Everett Emerson, Robert Rodney, and others have detailed Twain's creative productivity while he lived in England and other countries.[8] His travels within the United States were also extensive, covering diverse states (and territories) such as Montana, Missouri, Ohio, Minnesota, New Hampshire, Iowa, Connecticut, Oregon, West Virginia, California, Nevada, Louisiana, Utah and New York. Because his first book (*Innocents Abroad*) was a travel book and a financial success, and perhaps because it seemed so easy to do, Twain returned to travel writing throughout his life. He is often thought of as a regionalist of the South, having written so compellingly about his roots in Missouri in a variety of ways (in the books on Tom Sawyer and Huck Finn, as well as in so many short stories, essays, interviews, and lectures), but he is also a regionalist of the West (in *Roughing It*), and, for that matter, a regionalist of America as well, because he can represent the common citizen's perspective no matter which region he contemplates (even a southern-style Connecticut Yankee). His role of traveler allows him the pose of being a naive observer of the West, an experienced and wise writer on the Mississippi, or an old pundit experiencing India with an anti-imperialist eye. While he observes some of the characteristics of ordinary travel writing, these works about his travels prove to be much more than naive observations.

Twain, at 56 in Berlin, 1892 (courtesy of the Mark Twain Project Bancroft Library, University of California, Berkeley).

The tourist is curious about the basics of travel: food, lodging, transportation, sights, and exchange values for currency. Twain does provide some of that; he does know the genre of the travel text as it might be used by a traveler. In *Roughing It*, for example, he writes of the forms of horrible coffee to be found on the plains, the kinds of camp life beside Lake Tahoe, the long but fascinating ride on the stagecoach, the deserts across America and the vistas of Hawaii, and the inflated cost of hay in Nevada. A tourist might benefit from knowing these things, but Twain goes further. He considers and examines the nature of language, nostalgia, memory, time and space, religion, truth and fiction, the American family, the outsider or stranger, gender roles, the question of social identity, and the purpose of travel itself. And, of course, he uses humor, several types of humor, to consider these fairly serious themes; that, in itself, eclipses the kind of travel writing others practiced, writing that sometimes entertained but mostly informed the reader of the exotic places that the writer explored.

Huck Finn has long been recognized the voice of the people; Henry Nash Smith established the importance of this vernacular point of view. The travel works are equally involved in honoring the individual voices in America. In *Roughing It*, Scotty Briggs and his conversation with the minister about Buck Fanshaw's funeral contrasts Scotty's colloquialisms with the minister's elevated diction; Jim Blaine and the story of the old ram provide a rambling discourse on the power of humor; Horace Greeley's "turnip" letter contextualizes the necessity of interpretation. *A Tramp Abroad* catalogs the intricacies of the German language. A central focus in *Life on the Mississippi* is the language of the river. The language of tour guides in *Innocents Abroad* becomes fodder for practical jokes and one-liners. *Following the Equator* presents the fantasy of the Mark Twain Club though the language of its sole member, the letters, the short reports, and the summaries of imagined debates detailing the hoax and the tall-tale framework that language provides. Twain presents the idiosyncrasies of the Australian language: "One hears such words as *piper* for paper, *lydy* for lady, and *tyble* for table" (129).

There are two kinds of nostalgia for the traveler. Twain knows well the fondness for home, but knows that the backward glance forgives the threats and risks one has survived. Nostalgia blurs the edges of bad memories. The first nostalgia is apparent in *Roughing It* when Twain compares European sights with Rainbow Falls in New York's Watkins Glen; the American vista is better than the European one. Lake Tahoe is beautiful beyond words for an older Twain, despite the second nostalgia in which he remembers the time he started a forest fire on the edge of the lake, escaping the fire with a boat. Mono Lake threatens to remove his skin, but he recalls with excitement the adventure of the untied boat so close to shore on his barren island yet just out of reach. Twain escapes the Reconstruction of the South by returning to his childhood in *Huckleberry Finn*, in much the same dual-edged nostalgia, remembering the freedom of Jackson's Island and the tyranny of the Southern society along the shores of the mighty Mississippi. The ice storm episode in India — when Twain vividly contrasts the memorial building of the Taj Mahal with the ice storm in America — lets Twain temporarily transcend the death of Susy, the nostalgia for her and his memories of her.

Memory forms the basis for the oft-quoted passage on the Sphinx in Egypt in *Innocents Abroad*; similarly, memory is crucial for the riverboat pilot in *Life on the Mississippi*; in Jim Blaine's story of the old ram in *Roughing It*; and in Twain's recounting slavery in America and in South Africa in *Following the Equator*. Memory serves Twain well in his lecture tours when he is required to recall the adventures he had on the volcanoes of Hawaii, though he came to regret having to read some of the purple prose generated for the occasion. Memory can freeze a moment of time so that a picture of life is kept stable. A traveler needs those memories in order to make the trip worthwhile, though Twain is aware in *Following the Equator* that contemporary tourists are relying on the camera to capture those memories: "Crossed the equator. In the distance it looked like a blue ribbon stretched across the ocean. Several passengers kodak'd it" (66).

Memory transforms time and space so that one can better understand the experience of travel. The photograph can, of course, freeze the moment. Twain's memory can transcend the market square in South Africa, returning him in time and space to his childhood in Missouri when his father rebukes a slave in *Following the Equator*; the Sphinx in *Innocents Abroad* makes its memories eternal and "pitiless." The stagecoach Sphinx in *Roughing It* seemingly obliterates time with her conversational skills. The blue jay fills the cabin with acorns in *A Tramp Abroad*, the tall tale becoming a memory of the West as a limitless land of opportunity. *Life on the Mississippi* makes the romance of the river change into a map of the hazards of travel; the cub pilot's memory of his past life along the river becomes a list of the disappearing landmarks. The travel works associated with America in particular consider the Western landscape as a powerful set of memories, forcing the traveler to survive with natural skills rather than with traditional forms of education; the dictionary in *Roughing It* becomes a hindrance, an object thrown at their heads to use as a pillow in the stagecoach, otherwise generally useless for the trip. Twain discusses "pocket mining" in this text as a way to stop time, the aging prospector still trying to find fortune long after the flush times. He pillages a newspaper article to compare the stagecoach ride to contemporary train travel as a time frozen in a moment of memory, the traveler on the stagecoach relying on the native skills of the driver rather than on the train rails that transport him, a memory still carrying the grand excitement of the journey westward.

Religion, as many critics have noted, is one of Twain's targets for satire and personal attack. Livy's attempts to civilize him, of course, failed. Religion comes under scrutiny in *A Connecticut Yankee in King Arthur's Court*, to put it mildly, as well as other works of fiction. Superstition, as an offshoot of religion, has its place in *Huckleberry Finn* and *Tom Sawyer*, with the customary satire and occasional humor directed at it. Organized religion in the travel works equally finds rocky ground in Twain's comments. The tourist buying authentic pieces of the cross in *Innocents Abroad*, the misguided efforts of the Hawaiian missionary in *Roughing It*, the equally bad Thuggee and the Christian in *Following the Equator*: most religions are suspect because of the narrow-mindedness of some practicing their doctrines, particularly with those not in their congregations. The Mormons in *Roughing It*, the Pilgrims in *Innocents Abroad*, the Catholics generally: most Christians are humbugs and sham moralists in Twain's world. Jim's faith in superstition in *Huckleberry Finn* resembles the kind of foolish and desperate Christian faith in a deity who makes the world seem reasonable and orderly. His knowledge of rattlesnakes and how to counteract their venomous bite is parallel to the faith in Providence that the Widow Douglas demonstrates in her attempt to civilize Huck; both efforts attempt to harness the unknown without real knowledge of snakes or boys. Travelers in the worlds of Twain learn to appreciate the hypocrisy of religious fervor that lacks the pragmatic connection to reality.

Here the tall tale serves as an anodyne to religion, a substitute form of wisdom, since religion itself is a pretender, an impostor form of knowledge and wisdom. The tall tale declares itself to be purely fiction with no pretense of reality, though it may contain elements of truth and sometimes a kernel of advice. Tom Quartz the cat is blown skyward in *Roughing It* and learns the hazards of prospecting; the Morgan/Hyde lawsuit, the landslide property case, proves to be an elaborate practical joke as well as a tall tale, one that suggests that gullibility is a virtue reserved for the tenderfoot out West. In its most elaborate form, Huck's series of falsehoods at the Phelps farm become a template for truth, since he has found his new identity of Tom Sawyer, his lies the truths about a family he knows well. Huck lets Providence show him the way, a religion supplanted by a natural set of skills of lying for the sake of truth: "I went right along, not fixing up any particular plan, but just trusting to Providence to put the right words in my mouth when the time come; for I'd noticed that Providence always did put the right words in my mouth if I left it alone." The tall tale, in this sense, has replaced religion. Fiction supplants reality.

In his travel works, Twain seems to be searching for a way to use tall tales to explain the boundary layers between truth and fiction. The German folklore in *A Tramp Abroad*, the fight between Bemis and the buffalo in the tree in *Roughing It*, the nervous suitor without pants in a story without an ending in *Following the Equator*: these and many other tall tales force the act of interpretation, an act that makes the tall tale transparently an act of fiction while at the same time reaching some level of truth. The German tall tales of courtship and betrayal serve as models for Twain's reconstruction of Western myths in *Life on the Mississippi*, particularly the Karl Ritter story (chapters 31 and 32), where a fingerprint plays such a significant role, perhaps a foreshadowing, if not a genesis, for *Puddn'head Wilson*, where tragedy strikes those who do not know their true identities. Bemis concocts the battle with the buffalo in order to explain his missing horse and lasso, using specious logic and circumstantial evidence as a way to begin creating a myth about the Western hero. Twain and fellow passengers try to find a suitable ending for John Brown's dilemma with the lap robe in Chapter 2 of *Following the Equator*, a story without an ending, a chapter framed around the context of General Grant's remarkable memory.

The American family is at odds with itself in *Roughing It*, with the Mormon polygamous family representing a kind of bridge between religion and superstition for Twain, and with an assortment of orphaned relationships among families. Slade's family consists of himself and his wife, apparently, while Twain's own family seems absent from this text, with Orion disappearing entirely; exotic families, such as the Chinese and the Hawaiian, do appear, but nuclear families are largely untapped as sources of interest. The question of parentage is striking with the Mormon family, the possibilities for humor clear to Twain; Brigham Young apparently can't remember all of the children that he has. Families are equally disjointed or absent in *Innocents Abroad* and *A Tramp Abroad*; Twain refers to families, parents, and children, but these are rootless families, disconnected from America and from each other. *Life on the Mississippi*, with its fascination with death, seems awkward and ill at ease with any nuclear family, with most disintegrating because of war, pestilence, and poverty. *Following the Equator*, perhaps because of the tragedy of Susy's death, makes little reference to the American family, but does examine in passing an assortment of exotic family relationships, even though Livy and Clara were on this voyage with Samuel around the world. This is puzzling in some ways, because one ought to see in travel works an American family that is cohesive, relying on each other for comfort, food, and conversation; the typical tourist family travels together as parents and children. This splintered family has its place, of course, in Twain's major fiction, with Huck an orphan, Jim determined to buy back his children and wife, Hank a displaced time-traveler, and Chambers an uneducated slave/master (among other many families that lack a center of some kind).

The stranger or outsider is a common theme in literature; this person can represent threat, risk, death, and unwelcome news, and yet sometimes can suggest change, revolution, and a welcome rebirth of the community that may at first be suspicious. Slade in *Roughing It* is a powerful figure, necessary to tame the territory but as much a criminal as those he kills. Satan, the slippery and competent servant in *Following the Equator*, introduces God to Twain, one of the thousand in India, someone who wishes to discuss literary theory on Huck Finn's character, which reinforces the distance between not just the religion that allows for an earthly God and the Christian one that Twain knows about, but also the distance between the mysterious servant (named by Twain as Satan, because the real name is not easily pronounced) and himself, an obvious stranger to the culture of India. A "relic-hunter" in *Innocents Abroad*, a fellow passenger on Twain's journey to Egypt, attempts to chisel off a part of the Sphinx; this person, comic relief no doubt, represents an alien culture attempting to carry off an authentic sight (a piece of it, anyway) of a culture that has long faded into history, replacing that culture with the aggressiveness of the American tourist. He's a William Randolph Hearst intruding into ancient cultures. Huck Finn, Pap, David Wilson, and Satan (in *The Mysterious Stranger*) share some of the characteristics of this outsider figure. Huck is clearly the redemptive stranger, someone who can repair the soul of the community he escapes from. Twain himself, in

Roughing It, realizes that he can become a lecturer, even though feeling that he is an impostor on stage, a person with the power of rhetoric, someone who has enormous control and power over his audience.

Gender roles are occasionally examined in several of Twain's travel works, but these reviews are desultory in early work and fairly straightforward in later work. Judith Loftus in *Huckleberry Finn* and Roxy in *Puddn'head Wilson* are perhaps the most powerful women in Twain's fiction; Pap in *Huckleberry Finn*, Hank Morgan in *Connecticut Yankee*, and Satan in *The Mysterious Stranger* are perhaps among the most powerful men. Men in *Roughing It* tend to be either tenderfoot fools or powerful figures; women are curiously absent, though Slade's wife and the Sphinx-like passenger seem stereotypical, Slade's wife a strong, powerful, even romantic, figure, and the Sphinx a loquacious, rambling busybody. *Innocents Abroad, Life on the Mississippi* and *A Tramp Abroad* have equally stereotypical women and men, women romanticized and placed on pedestals, men burly and independent. *Following the Equator* does begin to challenge the notions of gender assignment; for example, one of Twain's servants in India seems so feminine that Twain is embarrassed to dress in front of him. The story of Dr. Barry in South Africa similarly presents a reversal of gender roles, when it is discovered that he was actually a she at her death (almost a throwaway anecdote at the very end of the text). Roxy and Chambers in *Puddn'head Wilson* more clearly show role reversal, and Huck attempts to mimic a girl in Judith Loftus' cabin.

The question of social identity — an identity formed by others — relates to gender roles, because stereotypes and assumptions can govern how people see themselves. Tom Sawyer sees himself within the tradition of romantic or Gothic literature, believing himself to be a part of the tradition that Twain rails against in *Life on the Mississippi* and the Sir Walter Scott world that he satirizes in *Huckleberry Finn*. Huck, of course, struggles to come to terms with himself within the spectrum of church, civilization, and his own tenuous family; he finds himself reborn at the Phelps farm as Tom Sawyer, an identity that allows him to proceed with his quest to free Jim. Throughout *Roughing It* Twain searches for a suitable identity and settles for a career as a journalist, the other occupations having escaped him, though he adds to this core other competencies as a lecturer and a humorist. In *Life on the Mississippi* Twain explores the creation of one of his identities, that of riverboat pilot; in his visit to Hannibal he is fascinated by the eventual fates (and formed social identities) of his former classmates, and is self-deprecating when one of the inhabitants of Hannibal refers to Twain (not knowing who he is talking to) as a damned fool. In *Following the Equator*, identity conflicts exist throughout the text; the Tichborne Claimant case (156–58) is just one of the impostor anecdotes in the text and is closely followed by another, a story that Twain writes about a mysterious letter claiming that he had given a lecture tour in Australia and had unfortunately died on that tour. Twain finds the letter to be a complete hoax when he actually does arrive in Australia (158–160). Much later Twain reveals the source of the letter, written by a Mr. Blank (real name not revealed) who had created a far greater hoax about a nonexistent Mark Twain Club of Corrigan Castle, Ireland.

Travel itself is healthy for opening the mind to new vistas and possibilities. The usual travel writer seeks out the oddities of nature, the unusual sights, and the culturally authentic facts that would amuse or teach a reader about the trip taken. Twain's general purpose for travel writing is familiar at times. The volcanoes of Hawaii, the local Hawaiian native, and living accommodations or clothing these inhabitants have — these are expected observations for a travel writer. It is also useful to suggest that the volcano is a threat, that nature is dangerous. Tourists thrive on some element of risk. Nature is also something to interpret. The comparison of the volcano Kilauea with biblical images in *Roughing It* is an example. But Twain also adds humor, considerable amounts of it, which is not traditional in travel writing. Humor can have a serious side to it; the chapter on Horace Greeley's impossible handwriting in the letter on turnips shows how bad interpretation can lead to insanity.

Humor has numerous ways to express the human condition so that people laugh at the unexpected witticism or event. Slapstick humor, for example, is physical, a pie thrown in the face, an embarrassment to a victim, a moment of reversal, someone who is slapped, poked, or kicked, a moment we do not expect. Most humor works that way: something happens that comes out of left field. A witticism works the same way, of course; a comment ends with a punch line that differs from the ordinary, upending the usual phrasing. Expecting a Benjamin Franklin profundity, the reader in Twain's world finds a Puddn'head Wilson calendar aphorism. Animal jokes or animal behavior that seems human is similar; we expect animals to do things that are ordinary, and we laugh when they act (or seem to act) like humans. The political joke (often satire) is a bit different in that all too often the politician does something that seems quite incompetent (we expect competent politicians, do we not?), becoming an easy target for a late-night talk show host; the unexpected is sometimes the expected behavior. Twain himself found Congress and criminals to be cut from the same cloth of humanity. The practical joke, humor wherein the audience knows what the unexpected event or behavior will be and the victim does not, is one of Twain's most common tools of the trade. His practical jokes, such as the Morgan/Hyde landslide case in *Roughing It*, are developed at length, so that the reader can chuckle at the complexity of the joke played on the gullible person, who usually understands the joke at last and is properly embarrassed. A variant of the practical joke is concrete in the example of the three prospectors (Twain included) lost in the snowstorm in Nevada, mere steps from the station, vowing to rid themselves of various vices, and, the next day, upon finding themselves alive and safe, returning to those vices; this practical joke includes the author, a kind of joke that allows the community of readers to share in the folly without embarrassment. A typical travel work might strive to be informative and entertaining, but Twain's snowstorm anecdote says more about the willingness of people to change their minds when their habits are at risk than about the pleasant accommodations one might find in the wilderness of Nevada; playing cards, smoking cigars, and drinking hard liquor: "absurdity could go no farther. We shook hands and agreed to say no more about 'reform' and 'examples to the rising generation.'" One could say that Twain's narrative framework, the "plank" system he devised for *Innocents Abroad*, insists that humor encase the serious point, and that this snowstorm adventure gives us something informative about relative morality. This is humor for humor's sake, however. Twain's use of humor makes his travel works an exploration of the genre of the travel work, so that most of his travel writings demonstrate a willingness to experiment with the form, to make it new in some way. *Huckleberry Finn*, it is well noted, breaks the traditional mold of literature, so that a vernacular voice rules and an elegant or nuanced world of literature is absent. Here, too, humor pervades in Twain's versions of the travel work, even in the admittedly lackluster *A Tramp Abroad*, where some experiments did not quite work and the humor was a bit forced.

Of course, the travel work includes a place and a time. *A Tramp Abroad* is loosely a jaunt about Europe, a pleasure walk among the vistas of a natural landscape, roughly the 1870s. The Alps beckon to the traveler as a monument to natural beauty; the cathedral at Chartres is a memorial to the worship of God. The reader expects to see something, particularly from Twain, that will entertain and inform in much the same way the earlier two travel works were written. (This it kind of does, but in attempting a new form of travel expression without repeating the old forms, *A Tramp Abroad* falters.) The reader wants and expects to read something that will explore the world outside of the confines of Syracuse, New York. That city the reader already knows. The reader also wants to learn something about a place that exists in the present; Twain satirizes the American tourist in *Innocents Abroad* who buys a relic of the past or who seems stupefied by the ancient art in a typical Louvre-like setting, suggesting in that travel work that the traveler ought to consider the modern train or hotel (particularly in America) a better tourist site.

London, Paris, Rome, Calcutta, Sydney: Twain comes to these urban centers of culture with several purposes in mind. He brings with him the American's experience, usually the competent capitalist, the prospector who strikes it rich — even when Twain himself is generally a poor businessman and unlucky at cards, gambling, and prospecting — and talks to large audiences in these cities about his American perspective. He also brings a curiosity about these foreign places, trying to absorb their culture. He weighs the merits and faults of the people who dwell there; he satirizes the inhumane, the inept, the foolish. He also learns to harmonize with these inhabitants, for it is the city itself that gives him a place to write and to think. Some of his best work occurs in these urban centers, sometimes as a result of financial necessity (having proved his lack of business acumen in America), but sometimes because he needs to be in a place that reveres his genius and a place that provides a neutral arena for his work. He can contemplate Susy's death in London with detachment and some grace, oddly enough, because he is utterly alone, utterly apart from his family and America. His efforts at writing *Following the Equator*, which bears little obvious evidence of the stress of his personal life, testify to that ability to detach, that ability to write without reflecting the inner turmoil. But he absolutely must travel to the foreign city; it represents ancient wisdom and history, a locus of stability. He enjoys the American city, of course, for he is at home there; the culture is familiar, the language accessible. By sneaking off the *Quaker City* in *Innocents Abroad* to see the Acropolis at night, though a quarantine prevents the tourists from visiting Athens, Twain plays the prankster, stealing grapes with his three companions, but is in awe of what he sees: "But what were sunsets to us, with the wild excitement upon us of approaching the most renowned of cities! What cared we for outward visions, when Agamemnon, Achilles, and a thousand other heroes of the great Past were marching in ghostly procession through our fancies? What were sunsets to us, who were about to live and breathe and walk in actual Athens; yea, and go far down into the dead centuries and bid in person for the slaves, Diogenes and Plato, in the public market-place, or gossip with the neighbors about the siege of Troy or the splendid deeds of Marathon?" Yes, because of the quarantine, most of his fellow passengers do not get to see that sight, but the thief of grapes can tell of the adventure he had.

The phenomenological structures, and, in part, the sociological structures that are found in Twain's travel works are not consistent and continuous throughout. If they were, that would suggest an intelligence about the nature of travel formed from the beginning. Rather, Twain's contemplations about nostalgia, time, place, identity, and other concepts, evolve over time. The quest motif, for example, is particularly strong in *Roughing It*, but is less apparent in *A Tramp Abroad* or even *Following the Equator*, and concepts about identity or nostalgia vary in complexity and intensity throughout Twain's writings about travel. However, one can find tracings of these phenomenological and sociological structures in almost all of his works, and one can see elements of the curious focus on travel as a major component of Twain's development as a writer.

2

Travel as a Method of Piloting the River of Life

When in doubt, tell the truth.
— Pudd'nhead Wilson's New Calendar.

In general, travel literature consists of a narrator who takes advantage of the context of traveling in order to describe natural surroundings, other cultures, and details of the journey itself. That narrator can take on the role of instructor.[9] Readers may learn how to travel the same route. (Travel literature can include works that dwell on static experiences, such as journals or diaries about vacation trips, where the trip means more to the narrator than the reader in terms of any pleasurable instruction, the point of many travelogues.[10] My study here has a separate focus on the rhetorical aspects that include the audience.) Modern travel guides fulfill that expectation, particularly if maps, descriptions of sites, phone numbers, web addresses, costs, and other details accompany the text. Rick Steves, to use his example again, can provide that level of information in one of his tour books of Europe or elsewhere. (His *Postcards from Europe* can be classified with travel works that, like Twain's, are autobiographical.) But that does not require that the reader be able to retrace the travel experience; the account need not be journalistically true or even accurate. Many works of travel literature, in fact, have an ideological or political basis. Often in European travel literature of the nineteenth century, the narrator is a superior being who examines the wilderness and its savages. This colonialist narrator may, in fact, bring back oddities of nature, even those savages from a foreign land, and, at least, attempt to explain nature from a civilized, often Christian and Western, perspective.[11]

While Twain occasionally comments on civilizations from this colonialist perspective, he also uses a humorist's perspective to undercut pretensions of the civilized traveler and occasionally to remark on the savage's superiority to Western civilization. Twain's search for success, literary fame and reputation may mirror the expectations of his audience that he be a moral guide to his readers, simply because he was aware of the commercial aspects of his early accounts of his travel experiences. *Innocents Abroad*, for example, arose from his travel letters as a correspondent, mostly tailored for the *Alta California* reader. Twain knew that he had to be new: while using the narrative persona of a moral guide in *Innocents Abroad* (in the sense that he chastises the Pilgrims and belittles the pretensions of Europe), Twain upends typical travelogues that praise the Grand Tour as a maturing experience and that glorifies the ancient cultures of the Old World. He was quite aware of the conventions used by travel writers, and observed some of those conventions. But he also felt threatened by the task of being a moral teacher, seeking through humor systems of evasion from the role of teacher, because, as a humorist and as a philosopher of sorts, he recognized that he did not wish to be just another travel writer who taught the reader how to travel with an appropriate spiritual or moral purpose. That had been done, perhaps overdone.[12]

The literary traveler is often bold, intelligent, and determined. In some travel literature, the narrator is a conqueror, such as Edward Whymper, who wrote about his successful ascent of the Matterhorn in 1865, *Scrambles Amongst the Alps*, a text which Twain used for *A Tramp Abroad*, appropriating, in fact, a number of illustrations from that text.[13] Twain's travels, however, rarely reflect a real sense of his being a conqueror, and, by contrast, often parody acts of heroism. For example, Twain's presumed conquest of the Riffelberg mocks the outlandish preparations made for that hike (in *A Tramp Abroad*, chapters 37–41). If anything, Twain's excursion up the Matterhorn reveals his own lack of superiority with the self-deprecating humor used to highlight the account of Whymper's real adventure (borrowing at length from Whymper's own words). In other works, Twain adopts a variety of narrative guises, sometimes bold and intelligent, as in parts of *Roughing It* and most of *Innocents Abroad*, but he generally avoids the conqueror's sense of superiority, although he shows some sign of that in a few portions of *Life on the Mississippi* (primarily when he

2. Travel as a Method of Piloting the River of Life   31

"The 'Baton Rouge'" in *Life on the Mississippi* (frontispiece). Illustration by Edmund Henry Garrett.

masters the river as a pilot), and he does appear on occasion in *Following the Equator* as an elitist voice of civilization among the savages in New Zealand, Australia, South Africa and India. Twain's acts of heroism are few, although it could be claimed that writing *Following the Equator* after the death of his beloved daughter Susy was itself an enabling act of courage (though not in the traditional sense of the adventurer overcoming great physical hardships).

Twain knew personally such travel writers as Bayard Taylor, and read others, such as Francis Parkman (historian and travel writer combined), William Cowper Prime, and Constance Frederica Gordon-Cumming. Twain may have used Andrew Carnegie's *Round the World* as a model for the diary structure of *Following the Equator*.[14] Clearly, Twain read other travel literature and knew the genre fairly well.[15] In one of his early letters from Hawaii, July 1866, Mr. Brown, one of Twain's narrative voices, says of travel literature written by missionaries: "They're the flattest reading — they are sicker than the smart things children say in the newspapers. Every preacher that gets lazy comes to the Sandwich Islands to 'recruit his health,' and then he goes back home and writes a book. And he puts in a lot of history, and some legends, and some manners and customs, and dead loads of praise of the missionaries for civilizing and Christianizing the natives, and says in considerable chapters how grateful the savage ought to be; and when there is a chapter to be filled out, and they haven't got anything to fill it out with, they shovel in a lot of Scripture" (*Letters from Hawaii*, 210–11). In general, this aptly describes his own travel works, particularly *Innocents Abroad*, with the inverted formula of debunking the efficacy of civilization and Christianity.[16] Twain's genius, in fact, rests in part on his ability to modify the genre of travel writing to suit humor's inversion of expected circumstances and to accommodate occasional satiric commentary.

It's been claimed that Twain's "geographical travels brought him little positive enlightenment"[17] and that Twain "could rely on the sequence of the journey itself to provide at least a simulacrum of coherence for his materials" (2). Further, "one need have neither a coherent worldview nor even a particular end in mind to write a travel book" (3). One can reach this conclusion by simply noticing Twain's seeming indifference to the travel work as a serious venture, because he soon understood after the success of *Innocents Abroad* that he could market this work to a mass public without regard for its place in popular culture, as a subscription book hardly to be compared with books of literature. But it's more likely to be the case that the travel writings inform, collect, and control the materials used in Twain's other writings, as suggested by Sherwood Cummings, who noted the "nuclear position of *A Tramp Abroad* with reference to the composition of *The Prince and the Pauper* and *Huckleberry Finn*. Along the dimension of time, its composition lies at the center of the two novels. The *Tramp* (1878–1880) nests within *The Prince and the Pauper* (1877–1881), which nests within *Huckleberry Finn* (1876–1883). Within days of finishing *A Tramp Abroad*, Twain was back at work on *The Prince and the Pauper*, writing with 'jubilant delight.'"[18] Travel writing for Twain allowed him to formulate positions, to practice writing on concepts and themes that he wished to explore or develop, and to think through life's mysteries, sometimes demonstrating a sharpened focus for the answers he may have sought. The act of travel, which may lack a definite purpose, acquires purpose by the act of writing about the experience. Twain may have felt the release necessary by writing about traveling, an act of recovery of his experiences, which then released his imagination for the art of writing fiction. More simply expressed, writing about a trip primed the writing of a novel. This does not suggest that the travel work is less valuable than the work of fiction. As Percy G. Adams argues, the travel work contains

2. Travel as a Method of Piloting the River of Life 33

many of the elements of a novel, including plot, character, style, and themes used in quest literature.[19] It can be said that Twain's lifework is a set of variations on the theme of travel. *The Prince and the Pauper* and *Adventures of Huckleberry Finn* contain elements of the journey as major structural components of character development and of plot, such as the river that helps reshape Huck's conscience or the journey to Court that helps define the conscience of the Prince. Other novels contain the journey as a central focus; *A Connecticut Yankee in King Arthur's Court* even uses time travel as a plot device.

Cummings' focus on science allows him to define well the aims of *A Tramp Abroad*, namely the application of Hippolyte Taine's method of analyzing a culture, and, as well, how Twain found a "deeper purpose of which he was unaware — that of clarifying his feelings about the legendary past" (96). I will examine the aims of Twain's travel writings in the same way, that of collecting information about life, about cultures, about one's own experiences, in order to understand the drift of oneself within a culture and within an era. Taine's method, however imperfectly it might have been applied, allowed Twain not to understand just a culture, the central purpose that Taine outlined, but also himself within the context of that culture (or other cultures). Taine reads as much material from as many different sources as he can in order to understand the old France and find a suitable political framework for contemporary France: "The Frenchmen of the ancient regime are still within visual range.... Through their literature, philosophy, scientific pursuits, gazettes, and correspondence, we can reproduce their feeling and thought, and even enjoy their familiar conversation."[20] In a similar way, Twain could examine history and culture from the outside as an observer yet also participate in creating that history and culture with the commentary that his travel works provide. As a naturalist, Twain's methods of observation were often suspect, but the results of his occasionally haphazard process of reasoning things out were provocative and sometimes profoundly unsettling, giving this running reexamination of himself and his place in a culture a set of deconstructive possibilities, often undercutting established thought and undermining his own sense of self.

Twain uses the "science of piloting," a method taught him by Horace Bixby well before Twain probably read Taine's work *History of English Literature* in the early 1870s (Cummings, 70), in writing out his travel experiences. Cummings writes, "The way a pilot learns the river is exactly like the Darwinian method of understanding nature. Relentlessly objective, indefatigably thorough, the pilot, like the scientist, comes to understand his subject only after months and years of assimilating and organizing data" (61). Twain found a philosophy written out for him by Taine, one that reflected his own early thinking and one that Horace Bixby provided as a practical exercise in mastering the river. Twain's practical experience as a cub pilot on the Mississippi River serves well as an analogy to the process of writing about traveling.

Cummings summarizes that "science of piloting" (61–67); I can only echo that summary with some amplification. In "Old Times on the Mississippi"(1874–1875), the cub pilot confesses his inadequacies to Bixby. Apparently Bixby's comments about particular points along the river have gone unnoticed by the cub. Bixby asks the cub why he supposes Bixby "told you the names of those points for?"[21] The cub's response, to "be entertaining," provokes a litany of curses from Bixby at first at him and then at some traders because Bixby had run over their oars ("blind" with the rage Bixby felt toward the cub). Drained from cursing others, Bixby turns to the cub and says "my boy, you must get a little memorandum-book; and every time I tell you a thing, put it down right away. There's only one way to be a pilot, and that is to get this entire river by heart" (87–88). From the notebooks that Twain kept throughout his life, particularly what we now call Notebooks Two and Three, covering the periods of April–July 1857 and November 1860–March 1861, we know that Twain did keep track of the points of the river. He had to write these facts down in preparation for memorizing them. Twain's memory was never as keenly developed as when he tried to master the river; Twain's memory was always suspect on other accounts, particularly when dictating his autobiography.

Bixby further trains the cub to transfer the facts of the notebook into his head, which had become a "confusion of meaningless names" (94). He wants the cub to "know the *shape* of the river" so well that "you learn it with such absolute certainty that you can always steer by the shape that's *in your head*, and never mind the one that's before your eyes" (104). Memory, here, becomes all-important. The cub pilot had to remember in great detail all of the facts which constitute the shape of the river. These facts become a platform of stability if they remain the same. During a night passage or during fog, the pilot must learn to trust what he already knows and not let the distortions of the dark or weather reshape the map he already has in his mind. Facts have become so assimilated that they become an internalized guide against which distortions of reality have no place.

The shape of the river, however, has many dimensions: "It was plain that I had got to learn the shape of the river in all the different ways that could be thought of,—upside down, wrong end first, inside out, fore-and-aft, and 'thort-ships,'—and then know what to do on gray nights when it hadn't any shape at all" (110). Bixby says that the cub must remember the changes to the river over time: "You mustn't get the shoal soundings and marks of one trip mixed up with shoal soundings and marks of another, either, for they're not often twice alike. You must keep them separate" (110). The river changes over time, and the pilot must keep track of all these shifting facts. Not only do facts have dimensions, differing perspectives from angles of time, place, and movement, these facts may shift according to the changing angles; the river's depth, path (currents and eddies), and direction can change over time, after a flood, or after a tree falls in the river.

In time, the cub learns to read the river water as well, anticipating the changes of the river from the surface. The cub needs to know the difference, for example, between a bluff reef and a wind reef, one dangerous, the other harmless, though they look just alike. As Bixby explains, the cub must learn the river as a process of "instinct," where "you will just naturally *know* one from the other, but you will never be able to explain why or how you know them apart" (118). Again, the cub pilot's memory needs to be solid yet fluid, retaining facts about the river while adjusting to changes along the river. The instinctual knowledge that Bixby presumes to have about a bluff reef and a wind reef is still knowledge, if not well defined as a body of facts concerning the difference between the two. One must assume that there really is a difference, perhaps so minute as to escape scientific observation, but a difference that the pilot recognizes at some level.[22]

Twain describes the process of reading the river in terms of reading a book, "which told its mind to me without reserve, delivering its most cherished secrets as clearly as if it uttered them with a voice." Further, "it was not a book to be read once and thrown aside, for it had a new story to tell every day" (118). It is a book of contradictions, at once pleasant and dangerous: "The passenger who could not read this book saw nothing but all manner of pretty pictures in it, painted by the sun and shaded by the clouds, whereas to the trained eye these were not pictures at all, but the grimmest and most dead-earnest of reading matter" (118–19). Piloting the river was serious business after all, with lives and property in the balance. Twain's travel books can carry the same weight of conviction, although the amount of instruction varies with the ability of the reader to understand the landscape of the text.

Twain realizes, however, that mastering the river as a pilot results in losing something, for "all the grace, the beauty, the poetry, had gone out of the majestic river" (119). After describing the river in fairly conventional poetic terms, Twain then describes how he "began to cease from noting the glories and the charms which the moon and the sun and the twilight wrought upon the river's face; another day came when I ceased altogether to note them" (119). He remarks, "The romance and beauty were all gone from the river" (120). This is a hyperbolic statement, considering how well Twain could describe the river — as well as other scenic vistas — long after he had become proficient as a pilot. But the nostalgia for innocence remains, albeit an innocence that Twain rejects anyway.

The process of learning to read the river thus entails a number of steps: first, recording the facts; second, memorizing these facts; third, adjusting to changes in those facts; and fourth, realizing these facts as instinctual portions of existence. The fourth step apparently cannot be taught rationally; it's as if a fact can only be felt, not expressed. This, of course, negates the process of reading the river as a series of facts, for the pilot depends on an internalized map of the river as well, and not just on the river that he sees. This internal map becomes especially important at night, when the points along the river are nearly impossible to see. Bixby's skill at navigating the river at night are clearly commendable; for example, he is able to land at Jones's plantation, at the upper or lower end of it, even though it may be a "dingy night," as the cub remarks to himself, "You'll have a good time finding Mr. Jones's plantation [on] such a night as this" (84). The anecdote of the pilot named "X," who pilots the boat while apparently asleep, further demonstrates the power of the instinct in knowing the river and the power of facts so well known that one can trust a pilot who walks in his sleep. And, too, a fifth step exists, that of accepting these forms of knowledge with a serene confidence.

Bixby plays a practical joke on the cub when crossing the "plainest and simplest" point in the "whole river," his fifth step of learning the river being that one must have absolute "confidence in that knowledge." Bixby leaves the cub in charge on one stretch of the river without any apparent bottom, and asks, "How much water is there in it?" The cub says, "I couldn't get bottom there with a church steeple." After saying, "You think so, do you?" Bixby leaves, only to hide behind a smokestack. The cub thinks, "the very tone of the question shook my confidence." Bixby arranges "fifteen or twenty people" to gather behind the cub to alarm him. "All my confidence in that crossing vanished," thinks the cub. The leadsman, who knows the joke, reads out incorrect (and increasingly shallow) depths of the river, until the cub shouts to the engineer, "Oh, Ben, if you love me, *back* her." Bixby then steps out of his hiding place, setting off a "thundergust of humiliating laughter." Bixby says, "I want you to learn something by that experience," that confidence in knowing the river must be certain and complete: "You shouldn't have allowed me or anybody else to shake your confidence in that knowledge" (160–165).

Twain also claims that having this knowledge results in a loss of innocence, as noted earlier. That kind of complete, instinctual knowledge of the river eclipses any "romance and beauty" that might be had with an uninformed imagination. It seems a paradox that this informed knowledge also becomes a kind of informed imagination as well, since the pilot must be able to change his perception of the river's facts as the river changes in time and space. Twain's descriptive passages which capture the romance and beauty of the river seems to deny any loss or lapse. He still has the power and the ability to see the river as an innocent observer. What he has lost is the uninformed innocence of observing facts that have no or little meaning. Everything connects or has a sense of meaningfulness because the facts contain the structure, the structure becoming a seamless web of meaning. In simpler terms, facts are the structure; the pilot does not need to depend on novelty or the uninformed guess; he knows where he is on the river (if his memory and his imagination are working that day). If anything, what Twain attempts to discuss as a loss of innocence becomes a strength of knowledge: at the same time facts convey meaning while they can become the romance and beauty of a higher kind, one that a trained observer (like a pilot) can express or understand. Linear thinking, then, dissolves in the paradox of an innocence of knowledge, the two seeming to contradict each other.

This kind of paradox strikes Twain late in life when he considers his autobiography. He finds it difficult to begin at the beginning and proceed down the river of his life; he would rather be the pilot starting his watch anywhere along the river. "The idea of blocking out a consecutive series of events which have happened to me, or which I imagine have happened to me — I can see that that is impossible for me. The only thing possible for me is to talk about the thing that something suggests at the moment — something in the middle of my life, perhaps, or something that happened only a few months ago" (*MELM*; Autobiography Dictation, January 9, 1906). Since all of life's facts can connect, or can be imagined or invented or made to connect, as long as the ship does not sink or run aground, life's pattern exists as a series of meaningful events. The pilot, similarly, controls the ship, its passengers and its cargo, within the meaningful pattern that the river has become; he also can, perhaps with reflection, understand the romance and beauty of the river better than the individual just along for the ride. Thus, too, the travel works that he writes do not necessarily have to reflect a chronology of events, because the events have been interwoven with other patterns that have coherence outside the fabric of time.

A pilot, with a confident mastery of the facts of the river, along with an elevated sense of imagination, controls the destiny of the ship and the passengers. As Twain notes, the pilot is the supreme master, whose orders cannot be lightly questioned, even by the captain. The few accidents that Twain himself as a pilot had along the river can largely be attributed to faults of the captains who wished to take charge.[23] Twain's choice of careers, as has been often noted, seemed to be between pilot and writer. The Civil War and other factors made his decision for him. Both occupations allow considerable control: while confined by the facts of the river or of life (such as reader response), the pilot and the writer can go where and when they wish. The level of talent possessed, including the confidence, judgment, and courage that are required to be in control, determines success in either occupation. Of course, either pilot or writer can run aground, depending on bad luck, poor decisions, or lapses in faculties.

This extended analogy of pilot and writer will work with Twain's travel writings if one maintains the illusion that they are the "little" memorandum books of Twain's memory, which allowed him to record observations, to manipulate those insights, and to reflect on life's possibilities. These travel works are not the kind of notes one sees in his notebooks about the river, for they are revisions, complete thoughts, and articulated observations about the relatedness of things. While some of these travel writings seem less successful in relation to each other, they still contain strategies of reading society, of understanding oneself within the context of the times. And, too, as many have noted, they reflect on what are

2. Travel as a Method of Piloting the River of Life   39

perceived to be Twain's greater accomplishments, his novels and short stories. His travel, in this sense, becomes a backdrop, a preparation for his fiction. It comes as little surprise that themes well expressed in (and well received by readers) *Huckleberry Finn, Connecticut Yankee,* and other fictional works are explored in the travel writings. Still, as a social critic and analyst of the human condition, Twain, in his guise of traveler, can use the pilot's training and ability to guide the reader among the changing patterns of life.

The pilot or writer—or, in the current framework, the traveler—needs to write the experience down in order to start memorizing the details. These details then become a shape inside one's mind, not just a memory of, but also a structure so that the "shape of the river" can be a trustworthy guide. As the facts change, and they will, the shape will change even as this shape becomes instinctual and matures over time. The original innocence about these facts may be lost, but a greater realization or recognition will emerge, one that offers a confident mastery of the shape, of the memory of the experience.

This can translate into a formula of remembering, albeit a formula that William Blake might not want, because it limits the imagination in terms of any kind of re-experience of the moment. Twain's formula is an inexact one, a guide to the phenomenology of his travel experiences that shifts over time, because he does not apply it formulaically nor does he neatly account for any contradictions in the formula. Nonetheless, Twain, as a traveler, does attempt to write the experience down, to memorize the pattern, to begin to use the details that he observes as a guide for other travel experiences, and to find a recognizable pattern that will allow him to travel with the perspective of a mature traveler, one who knows the shape of the travel experience, something that will allow him to travel with a confident mastery of that shape. As the travel changes, the facts will change; the traveler can proceed to adapt, serene in knowing the travel experience as a set of paths of knowledge, paths encountered before, measured, observed, internalized, and reshaped to one's necessary ways of encountering new experiences as old ones, modified and transcended while still the same shape. Thus the Grand Tour of Europe or of India can become a comfortable extension of one's expectations about the journey, a journey with few surprises because the traveler has been given not only the facts of the experience but also the method by which these facts can be incorporated into a perspective that allows for the exotic as the familiar.

Twain fulfills the travel writer's general functions as an instructor or guide by providing these facts of the journey within the context of an internalized shape that one can follow as a fellow traveler.

Travel in the abstract consists of the traveler, the journey, and the sites visited. One can, as a number of theorists on the travel experience have done, examine these elements in a number of ways: the ideological, political, rhetorical, and psychological purposes of the traveler; the symbolic, the semantic, and the semiological nature of the trip (manner and mode of the transportation, lodging and payment systems); and the cultural, symbolic, political, and semiological nature of the objects of reverence (artifacts, significant locations, scenic vistas, and so forth). Twain pretends, for example, to be a naive youth on his way to join his brother Orion in Nevada, using the adventurous and dangerous stagecoach, while eating and lodging at frontier way stations and seeming awed and amazed at the notorious outlaw Slade in *Roughing It*. Much of this text focuses on the trip out West as a symbolic quest of the youth becoming a writer, discovering the qualities of the West as a symbolic realm and learning how to adapt to it. It is useful to classify the structures in *Roughing It* in terms of the traveler, the journey, and the sites encountered along the way, because these structures impose themselves on each other, changing and evolving as the journey progresses. The coyote becomes a noble, even mythic, creature, while the youth becomes less naive, more confident; the stagecoach acquires a nostalgic power that the train lacks; the prospector becomes the symbol of capitalism in the wilderness. Travel in Twain's concrete world contains abstract lines that intersect as a map of the West, verifying its place in the text as a frontier where anything is possible.

In his other travel works Twain returns to a common shape of the river, one that allows him (and us as readers) to navigate within the journey, informed about the places and the people we encounter. This helps to explain Twain's penchant for rewriting some of the travel guides that he read. As Dewey Ganzel and others have shown, Twain padded his work with quotations and extensively paraphrased commentaries of other travelers in order to meet publication demands; however, Twain transcends that material because he has appropriated it as an experienced traveler and riverboat pilot. He makes that reading material his own within the context of his shape of the river/life. Hence, his famous description of the Sphinx, which delights in the somber analysis of memory, is written nearly a year after the experience, based on Twain's notoriously fickle memory,

2. Travel as a Method of Piloting the River of Life   41

with few notes taken and no letter written to the *Alta California* about Egypt. Thus Twain can re-create the experience as a traveler might, as a moment of authenticity, of awe, and of reverence.

As a number of critics have observed, one can also take delight in the description of the Sphinx as an elaborate critique of the tourists' expectations, even as a rhetorical flourish meant to parody the usual tourists' search for authenticity. Dewey Ganzel notes, in fact, that Twain had few notes about the Sphinx, that he did not seem overwhelmed at the time, and that other passengers were noticeably unmoved by the sight.[24] Tourists, however, in their search for authenticity, seek to verify their notions of the authentic sight as a memory, even as a photographic frozen moment in time.[25] Twain's parody of the Sphinx description occurs elsewhere in *Innocents Abroad*, using the same rhetorical devices, but this description of his memory serves him well as a recreation of what it might mean to be authentic, that the Sphinx can turn into a sentient being that can recover the lost memories of time, even if it is apparent that stone cannot speak or think. An authentic sight moves tourists into creating that memory, one that a photograph will not capture, except as a reproduction that all tourists realize as something not authentic. The authentic becomes a spiritual moment that can only be generalized as a concept best understood in silence, one that transcends its moment of parody to become something understood by all who share in Twain's vision of the Sphinx.

Twain's travel books, whatever the flaws that a number of critics have noticed, are the little memorandum-books of Twain's imagination, the published versions, the sometimes fairly coherent reflections of his notebooks kept during his lifetime. These texts also reflect different kinds of journeys that Twain takes in order to understand history, tradition, cultures, and the American perspective. That he may not have fully understood what he undertook does not diminish his own realization of what he found, namely a better sense of himself within a complex web of physical and moral elevations, internalizing what he saw in order to develop an internal map of his own. While his travel writings can be compared to traditional travel works of earlier travelers, those individuals who carried civilization to the wilderness, often examining the distance and exploiting the difference between themselves and the savages that they encountered, Twain's work becomes less an examination of Africa or Europe or India than an internalization of what America has become and a record of what he found in himself. The travel works, while they still operate on the level of parody (stretching the bounds of the genre of travel literature), continue to observe traditional elements of the genre. They transcend the travel account meant as pleasurable instruction so that others may benefit from Twain's perspectives on the travel experience, becoming an examination of the human condition. In short, they become a serious dialogue with himself and the reader about what it means to be human, encountering cultures and civilizations that challenge the American experience and received wisdom of what that entails. It is serious stuff, remarkably aligned with his philosophies and his works of literature.

One of the key elements of the travel narrative, as Fussell and Adams argue, is the quest or the journey itself. The narrator goes somewhere deliberately to find something new, to find something that is not familiar, something that is not the home one has gotten overly accustomed to. Fussell devotes a chapter to the sense of loathing toward England, "I Hate It Here" (*Abroad*, 15–23). Fussell's travelers seek refuge from the familiar. Twain writes to his mother: "All I do know or feel, is, that I am wild with impatience to move — move — *Move!* Half a dozen times I have wished I had sailed long ago in some ship that wasn't going to keep me chained here to chafe for lagging ages while she got ready to go ... I wish I never had to stop *any*where a month" (June 1, 1867, Letters, 49–50). Adams suggests, among other things, that this quest can take on mythic proportions of a hero who encounters challenges and overcomes these obstacles, sometimes expelled from his home: "After being driven from home, after escaping an undesirable environment, or after succumbing to curiosity or a restless nature, the continuance of the journey nearly always involved some kind of quest ... involving religion, war, a golden or social utopia, exploration, monetary gain, a person, and a knowledge of the world or oneself" (*Travel Literature*, 153). Adams discusses these seven goals for a traveler as sets of possibilities for the overall quest motif, one used in fiction as well, where the "real traveler, whether a questor from the start or perhaps turning from a motiveless going forth to a quest or pilgrimage, engaged in contests that were more or less frightening, descended into physical or mental hells, and finally underwent rebirth or resurrection to make the ascent or return journey on the river, across the ocean, or through the wilderness" (160). According to Adams, "the traveler-hero finally turns home, the conqueror of great forces, wiser, perhaps sadder, but invariably master of the world he started from as well as all those worlds he encountered during his heroic or adventurous or knowledge-seeking years of wandering" (160).

Twain rarely resorts to a denial of home; rather he demonstrates the opposite, nostalgia for home or place, even to the point of negating past memories in order to resolve conflicting cultural values or re-remember these events in positive ways. His quest offers the anti-heroic stance that the journey is sometimes less important than the arrival at home; he compares Europe, for example, to America and finds that America wins in the comparison (as in *Innocents Abroad* and *Roughing It*). His quest can offer the opposite heroic stance as well, making the journey an indictment of American values. He can realize that technological progress may not lead to moral enlightenment, which he alludes to in *Following the Equator*. Twain's traveling hero, unlike the heroes that Adams finds, does not always find himself; indeed Twain suggests that by traveling one can lose one's identity. Twain finds it difficult to locate a stable reality in a world of uncertain realities. Twain does not always find himself a traditional hero, as Adams claims for that hero someone who is "master of the world he started from as well as all those worlds he encountered" (*Travel Literature*, 160).

As a detached yet involved traveler Twain demonstrates the following characteristics, however unevenly, throughout his travel works. He shows a nostalgia for home or place at the same time he remains uneasy about conflicting cultural values, sometimes negating past memories in order to retain the nostalgia as a positive point of return. He has despair about moral growth in American values, which surfaces sometimes as an awareness that technological progress may not lead to moral enlightenment, sometimes as a notion that civilization itself lacks a foundation of moral enlightenment. He fronts a false bravado that he can retain a stable identity, even as he realizes that society creates a self as much as the self creates an identity. He recognizes that different cultures are very different because each creates a reality that the others can only sometimes understand or barely perceive, each culture parallel (even similar) yet occasionally unfathomable to each other. Twain finds he is unable to understand how these cultures allow any stable moral certitude about one's religion or philosophy. He develops strategies of moral withdrawal that allow him to accept these uncertainties of identity, of comprehension, and of moral righteousness. He develops a method of reacting to these perplexing contradictions and uncertainties by examining the relative nature of "truth." He yearns for and occasionally finds a timeless moment in which to find solace or safety from these complexities of life, realizing most of the time that while one cannot create a timeless moment, hope can mimic its essence. Within this world of piloting the river, Twain learns about the unstable realities of the river, the flux and change that occurs each day, and how to master these unstable realities with an unshakeable confidence in the knowledge (real and instinctual) that he can make time stop — long enough, anyway, so that he can make safe passage. His travel works demonstrate the themes he finds along the way, which create a coherent pattern of belief: nostalgia, insufficient moral American values, rootless identities, strategies of avoidance, and acts of defiance toward time. Some of these themes materialize in the travel works as partially explored concepts, others as evolved frameworks by which to understand the river of life. It is remarkable that the patterns suggested here exist throughout, sometimes just apparent, sometimes overwhelming, as a coherent structure of relationships and ideas within the travel works. Bixby, it seems, may have trained the cub pilot to fathom the rules of life along the river that serve as guidelines for experiencing the world. Of course, it is Twain, not the fictive cub pilot, who learns the river, but it is Twain who formulates these guidelines in the travel experiences that he labors to write about.

3

Innocents Abroad: *A Parody of Tourist Books*

> *Let us be thankful for the fools.*
> *But for them the rest of us could not succeed.*
> — Pudd'nhead Wilson's New Calendar.

Innocents Abroad (1869), Twain's first sustained effort at a book, shows an evolving complexity in his outlook toward the American landscape, which, at first glance, seems to have little to do with his travels in Europe and the Holy Land. This travel book becomes a record of his revision of the memorandum-book that he kept while on the trip, a revision of the 50 letters that he sent to the San Francisco *Alta California* and of some other letters to the New York *Herald* and the New York *Tribune*. Twain had, in fact, revised some of these letters on board the *Quaker City* excursion, with the prompting and influence of Mrs. Mary Fairbanks, a shipboard companion and friend for life, someone who represented civilization and respectable culture to Twain.[26] Later, after contracting with Elisha Bliss of the American Publishing Company in 1868 to write a book about his travels, Twain began using these letters to construct the core of the book, while adding material from his notebooks and travel writings from fellow passengers. While he was in San Francisco to persuade the *Alta* to grant him rights to the letters already published, Bret Harte suggested revisions to make the text less irreverent, more relevant, and more proper.[27] Twain began to edit out "chief faults of construction and inelegancies of expression," in his mind at least, in his letter to Bliss (December 2, 1867), before starting on the project (*MTL*, Vol. 1).

Thus it is that Twain's effort on his first major book becomes a series of revisions of the text until the changing "shape of the river" modifies his thoughts on the trip. A number of commentators have observed that Twain's travel literature did not require much more than a chronological series of events to construct a structure for a coherent text; also, Twain discussed a "running narrative–plank" in a letter to Livy (November 27, 1871), which would provide an alternate series of serious and humorous "plugs" in this narrative structure, allowing another kind of coherence to his published travel notes.[28] In a letter to Michael Laird Simons (January 27–28, 1873), he remarks that "humor cannot do credit to itself without a good background of gravity & of earnestness" (*MTL,* Vol. 5, 284). Hence Twain's revisions in order to provide a narrative structure change the pattern, the tone, and the level of satire in the text. Twain drops much of the sarcasm about his fellow travelers; he reduces the amount of irreverence about locations and ideas; he dispenses with Mr. Brown as a fellow narrator (a useful device in his Hawaiian letters, and also in the *Alta* letters). But the craft of revision has changed the text, so that the original notes on his trip transform Twain's work into what Smith calls "an archetypal fable with elements of epic, tragedy, comedy, and farce depicting the return of the American prodigal to his old home" (*Development,* 37). It is more than just a fable, however. As Smith suggested, *Innocents Abroad* "is partly a journalist's account ... partly an autobiography ... and partly ... an embryonic novel" (22). Twain had not yet written about the strategy of reading the river, but this text demonstrates how he internalized the shape of the river, accumulating sundry facts and generating a map of the journey as a way to negotiate confidently, even imaginatively, through the complexities of the American experience, one that encounters the past while maintaining a stable relationship with the present. Strategies of the narrative structure help create the thoughts expressed; in other words, the style becomes Twain's way to understand what he sees. These revisions generate something greater than the simple travel text, something akin to Smith's "embryonic novel," a reformulation of facts into imaginative discourse that reveals the pattern Twain discovers well after his *Quaker City* excursion. In terms of the traditional quest that some travelers pursue (see Percy G. Adams, *Travel Literature and the Evolution of the Novel*), Twain's trip abroad becomes a journey within himself and a discovery of the terrain that exists in the American psyche. His is a quest to find himself and to find America.

Twain transforms the narrator so that he becomes a spokesman for a set of evolving American concepts about home, moral enlightenment, stable identities, moral uncertainties, and shifting definitions of truth. The created persona, Mr. Brown, so useful as an American innocent in the letters from Hawaii and the original letters to the *Alta*, vanishes in the new, internalized map of his trip, becoming Blucher and Jack, perhaps Twain's internalized voice at times. The narrative voice changes from a relatively innocent one to a mature and well-seasoned one, reflecting an evolution in the narrative voice as the text proceeds. This does not mean that the roles that the narrator plays out remain stable at all; these roles shift from innocent to wise to self-reflexive commentator. The original letters had more venom in them concerning fellow travelers, and in the later full text this sarcasm is changed into introspective analysis. The hostile, even vindictive, attitude toward fellow pilgrims becomes muted in favor of a satirical and self-critical analysis of American egocentric attitudes. The narrator acquires experience but reflects that experience as it happens, appearing as an observer not just of the trip but also of the supposed record of the trip: "But the surest way to stop writing about Rome is to stop. I wished to write a real 'guide-book' chapter on this fascinating city, but I could not do it, because I have felt all the time like a boy in a candy shop — there was everything to choose from, and yet no choice. I have drifted along hopelessly for a hundred pages of manuscript without knowing where to commence" (307). Here the narrator pretends to be a novice at writing a "guide-book," and Twain is, but he is also the mature writer thinking backward on his experiences in Rome. While the "running narrative–plank" of serious and then humorous reflections does create a movement between reverence and undercutting recognition, the narrator seems relatively stable throughout the text.[29]

Innocents Abroad begins innocently enough with a description of the impressions of what the trip should be or become, a "picnic on a gigantic scale" (19). These travelers would "read novels," "watch for the jellyfish," "dance in the open air," "make love," "search the skies for constellations," "see the ships of twenty navies" and [see] the customs and costumes of twenty curious peoples — the great cities of half a world — they were to hobnob with nobility and hold friendly converse with kings and princes" (19–20). Twain includes the program, an extended advertisement for the excursion. Supplements to this glowing description suggest that all is prepared: "excursionists" with "musical instruments," "saddles for Syrian

THE INNOCENTS ABROAD,

OR

THE NEW PILGRIMS' PROGRESS;

BEING SOME ACCOUNT OF THE STEAMSHIP QUAKER CITY'S PLEASURE EXCURSION TO EUROPE AND THE HOLY LAND; WITH DESCRIPTIONS OF COUNTRIES, NATIONS, INCIDENTS AND ADVENTURES, AS THEY APPEARED TO THE

AUTHOR.

WITH TWO HUNDRED AND THIRTY-FOUR ILLUSTRATIONS.

BY

MARK TWAIN,
(SAMUEL L. CLEMENS.)

(ISSUED BY SUBSCRIPTION ONLY, AND NOT FOR SALE IN THE BOOK-STORES. RESIDENTS OF ANY STATE DESIRING A COPY SHOULD ADDRESS THE PUBLISHERS, AND AN AGENT WILL CALL UPON THEM.)

HARTFORD, CONN.:
AMERICAN PUBLISHING COMPANY.
BLISS & CO., NEWARK, N. J.; R. W. BLISS & CO., TOLEDO, OHIO.
F. G. GILMAN & CO., CHICAGO, ILL.; NETTLETON & CO., CINCINNATI, OHIO.
F. A. HUTCHINSON & CO., ST. LOUIS, MO.
H. H. BANCROFT AND COMPANY, SAN FRANCISCO, CAL.
1869.

Title page of *Innocents Abroad*

travel," "green spectacles and umbrellas," "veils for Egypt," and "substantial clothing to use in rough pilgrimizing in the Holy Land" (24). The Holy Land, in fact, "was part of the excursion and seemed to be its main feature" (24). A number of the illustrious fellow passengers, such as Rev. Henry Ward Beecher and General Sherman, were "to have accompanied the expedition," but bow out (24). There is little sense of risk or danger; the savages on this journey will apparently be a number of the travelers rather than the people they will visit. Twain's opening chapter outlines the promise of a relaxed, unhurried, organized, and focused vacation trip. These excursionists will learn about different cultures, visit with royalty, and do the Grand Tour of the Holy Land. It is a quest for knowledge, secular and religious. With the Civil War just ended, it seems an escape from the horrors of that conflict and a mythic return to the Christianity that should have sustained these travelers during that war. It seems appropriate that Sherman and Beecher stay behind as major symbols of war and religion, because the travelers need to find stable markers of civilization assumed to be abroad rather than at home. Twain soon finds that most of the passengers are too puritan in their attitudes and their values.

The opening scenes shift from the "happiness of being for once in my life drifting with the tide of a great popular movement" (11), the naive passenger and narrator filled with expectation, to troubled waters, literally, as the ship is stalled in the harbor, waiting out a storm at sea. Packing for the trip and the accompanying rain had dampened the spirits of the passengers; Twain remarks that he passes his first night on board, "rocked" and "lulled by the murmur of the distant surf," and "soon passed tranquilly out of all consciousness of the dreary experiences of the day and damaging premonitions of the future" (15). "As America faded out of sight," Twain feels a "spirit of charity," "boundless ... as the broad ocean that was heaving its billows about us" (17). Soon enough, many of the passengers, except for Twain, become seasick. Throughout these opening chapters of *Innocents Abroad*, a sense of nostalgia for home pervades, which contradicts the high expectations that Twain suggests the travelers had before embarking on this journey.

Twain seems to be purging these travelers of their past, "so many venerable people" (16). Through the process of traveling on board a ship, he begins to create new identities for them, giving them additional aspects to their stereotypical characters, as well as reimagining them as a collection of societies. The monotonous life on board ship seems to force these pilgrims into creating a community of selves; they learn "sailor terms," "a sign that they were beginning to feel at home" (21). They begin to create routines, playing new shipboard games, following the activities of the crew, and adjusting to the ship's movements. The Christians devote part of their evenings to prayer and to hymns on a regular basis. Twain describes at length the diligent journal-writers who keep track of the trip, which he, in his letters to the *Alta*, joins in spirit. The travelers even try charades and conduct a mock trial. Twain sketches out the individual members of this larger community, such as Jack and George, both naive and young and a bit foolish, and alludes to the Christian pilgrims and their activities. Thus Twain attempts to create the fiction that these different selves have a common purpose, aside from that of traveling to the Mediterranean and the Holy Land, that being the purpose of constructing an American community which will deny the nostalgia felt on leaving America. Much later, on the separate journey to the Holy Land, a number of travelers will further be distinguished as "pilgrims" and another group as "sinners."

Twain describes Mr. Blucher, in particular, "who is from the far West," as a good deal worried about the "constantly changing 'ship time'" (32). Akin to the river changing shape over distance and time, this description follows Blucher's consternation about his watch, which apparently loses time as the ship gains "a full hour every three days" (32). He sets the "regulator up faster and faster ... but it don't do any good" (32). The captain eventually explains "ship time" to him, so Blucher can "set his troubled mind at rest" (33). This brief anecdote simply amplifies the American need for stability despite seeming chaos; it also seems to reflect how these travelers are trying to make adjustments to their lives in order to make stable the shifting realities around them. Blucher wants time to stand still for him, particularly the $150 watch he purchased in Illinois. Some Americans seem obsessed by time. (Indeed, typical cultural simplifications include this notion that American business leaders appreciate punctuality.) Each of these travelers seems wary of losing a sense of place and home, of being adrift in time, a condition familiar to most travelers. George Ritzer and Allan Liska argue that some of the modern tourists of our century wish to have their travel experiences resemble comfortable surroundings, in what they term a "McDonaldized lifeworld."[30] These tourists apparently want to have "highly predictable vacations," "highly efficient vacations," "highly calculable vacations," and "highly controlled vacations" (Ritzer, Liska, 99–100). That is, these tourists wish things to be as familiar as home, time and money spent without waste, itineraries and costs specific in advance, and events and local inhabitants' behavior occurring according to expectations. Blucher's watch by itself is not that significant, but his anxieties are.

This concern for stable time changes the travelers' perspective toward their first stop, the Azores Islands. They are awakened at the inconvenient time of three o'clock in the morning, leaving them "huddled about the smoke-stacks," "looking sleepy and unhappy in the pitiless gale and the drenching spray" (34). The island they first see is Flores, "a mountain of mud standing up out of the dull mists of the sea" (34). They are thwarted by yet another story from their destination, San Miguel, and anchor off Fayal. What they see from a distance through "opera-glasses" seems a "beautiful picture," and "no village could look prettier or more attractive," (35) — until they meet the inhabitants. "A swarm of swarthy, noisy, lying, shoulder-shrugging, gesticulating Portuguese boatmen, with brass rings in their ears, and fraud in their hearts" climb on board to negotiate a tour of Horta, the town they see (35–36). "Beggars" follow the tourists on shore, and "never more, while we tarried in Fayal, did we get rid of them" (36). Described as "vermin" (36), these beggars surround the pilgrims. These pirates reinforce the cultural distance the pilgrims feel from a society other than their own. Not only are they inconvenienced by the time of their arrival, these pilgrims are also jostled by the differences in culture and find themselves uneasy about being enclosed or surrounded by a culture they do not understand. Although Ritzer and Liska refer to tourists of our time, the attitudes that they discuss about a "McDonaldized lifeworld" are applicable to Twain's tourists. Their "beautiful picture," that of the town seen through a sanitized set of expectations, through a boundary layer of civilized opera-glasses, is the postcard that tourists expect to send.[31]

Blucher makes yet another miscalculation, this time about the exchange rate between the Portuguese *reis* and the American dollar. He feels financial ruin when receiving a bill for a dinner for nine of his fellow travelers. He feels he cannot afford the bill of 21,700 *reis*, which he seems to have assumed to be an equivalent amount in dollars. Blucher is relieved to find that the bill is actually only $21.70, so "more refreshments were ordered" (38). The pilgrims are learning, it seems, to adapt to changing circumstances, even if they feel cultural isolation. Here, too, Blucher reminds us of the modern traveler who wants a "highly predictable" and "calculable" vacation (Ritzer, Liska, 99–100).

They are also learning to feel superior to other civilizations and cultures; the community in the Azores "is slow, poor, shiftless, sleepy, and lazy" (39). Here, too, exists a presumed fragment of Christ's cross, described as a "Jesuit humbuggery," and it's noted that "these confiding people believe in that piece of wood unhesitatingly" (41–42). A cathedral contains "a swarm of rusty, dusty, battered apostles ... crippled and discouraged, and fitter subjects for the hospital than the cathedral" (42). While condescending to these people and their religion, the pilgrims try riding donkeys, "making a ridiculous spectacle of ourselves through the principal streets" (43), adding a counterpoint of self-ridicule, though Twain adds, "it was fun ... it was a fresh, new, exhilarating sensation, this donkey-riding, and worth a hundred worn and threadbare home pleasures" (44). Twain seems particularly impressed with the highway system: "The roads were a wonder" (44). He describes the contrast of the "lower classes" in hygienic terms, for they "are not clean," but the "town and the island are miracles of cleanliness" (46). Still, the pilgrims feel morally superior to these inhabitants of the Azores, who attempt to cheat the travelers when it comes time to pay for the donkey ride.

Later, Twain reflects on the nostalgia that the French must surely feel upon being separated from France: "I have observed that Frenchmen abroad seldom wholly give up the idea of going back to France" (98). He does seem particularly impressed with the sense of orderliness in France: "All is clockwork, all is order" (101). But he does not appreciate the railway system, because it does not have a sleeping car or water to drink or "heating apparatus for night travel" (100). Twain also feels nostalgic for America; he describes his trip west on a stage as "infinitely more delightful" (98). "All my pleasure trips," he writes, "must be measured to that rare holiday frolic" (98). He describes this earlier trip in detail:

> The first seven hundred miles a level continent, its grassy carpet greener and softer and smoother than any sea, and figured with designs fitted to its magnitude — the shadows of the clouds ... it was worth a lifetime ... to scan the blue distances of a world that knew no lords but us; to cleave the wind with uncovered head and feel the sluggish pulses rousing to the spirit of a speed that pretended to the resistless rush of a typhoon! Then thirteen hundred miles of desert solitudes; of limitless panoramas of bewildering perspective; of mimic cities, of pinnacled cathedrals, of massive fortresses, counterfeited in the eternal rocks and splendid with the crimson and gold of the setting sun; of dizzy altitudes among fog-wreathed peaks and never-melting snows, where thunders and lightnings and tempests warred magnificently at our feet and the storm-clouds above swung their shredded banners in our very faces! [99].

This shows Twain's admiration for the western landscapes of America and the deconstruction of the benign neglect of the French railway system: "I am in elegant France, now.... It is not meet that I should make too disparaging comparisons between humdrum travel on a railway and that royal summer flight across a continent in a stage-coach" (100). This contrast between America and France seems always to be there as a nostalgia for what the travelers miss most on their trip, a natural world rather than the corrupted one of supposed civilization (represented by the culture in the Azores).

Little amuses these travelers, it seems, while they become "foreignized" (90). They are learning to be better travelers, perhaps, by realizing that they need to carry their own soap (90–91); by "getting reconciled to halls and bed-chambers with unhomelike stone floors, and no carpets" (90); by "getting used to tidy, noiseless waiters, who glide hither and thither" (90); and by learning the "lingering routine" of dinner (91). But the conduct of a few Americans is suspect, particularly one "who talked very loudly and coarsely, and laughed boisterously where all others were so quiet and well behaved" (91–92). In Marseilles they visit the "great Zoological Gardens" and find "a sort of tall, long-legged bird with a beak like a powder-horn, and close-fitting wings like the tails of a dress-coat ... such tranquil stupidity, such supernatural gravity, such self-righteousness, and such ineffable self-complacency as were in the countenance and attitude of that gray-bodied, dark-winged, bald-headed, and preposterously uncomely bird" (92–93). Recognizing that the bird resembles some of their own fellow travelers, they name him "'The Pilgrim'" (93). This bird makes "Dan and the doctor laugh — such natural and such enjoyable laughter had not been heard among our excursionists since our ship sailed away from America" (93). This self-reflexive laughter suggests awareness that the travelers can recognize themselves in other cultures as American types, here as the vulgar American and the pretentious American. Twain amplifies this with a brief anecdote about a cat that wishes to be a companion to an elephant; the elephant is first annoyed but the patient cat perseveres, and sits on his back in the sun; they are now "inseparable friends" (94). This suggests that the laughter is at themselves as well as others; just as the cat and the elephant learn to get along with each other, the travelers begin to adjust to each other, even at the expense of decorum.

It's clear, then, by this preliminary analysis, that Twain's claim in the preface that he has not intended to teach the traveler is somewhat misleading: "I make small pretense of showing any one how he *ought* to look at objects of interest beyond the sea — other books do that, and therefore, even if I were competent to do it, there is no need." If there is a purpose at all, Twain writes, it is "to suggest to the reader how *he* would be likely to see Europe and the East if he looked at them with his own eyes instead of the eyes of those who traveled in those countries before him." The one statement contradicts the other; while they are becoming "foreignized," simply adjusting to different customs, these tourists begin to learn the shape of the country by way of Twain's instructive anecdotes and tales. Twain attempts a paradox in his preface; he is showing a method of deciphering the differences among fellow travelers, namely the pilgrims from the sinners, by the bird in the Zoological Gardens of Marseilles, while pretending not to show the reader how to interpret the signs, the way the bird presents itself to Twain and his fellow sinners. It takes an animal analogy, that of the bird, the cat, and the elephant, but the method of comparison, of analogy, appears to be the way the reader "ought" to understand exotic cultures and fellow travelers. The same holds true for Twain's analysis of France's railway system as it compares unfavorably with the scenic ride of the stagecoach, the short stay at the Azores (the exchange rate, the "humbuggery" of Christian relics), and the feeling of nostalgia that pervades as they set sail. Aside from the "narrative-plank" scheme as a structural device, Twain also employs analogy and comparison as ways to understand the traveling experience. Perhaps, once the method is used, the reader then can apply it through his or her own eyes, but the method is taught, despite Twain's claim that he is merely creating "a record of a pleasure-trip." He is, in fact, teaching us how to travel and what to see.

For example, on the question of timeless states in his travels, Twain writes of the Wandering Jew, a figure condemned to wander the planet because of his rudeness to Christ on the "memorable day of the Crucifixion" (576). This mythical figure "looks always the same," perhaps "looking for some one, expecting some one — the friends of his youth" (577). He is compared to the travelers as well: "The old tourist is far away on his wanderings, now. How he must smile to see a pack of blockheads like us, galloping about the world, and looking wise, and imagining we are finding out a good deal about it! He must have a consuming contempt for the ignorant, complacent asses that go scurrying about the world in these railroading days and call it traveling" (578). This timeless traveler appears throughout in other guises, such as in the occasional biblical story that Twain uses to frame his travels within the context of ahistorical time. Twain writes at length about Joseph and the pit that his brothers throw him into, a pit that "is there in that place, even to this day; and there it will remain until the next detachment of image-breakers and tomb-desecraters arrives from the *Quaker City* excursion, and they will infallibly dig it up and carry it away with them. For behold in them is no reverence for the solemn monuments of the past, and whithersoever they go they destroy and spare not" (493). This sketch about Joseph continues, making this aside about the timeless *Quaker City* excursionists stand out (within its own biblical phrasing as well), not just because of the cynical comment about those pillagers throughout the book, but because it suggests that a universal and timeless ship named the *Quaker City* will arrive again sometime in the future. Twain, in the last chapter of the book, is "moved to confess" that despite all of the difficulties on the trip, "if the *Quaker City* were weighing her anchor to sail away on the very same cruise again, nothing could gratify me more than to be a passenger. With the same captain and even the same pilgrims, the same sinners" (649). There are many moments when time ceases: "There was no sound, no motion. Above the date-plumes in the middle distance, swelled a domed and pinnacled mass, glimmering through a tinted exquisite mist; away toward the horizon a dozen shapely pyramids watched over ruined Memphis: and at our feet the bland impassible Sphynx looked out upon the picture from her throne in the sands as placidly and pensively as she had looked upon its like full fifty lagging centuries ago" (623).

While these appear to be observations about the trip, these comments about time are showing the reader how to remember these isolated images and scenes. Throughout Twain's travel literature the notion that one must recover these moments of time as a static memory, one pure without any regret or pain, helps the reader to best experience the sights along the journey. As Twain writes: "Our experiences in Europe have taught us that in time this fatigue will be forgotten; the heat will be forgotten; the thirst, the tiresome volubility of the guide, the persecutions of the beggars — and then, all that will be left will be pleasant memories of Jerusalem, memories we shall call up always increasing interest as the years go by, memories which some day become all beautiful when the last annoyance that incumbers them shall have faded out of our minds never again to return" (585). Twain continues with an analogy about our own youth: "Schoolboy days are no happier than the days of after life, but we look back upon

"The Quaker City in a Storm "in *Innocents Abroad* (frontispiece). Elisha Bliss, the publisher, used a stock illustration from his firm. The illustrator is unknown.

them regretfully because we have forgotten our punishments at school, and how we grieved when our marbles were lost and our kites destroyed — because we have forgotten all the sorrows and privations of that canonized epoch and remember only its orchard robberies, its wooden sword pageants and its fishing holydays" (585). Memory will create this golden moment of timelessness: "To us Jerusalem and to-day's experiences will be an enchanted memory a year hence — a memory which money could not buy from us" (585). As Carol Crawshaw and John Urry realize, "tourism is the appropriation of the memories of others ... it is the visual images of places that give shape and meaning to the anticipation, experience and memories of traveling" (179).

This method of analogy and timeless memory serves Twain well to compare his past with his present trip. The shape of the river becomes clearer to the reader as well. When measuring out the Pyramid of Cheops Twain returns to his own land: "The first time I ever went down the Mississippi, I thought the highest bluff on the river between St. Louis and New Orleans — it was near Selma, Missouri — was probably the highest mountain in the world. It is four hundred and thirteen feet high. It still looms in my memory with undiminished grandeur. I can still see the trees and bushes growing smaller and smaller as I followed them up its huge slant with my eye, till they became a feathery fringe on the distant summit" (627). The Pyramid of Cheops is higher yet. And, not done, Twain returns to his memory of Holliday's Hill, where he and another boy persuaded a boulder to tumble down some three hundred feet, crashing through the trees, narrowly missing one wagon and driver and crushing a "frame cooper-shop" (628). "That mountain," writes Twain, "was nothing to the Pyramid of Cheops" (628). This technique of showing something familiar, something held in timeless memory, and relating this comparison to the sight found along the journey allows Twain to move between the past and the present as a strategy of familiarization and as a strategy of instruction to the reader.

In Chapter 58, Twain writes a description of the Sphinx that parodies travel writing and punctures a notion of history which glorifies the past:

> After years of waiting it was before me at last.... It was gazing out over the ocean of Time.... It was MEMORY — RETROSPECTION — wrought into visible, tangible form. All who know what pathos there is in memories albeit only a trifling score of years gone by — will have some appreciation of the pathos that dwells in these grave eyes that look so steadfastly back upon the things they knew before History was born — before Tradition had being ... and there is that in the overshadowing majesty of this eternal figure of stone, with its accusing memory of the deeds of all ages, which reveals to one something of what he shall feel when he shall stand at last in the awful presence of God [628–9].

Into this reverie appears a "wart or an excrescence of some kind" on the jaw of the Sphinx. One of Twain's companions, "one of our well-meaning reptiles," "had crawled up there and was trying to break a 'specimen' from the face of this the most majestic creation the hand of man has wrought." This American, typical in *The Innocents Abroad*, wants to take home a piece of history, much as *The Innocents Abroad* attempts to chisel away at the traditions which allow Twain to gaze so sincerely at the Sphinx, a sincerity doubtful in its final strength. Twain knew full well what his readers wished, aside from the humorist's view of Europe or Egypt, a mocking of that sense of timeless history. By way of the revision process, one that included his fiancée, Livy, and Bret Harte, Twain kept the irreverence in while keeping the anger out.[32] Twain also wrestles here with a sense of that timeless history, one that confounded him throughout his career, because he truly wished to have an achievement of timelessness, a merging of past, present, and future, a statement that only partially makes its way into this discourse on time. Later travel writings, particularly *Life on the Mississippi* and *Following the Equator*, also address the nostalgia that he feels about stabilizing time.

Twain practices this stylistic parody of the Sphinx description in other places that he visits. For example, while in Pisa, Italy, he describes "an ancient tear-jug," used by a "bereaved family in that remote age when even the Pyramids of Egypt were young," which received "the tears wept for some lost idol of a household": "It spoke to us in a language of its own; and with a pathos more tender than any words might bring, its mute eloquence swept down the long roll of the centuries with its tale of a vacant chair ... a tale which is always so new to us, so startling, so terrible, so benumbing to the senses.... No shrewdly worded history could have brought the myths and shadows of that old dreamy age before us clothed with human flesh and warmed with human sympathies so vividly as did this poor little unsentient vessel of pottery" (252). The "tear-jug" can hardly stand the test of reverence that the Sphinx might survive.

Elsewhere he describes his visit to Milan's "renowned Cathedral" (171) in much the same way: "At last, a forest of graceful needles, shimmering in the amber sunlight, rose slowly above the pygmy housetops, as one sometimes sees, in the far horizon, a gilded and pinnacled mass of cloud lift itself above the waste of waves, at sea,—the Cathedral. We knew it in a moment" (171). He continues: "What a wonder it is! So grand, so solemn, so vast! And yet so delicate, so airy, so graceful! ... It was a vision!—a miracle!—an anthem sung in stone, a poem wrought in marble! ... Surely, it must be the princeliest creation that ever brain of man conceived" (172).

While in the cathedral, Twain takes note of a sculpture of a "man without a skin," "with every vein, artery, muscle, every fiber and tendon and tissue of the human frame, represented in minute detail" (175). He remarks that it "was a hideous thing, and yet there was a fascination about it somewhere ... I shall dream of it" (175). The sculpture reminds him of a youthful escapade when he decided to sleep in his father's office rather than go home to face the consequences for being out late at night; he remembers seeing a corpse (James McFarland, killed in Hannibal, Missouri, September 1843) on the floor, and then fleeing from the scene: "I have slept in the same room with him often, since then—in my dreams" (177). Twain merges past and present in his dreams, preferring, it seems, the horror of his youthful trauma to the artifice that he sees in Milan, which only fascinates him. By this contrast Twain intensifies his mockery of European artistry, even as it reminds him of his own past. It can be said that many of the sublime human-made scenic vistas that Twain viewed carry with them the threat of death, of human time at an end.

3. Innocents Abroad 59

Twain, in *Roughing It*, seems to back off from mockery when he visits Kilauea (Chapter 74), and when he views the volcano: "I thought it just possible that its like had not been seen since the children of Israel wandered on their long march through the desert so many centuries ago over a path illuminated by the mysterious 'pillar of fire.' And I was sure that I now had a vivid conception of what the majestic 'pillar of fire' was like, which almost amounted to a revelation" (533–34). The Sphinx, an artifact created out of Egyptian granite which has "defied the storms and earthquakes of all time," and "has nothing to fear from the tack hammers of ignorant excursionists," is human, yet the volcano is a natural occurrence. The two both propel Twain to write about them as "the awful presence of God" and as a "revelation." As noted, however, the human sublime event or scene provokes thoughts of mortality, while the natural vista seems to present images of eternity. Also, the Hawaiian volcano description is "smouched" from Twain's earlier letters to the *Alta*, and represents, perhaps, a different stage of appreciation for nature, besides the lessened venom for annoying tourists; these letters do not have the same origin of writing, that of memory for Twain (remembering being a different method), the letters representing a set of descriptions without time for reflection. *Innocents Abroad* is a revisionist history, a revising of letters with a changed purpose, that of comparing Europe to America.

Thus it is that in *The Innocents Abroad* Twain follows up his seeming reverie with a capitalistic, nineteenth-century American response, that of measuring the Sphinx and comparing its relative size with "the Fifth Avenue Hotel," and with a remark on the time it took to carve it, "a hundred years of patient toil." In *Roughing It*, the volcano provides "room for the imagination to work!" and was the "idea of eternity made tangible," a volcano erupting in Twain's text (Chapter 75) as an event from 1840, the "devastation consummated along the route traversed by the river of lava," "complete and incalculable" (543). True, *Roughing It* also presents a few facts, the width and depth of the lava stream and its length of its destruction, but the final comment in Chapter 75 reverts to a sense of timelessness: "Only a Pompeii and a Herculaneum were needed at the foot of Kilauea to make the story of the eruption immortal" (543). At the end of Chapter 58 in *The Innocents Abroad*, Twain's narrator returns to a reverie, one that praises the accomplishments of Egypt, the "mother of civilization," an "advanced civilization" which had "built temples which mock at destroying time." The contrast to the Egypt of Twain's time, a civilization no longer on the rise but on the decline, makes clear the frailty of human endeavor.

On the surface it appears that Egypt's accomplishments are also timeless, as much as the natural event in Hawaii. But the traveler in Egypt records events that occurred long ago, while the traveler in Hawaii records current events. There is a distinct difference in terms of relative praise. An intruding traveler can chip the Sphinx away, while nature resists mockery of any kind. In Chapter 76 of *Roughing It*, Twain describes a cataract "leaping from a sheer precipice fifteen hundred feet high; but that sort of scenery finds its staunchest ally in the arithmetic rather than in spectacular effect" (546). Twain writes, "If one desires to be so stirred by a poem of Nature ... he need not go away from America to enjoy such an experience" (546). He uses the "Rainbow Fall, in Watkins Glen (N.Y.)" as an example: "It would recede into pitiable insignificance if the callous tourist drew an arithmetic on it; but left to compete for the honors simply on scenic grace and beauty — the grand, the august and the sublime being barred the contest — it would challenge the old world and the new to produce its peer" (546).

Rather than find fault with America's lack of history, Twain here provides yet one more reason to praise America as a process of discovery. As each vista in the West is visualized, it becomes greater than time itself. The Sphinx represents that portion of the past now recovered as "MEMORY"; it may move us yet, but only without a sense of movement, the kind that makes *Roughing It* a journey while *The Innocents Abroad* becomes a visit. In Chapter 59 of *The Innocents Abroad*, Twain rests after the trip to the Sphinx and describes the traveler as "lazy and satisfied," having little to do on board ship for several weeks: "What a stupid thing a notebook gets to be at sea anyway." The memory of the Sphinx becomes insipid. The trip itself becomes a useful memory for Americans, allowing the younger culture to admire the older one but with the realization that America itself will prove to be the truest adventure.

4

Roughing *It:* Travel as a Way to Find an Identity

There are two times in a man's life when he should not speculate: when he can't afford it, and when he can.
— Pudd'nhead Wilson's New Calendar.

Roughing It and *Following the Equator* present differences in spatial and temporal concepts. The difference in years between these two works amplify the nature of Twain's sense of risk, chance, and the unknown; and the growth in consciousness about identity, maturity, culture, society, race, and travel. For example, *Following the Equator* emphasizes identity, maturity, race, and travel, while the earlier work more sharply defines and describes risk, chance, the unknown, and society, the later work providing a penetrating analysis of culture, race and travel, the earlier providing conventional schemes of discussing culture, race, and travel. *Roughing It* demonstrates the energy of involvement within a wilderness, while *Following the Equator* shows the apathy of hidden and unrealized despair, having lost some of the nostalgia for nature. In both, however, Twain reveals aspects of the traveler, one who observes, participates, and learns from the experience of the adventure. Twain's response in both works toward space, the human involvement within spaces, territorial and cultural, reveals the history of the times while participating in the transformation of American cultural attitudes. America's energy in conquering the wilderness and the western landscape had faded in the latter part of the century. No longer did the frontier present itself as a domain to be

ROUGHING

IT

BY

MARK TWAIN.
(SAMUEL L. CLEMENS.)

FULLY ILLUSTRATED BY EMINENT ARTISTS.

(ISSUED BY SUBSCRIPTION ONLY, AND NOT FOR SALE IN BOOK STORES.)
(RESIDENTS OF ANY STATE DESIRING A COPY SHOULD ADDRESS THE PUBLISHERS AS BELOW.)

HARTFORD, CONN.:
AMERICAN PUBLISHING COMPANY.
F. G. GILMAN & CO., CHICAGO, ILL.; W. E. BLISS, TOLEDO, OHIO.;
NETTLETON & CO., CINCINNATI, OHIO.; D. ASHMEAD, PHILADELPHIA, PENN.;
J. W. GOODSPEED, NEW ORLEANS, LA.;
A. ROMAN & COMPANY, SAN FRANCISCO, CAL.
1872.

Title page of *Roughing It*

conquered (except, perhaps, for Alaska). Railroads and civilization tamed the natural wilderness. Twain would suggest in *Following the Equator* that the earlier dependence on moral superiority and the earlier confidence that technological and colonial progress would benefit all had faded as well. These spatial and temporal differences seem vast, but *Roughing It* proves to be an evolutionary process from *Innocents Abroad*, a process leading toward *Following the Equator*.

Roughing It (1872) came on the heels of the success of the first travel book, although Twain thought a book on Hawaii might be more promising. He did have some 25 letters that he had written on the topic of the Sandwich Islands (as they were called then) for the *Sacramento Union* in 1866. He would, much later, consider and start a novel on Hawaii in 1884; much of his early fame derived from his lecture tours based on material concerning his Hawaiian letters. But he changed the general topic to his western years, borrowing Orion's notebook about the trip, and using a scrapbook of his western newspaper and magazine articles. During the summer of 1870, Twain negotiated a contract with Elisha Bliss, of the American Publishing Company, and started writing the manuscript. His progress with the text was slow; his father-in-law, Jervis Langdon, died in August, his wife Livy became ill (while pregnant), Livy's friend Emma Nye died in Twain's Buffalo home in September, and in November, their first child was delivered prematurely. But by July of 1871, he had progressed to his trip to Hawaii; short of material for the subscription book, he appropriated his earlier letters for the *Union*, and finished the manuscript in August of 1871. *Roughing It* finally appeared in February of 1872.

The letters that he had written for the *Sacramento Union* in 1866 were incorporated in revised form of chapters 62–73 of *Roughing It*, leaving out a dialogue with Mr. Brown, a foil and companion for these letters, some history of Hawaii, an account of the *Hornet*'s sinking in the Pacific (and the heroic struggle of its captain to take survivors to Hawaii), an account of Honolulu's prison, notes and statistics on the sugarcane and whaling industries, and other facts about Hawaii's social life. A. Grove Day's edition, *Mark Twain's Letters from Hawaii*, is a useful reprinting of these letters. Some of the data on sugar production may be historically interesting (or even accurate) but would surely be out of place in *Roughing It*, so the cumulative revisions of these letters for the end of that later text make a good deal of sense. *Roughing It*, as many readers have noted, seems uneven with the addition of the Hawaiian material, which Twain used to pad the text to meet his contract with Elisha Bliss. Twain would certainly profit from his many lectures that included a description of the volcano Kilauea.

The *Hornet*'s sinking in the Pacific is an omission from *Roughing It*, one that perhaps omits the narrator entirely, thus making its absence suitable for the longer text. The nature of this sketch, however, contains several elements that are well within the scope of travel literature. Some travel works emphasize the nature of risk, which certainly can be found in the hazardous journey of the survivors who manage to sail in their lifeboat some 3,000 miles to Hawaii under the capable leadership of Captain Josiah Mitchell. The traditional aspects of travel are detailed by Twain; he describes their food, their transportation, their lodging, their sights along the way, all being quite dreary and desperate. Food consists of whatever they had on hand and whatever they can catch from the sea. Their transportation and lodging are basic and uninviting. Their sights are few, mainly the pitiless ocean during the day and some stars at night. The sense of nostalgia for home and for safety is clear; their loss of time as a guide is ample; their identities begin to merge into each others as desperate individuals. They are welcomed back into society, the public eager to hear their stories, reconstructions from their memories put into words by the still-new journalist Samuel Clemens. Twain used material from Mitchell and other survivors to write "Forty-three Days in an Open Boat," published in *Harper's Magazine* in December, 1866. Stephen Crane's version may be more literary, but Twain's is the story that captured attention, being true and exciting.

As noted earlier, Twain's reading of the typical tour guide format is astute. Mr. Brown, the fictional companion, remarks that a missionary returns to the mainland determined to write a travel book: "You just look at Rev. Cheever's book and Anderson's — and when they come to the volcano, or any sort of heavy scenery, and it is too much bother to describe it they shovel in another lot of Scripture, and wind up with 'Lo! What God hath wrought'" (*Letters from Hawaii*, 210–11).[33] Twain is conversant with traditional travel literature such as Anderson's and Cheever's works, and these letters demonstrate a neutral response to the kinds of oppression that the Hawaiian natives face with the Christian morality that would civilize them.

Twain's letters also show the two voices that would later become one angry anti–Pilgrim of *Innocents Abroad*; the persona of the journalist responds to Mr. Brown with an elevated diction and stilted response to the affront just offered: "Mr. Brown, I brought you with me on this voyage merely because a newspaper correspondent should travel in some degree of state, and so command the respect of strangers; I did not expect you to assist me in my literary labors with your crude ideas. You may desist from further straining your intellect for the present, Mr. Brown, and proceed to the nearest depot and replenish the correspondent fountain of inspiration" (*Letters from Hawaii*, 211). Mr. Brown's voice seems to reflect the kind of vulgar regard for religion that Twain perhaps shares, while the journalist's voice is that of the literary elitist that Twain comes to loathe. Mr. Brown speaks sarcastically of the travel writer's need to praise the effects of the Christian missionary on natives, to describe native customs and legends, and to use the Bible to describe nature instead of using vernacular language. The travel writer here is Twain, of course, and, while there are occasional biblical references, the deference to religion is slight, as in his reaction to Kilauea's sounds and smells: "The smell of sulphur is strong, but not unpleasant to a sinner" (297). Twain's actual description of the volcano depends on the purple prose style that he could easily emulate: "For a mile and a half in front of us and half a mile on either side, the floor of the abyss was magnificently illuminated; beyond these limits the mists hung down the gauzy curtains and cast a deceptive gloom over all that made the twinkling fires in the remote corners of the crater seem countless leagues removed — made them seem like the campfires of a great army far away. Here was room for the imagination to work! You could imagine those lights the width of a continent away — and that hidden under the intervening darkness were hills, and winding rivers, and weary wastes of plain and desert — and even then the tremendous vista stretched on and on and on!— to the fires and far beyond! (294).

Mr. Brown appears again in a series of letters written for the *Alta California* for the period between Twain's departure from San Francisco in 1866, his journey to New York, and his trips to Missouri and locations in the Midwest, letters written before he began his travel adventure on the *Quaker City* in 1867. These are collected in an edition by Franklin Walker and G. Ezra Dane entitled *Mark Twain's Travels with Mr. Brown*. Brown appears again for the letters written while on the *Quaker City*, but disappears in the revisions for *Innocents Abroad*. Brown does serve the purpose of disguise; he is Twain to the degree that his is the vernacular voice, the practical Yankee and the uncouth American, someone independent in spirit and conversant with the virtues of the American frontier. The other voice, that of the journalist, is folksy as well, but pretends to be a bit more cosmopolitan and urbane.

The letters written before the *Quaker City* excursion have merit, certainly, but they lack a structure, a perspective or slant, something the Hawaiian letters have — an uncertainty about the missionary work that is changing Hawaiian culture. The *Quaker City* letters have sarcasm about the pilgrim passengers, a resistance to the traveler's deification of Europe, and a stubborn American independence from the refined sensibilities of the wealthy class or self-indulgent artist. There are hints of this reluctance to admire uncritically some of the values of high culture in these American tour letters of 1866–67. In a letter dated June 2, 1867, from New York City, where he is contemplating the expected extravaganzas of the *Quaker City* tour, he analyzes the features of Alfred Bierstadt's painting of the Yosemite Valley, suggesting that these are "natural" and "correct," but that the "atmosphere" (or sky) seems quite unrealistic, that it has modified the mountains and the natural landscape too greatly: "We do not want this glorified atmosphere smuggled into a portrait of the Yosemite, where it surely does not belong. I may be wrong, but still I believe that this atmosphere of Mr. Bierstadt's is altogether too gorgeous" (*Travels with Mr. Brown*, 251). This tentativeness about his opinion — "I may be wrong" — dissipates with later travel works. Twain felt these letters lacked substance; he writes to his mother the day before he departs on the *Quaker City* that "I haven't got *any*thing to write else I *would* write it. I have just written myself clear out in letters to the *Alta*, & I think they are the stupidest letters that were ever written from New York. Corresponding has been a perfect drag ever since I got to the States. If it continues, abroad, I don't know what the Tribune & Alta folks will think" (*MTL*, Vol. 2, 57; June 7, 1867).

Solving that problem of writer's block in *Innocents Abroad* — by finding a way to visualize the *Quaker City* excursion as an attack against the pretensions of the Christian traveler and as an exploratory revision of the genre of the traditional travel book — leads him back to the comfort of the States, and lets him overcome his first meager attempt at looking at America. *Roughing It* returns him to a new way of examining the role of the wise traveler, not from the vantage point of the already-formed narrator of *Innocents Abroad*, but from an evolving consciousness of the riverboat pilot he clarifies in *Life on the Mississippi*. Twain still lacks a traveler's roadmap of how to look at the landscape of life, but the outlines of that roadmap are becoming clearer. For *Innocents Abroad* Twain had the 50 letters that he sent to the San Francisco *Alta California*, and some other letters to the New York *Herald* and the New York *Tribune*. He borrowed from the notebooks, letters, and journals of other passengers; he appropriated material from contemporary travel works. These form the core of the "facts" of the river. *Roughing It* proved a bit more challenging; he needed Orion's thin journal; he needed to rely on his memory, that all-important facility of the riverboat pilot's confident mastery of the river. Twain did not have letters from the West to rely on, merely to revise and to add material as needed. He required an imaginative reconstruction of the "shape" of the trip, of the "shape" of the experience that helped form his identity as a writer.

Roughing It differs from *The Innocents Abroad* from the beginning preface in each text; Twain pretends to offer the European traveler "how he would be likely to see Europe and the East if he looked at them with his own eyes instead of the eyes of those who traveled in those countries before him," and claims in *Roughing It* the book "is merely a personal narrative," with a purpose of helping the "reader while away an idle hour," providing "a good deal of information" about the West. Clearly *The Innocents Abroad* does give the reader a roadmap to understanding the European experience from the American perspective, but *Roughing It* does much the same with the American experience, that is, attempting to explain the West from an Easterner's eyes (here, too, a European outlook).

Twain makes a point, after the specious claim of not meaning to write "pretentious history," to write his own "history" of the "rise, growth, and culmination of the silver-mining fever in Nevada" (iv). Indeed, it is curious to see Twain point at that one set of circumstances when so many episodes and details occur on a wide variety of topics in the book, such as his side-trip to Hawaii, his discussion of Mormon history, his description of Jack Slade, and his stay in San Francisco. This text becomes much more than a rambling history of capitalism at work in the West; Twain moves further West in terms of the frontier perspective, attempting to explain what the West is in terms of its boundaries, both physical and moral. If indeed Twain needs to write out this "history" without using his usual means of revising from travel letters—a strategy that, of course, he developed earlier for *Innocents Abroad*—he must depend on his memory, a memory that is a decade or more old. He reconstructs the past by revising his own sense of his identity, recognizing that this pivotal period of his life reflects not just the prospecting fever in Nevada but parallels his own development as a writer living on the frontier.

Much informs us in *Roughing It* of this frontier perspective. At the end of Chapter 6, one anecdote, which captures the spirit of *The Innocents Abroad* as well as referring directly to his earlier work, shows Twain's interest in contrasting the West to the East. Twain, in this chapter, seems to be relating the details of the Western transportation system, including the responsibilities of the conductor and driver of the stage coach, and to be admiring the sense of control that one "Ben Holliday" has over this "great portion of this vast machinery" (57). Twain also relates (from his "Holy Land note-book"— an entry which cannot be found in the surviving notebooks) the story of "a young New York boy by the name of Jack" who does not recognize the name of Moses, "the great guide, soldier, poet, lawgiver of ancient Israel," who, as an "elderly pilgrim" reminds Jack, "brought the children of Israel" over the course of forty years some three hundred miles to the "Promised Land." (58–59). Jack responds: "Forty years? Only three hundred miles? Humph! Ben Holliday would have fetched them through in thirty-six hours!" (59). As Twain remarks, "The boy meant no harm. He did not know that he had said anything that was wrong or irreverent" (59). While capturing the essence of *The Innocents Abroad*, that is, mocking a European tradition or custom or notion with an American sentiment, this brief story about Jack suggests the myth of the western giant, someone so competent and so powerful, that he can compete successfully with a biblical hero. This theme runs throughout *Roughing It*: the West (as a boundary region) ennobles those individuals who can tame it.

The Innocents Abroad differs principally as an earlier work simply because it does something which *Following the Equator* will later diminish, that of collapsing pretensions of European tradition with the innocent eye of the traveler, as presented through the tale of Jack and Ben Holliday. This apparent fiction — the tale of Jack in the Holy Land — reminds us of Twain's commercial success with *The Innocents Abroad*, relying on his readers to remember one of the threads of that earlier travel work, that Europe is a civilization on the decline while America is a civilization progressing toward a positive future. This new America will also leave behind old notions of history and biblical myth.

Roughing It emphasizes this new America, one dominated by nature, a spirit of the West. Twain seems absorbed by the splendor of nature at the dead volcano of Haleakala, where the narrator seems absorbed by the splendor of nature. Clouds then build, "the snowy floor stretched without a break ... the impressive scene overawed speech. I felt like the Last Man, neglected of the judgment, and left pinnacled in mid-heaven, a forgotten relic of a vanished world" (550). The sun breaks through, "glorifying the massy vapor-palaces and cathedrals with a wasteful splendor of all blendings and combinations of rich coloring" (550). Twain continues, "It was the sublimest spectacle I ever witnessed, and I think the memory of it will remain with me always" (550). One might then assume that the sphinx, as a memory, is overshadowed by this Western spectacle. There is no Blucher or any other "excrescence" marring the surface of the vision, chipping away at any notion of history. If the Western landscape on the journey in *Roughing It* rivals or even eclipses European vistas, then what can we find concerning the moral boundary between America and the rest of the world? The relic-hunter in *The Innocents Abroad* represents one aspect of the American self, the innocent who lacks a moral center when it comes to the past. One may appropriate souvenirs from history without respect for that history. However, a much different kind of Blucher-figure becomes apparent, one threatening violence and death.

This difference becomes more apparent and alarming in *Roughing It* when figures such as Jack Slade appear. In Chapter 10, Slade's exploits are detailed (sometimes with the pretense of being fictionalized) as if the man were a hero, but a hero of betrayal and violence. Slade kills enemies without warning, once shooting a "Frenchman who had offended Slade" sometime after the offense, "pushed the corpse inside the door with his foot, set the house on fire and burned up the dead man, his widow and three children" (86). When the narrator meets Slade, he writes "Here was romance, and I sitting face to face with it!—looking upon it—touching it—hobnobbing with it, as it were! Here, right by my side, was the actual ogre who, in fights and brawls and various ways, had taken the lives of twenty-six human beings, or all men lied about him! I was the proudest stripling that ever traveled to see strange lands and wonderful people" (87–88). Indeed, the narrator finds Slade to be "friendly" and "pleasant" (88). In Chapter 11, Slade's eventual demise is detailed, using an account by one Thos. J. Dimsdale. Twain writes, "The true desperado is gifted with splendid courage, and yet he will take the most infamous advantage of his enemy" (95). Twain believes that it is a "conundrum worth investigating" how Slade could demonstrate courage without moral backbone (96); Slade begs for his life at the end as well. This puzzle appears in one guise in *Adventures of Huckleberry Finn* with the familiar story of Colonel

Sherburn shooting Boggs in cold blood and facing down a lynch mob. This Western hero, evil and courageous, has other avatars in *Roughing It*, notably with the tale about the Western coyote and the Eastern dog, and the references to Mormon culture.

In Chapter 5, the coyote (spelled cayote in the text) is "not a pretty creature or respectable either," a "sorry-looking skeleton," with a "tail that forever sags down with a despairing expression of forsakenness and misery, a furtive and evil eye," a "living, breathing allegory of Want," and is "spiritless and cowardly" (48–49). Twain as narrator describes how one cannot easily shoot this pathetic creature, because the animal is so clever and fast. He then imagines a "swift-footed dog after him," "especially if it is a dog that has a good opinion of himself," and shows how the dog cannot catch him (50). The coyote "will go swinging gently off on that deceitful trot of his, and every little while he will smile a fraudful smile over his shoulder that will fill that dog entirely full of encouragement and wordly ambition" (50). The dog begins "to get aggravated," especially when he sees "how gently the cayote glides along and never pants or sweats or ceases to smile" (50). At the end of a frantic chase, the coyote finally departs with a "sudden splitting of a long crack through the atmosphere," leaving the dog "solitary and alone in the midst of a vast solitude" (51). The dog seems to have lost his enthusiasm, taking up a "humble position under the hindmost wagon," feeling "unspeakably mean" (51). Twain discusses the hardships of the coyote as a carrion eater with respect and admiration: "Remembering his forlorn aspect and his hard fortune, [we] made shift to wish him the blessed novelty of a long day's good luck and limitless larder the morrow" (53).

This brief anecdote about the coyote and the dog (described as a "town-dog," probably an eastern one) serves well as an analogy for the traveler in *Roughing It*, notably Twain's persona. In Chapter 1, Twain describes himself as "young and ignorant" in his trip West with his brother Orion (19). Travel "had a seductive charm for me" (19). Orion "would see buffaloes and Indians," "have all kinds of adventures," and "write home and tell us all about it, and be a hero" (19). Twain jumps at the chance when offered a position of secretary to his brother, in order to travel with Orion (actually, this position did not materialize until later in Nevada). Throughout *Roughing It* this "young and ignorant" traveler encounters a number of Western characters, such as the coyote and Slade. When confronted, the traveler appreciates the survival instincts, even the "cowardly" aspects, the native skills and "splendid courage" that he sees, while remarking on the brutality of life; this apparent contradiction — fearing the character of Slade, an "ogre," yet being the "proudest stripling that ever traveled to see strange lands and wonderful people"— constructs the landscape of the American West in *Roughing It*. Twain also tries to capture the "vigorous new vernacular" of the West (Chapter 4), the language used to express the frontier's energy and new morality. Terms used for the coyote, for example, "allegory of Want," "spiritless," "cowardly," are turned upside down to reflect positive qualities — the coyote becomes a force in nature to be admired.

Thus it is that Twain's encounters with Mormon culture betray this contradiction. Twain has supper with a Mormon Destroying Angel, "Latter-Day Saints who are set apart by the Church to conduct permanent disappearances of obnoxious citizens" (106). This Destroying Angel, "alas for all our romances," "was nothing but a loud, profane, offensive, old blackguard"(106). Twain asks, "Could you respect an Angel with a horse-laugh and a swagger like a buccaneer?" (106). Other travelers have written that this Destroying Angel, Eph Hanks, was actually the opposite to Twain's description, while Heber C. Kimball's son, briefly mentioned, fits it well. In any case, Twain inverts the expectation that the Destroying Angel was to be feared. The Stranger, in Twain's fiction, is often someone who seems to have a dual personality, one with a heart of gold and the other with a black heart, similar to Hank Morgan (who destroys his civilization) or Huck Finn (who needs to decide between the laws of his time and the code of his developing conscience).

As Twain walks the streets of Salt Lake City, "a land of enchantment," an "awful mystery," he wishes to ask each child "how many mothers it had, and if it could tell them apart," providing the stereotypical response some Americans had toward polygamy and the Mormon religion in general (108). While Twain pokes fun at polygamy, particularly at the jealousy of many wives and the annoyance of many tin whistles among a large flock of children (Chapter 15), his two appendices to the book reveal a good deal of common prejudice and some misinformation. Appendix A is largely a paraphrase of Waite's *The Mormon Prophet*, in fact a technique of historical transcription that Twain uses elsewhere to pad the text, either because he wishes to add verisimilitude to his narrative or to fulfill the obligations of his contract with a publisher. There does seem to be a hard edge to Twain's comments about the Mormon religion, but this accords well with Twain's comments about any culture which seems to tolerate polygamy in any form. He writes in a discarded chapter on France in *A Tramp Abroad* that "in clean-mindedness & in certain departments of social morals, the Frenchman compares quite favorably with the Turk, the Mormon, the Fijian, the early Sandwich Islander, & the inhabitant of Dahomey" (*MELM*; formerly Box 6, # 55). His claim is that all French households have a "harem." Religion and its culture create a morality that differs from preconceived concepts about any civilized religion, mainly that the family consists of one father, one mother, and any children born to that couple. Here, Twain sides with the stereotypical reaction to the Mormon religion, that it is suspect in its origins and a sham.

Chapter 16, in particular, attacks the Book of Mormon as a "prosy detail of imaginary history, with the Old Testament for a model; followed by a tedious plagiarism of the New Testament" (127). Twain reviews the use of language in the Book of Mormon at great length, using quotations freely to show how false the text is, and how it is "rather stupid and tiresome to read" (135). He ridicules Brigham Young for having had a revelation allowing polygamy, quoting a passage which declares polygamy as an "abomination" (132, Twain's phrasing). He does write that "there is nothing vicious in its teachings," and that "its code of morals is unobjectionable" (135). His response, however, mirrors the doubt that many Americans shared, not just about the religion but also about the morality of those practicing it in Utah.

As a counterpoint to this apprehension, Chapter 13 shows an admiration for the sense of industry and civilization, "a grand general air of neatness, repair, thrift, and comfort," with "workshops, factories, and all manner of industries," and "with the ceaseless clink of hammers, the buzz of trade and contented hum of drums and fly-wheels" (109–10). Twain claims to have "talked long with that shrewd Connecticut Yankee, Heber C. Kimball (since deceased), a saint of high degree and mighty man of commerce" (112). (One wonders how much of this admiration spills over into the later novel *A Connecticut Yankee in King Arthur's Court*.)

In the same chapter (13), Twain demonstrates how powerless he may have felt in this land of "enchantment" and moral denial (doubting the religion and the morality of its leaders). Orion had been asked by the U.S. State Department to clarify Brigham Young's intentions during the Civil War, so Twain accompanies his brother with other government officials for a visit with Young. Twain makes several attempts at conversation with

Young, "but he merely looked around at me, at distant intervals something as I have seen a benignant old cat look around to see which kitten was meddling with her tail." While departing, Young "beamed down on me in an admiring way and said to my brother: 'Ah — your child, I presume? Boy, or girl?'" (113).

Thus the traveler seems deflated by his inability to converse with Young, suggesting the inability to understand his admiration for Young's "absolute monarchy" while fearing it. This impasse of conversation spells out Twain's apparent blank wall of comprehension, which most Americans felt concerning the inhabitants of Utah. Chapter 15 begins with a statement about Utah being a "luscious country for thrilling evening stories about assassinations of intractable Gentiles," and, later, about "how heedless people often come to Utah and make remarks about Brigham, or polygamy ... the very next morning at daylight such parties are sure to be found lying up some back alley, contentedly waiting for the hearse" (119).

All of this may have been titillating information for the reader, but it also formed part of the consciousness of Twain as traveler. He both feared and respected the Mormons. The sense of organization and power that they possessed seems to have galvanized him, while the apparent treachery they also demonstrated seems to have left him uneasy at best: "I left Great Salt Lake a good deal confused as to what state of things existed there — and sometimes even questioning in my own mind whether a state of things existed there at all or not" (136–37). Twain does not suggest that he might wind up in "some back alley" for his remarks, but that Utah provides "thrilling evening stories." By dismissing the Book of Mormon as a work of plagiarists and by being dismissed himself by Brigham Young, Twain senses the moral risks that he faces by not understanding fully his experiences as a traveler in Utah: He does not understand how a fraud like Brigham Young could also be such a powerful leader. In other words, how can Twain justify a lapse in morality with the apparent prosperity and industry that it produces? Religion is confounding to Twain at times; Catholics, though reviled elsewhere and often, occasionally have redeeming characteristics.

The physical risks Twain took in *Roughing It* elsewhere seem less threatening than those moral risks he confronted in Utah. In chapters 30 and 31, Twain and his party do face the rising waters of the Carson River, but there is little sense of doom about being trapped for eight days. Once Twain's group decides to leave Honey Lake Smith's, the way station on the

Carson, there is a brief moment of danger, as Twain and his company are almost swept away into the still raging waters, but "we managed to push the boat ashore and make a safe landing" (227).

Chapter 32, however, presents the greatest risk to Twain, when all seems lost in a snowstorm, the horses gone with just four matches left. When all fail to light a pile of sticks successfully, the last flame giving off "a sort of human gasp" before going out, all members of the group feel "that this was our last night with the living" (235). Ollendorff, Ballou, and Twain forgive each other past sins, while renouncing individual ones, such as drinking, gambling, and smoking. The snow continues to cover them, and "we bade each other a last farewell" (237). "A delicious dreaminess wrought its web about my yielding senses, while the snow-flakes wove a winding sheet about my conquered body," writes Twain (237). Then in the following chapter Ballou realizes that the stage station is "not fifteen steps from us," with their missing horses "under a shed" (238). Miffed and "sullen" that the "whole situation was so painfully ridiculous and humiliating," the intrepid travelers seek shelter, "angry at ourselves" (238). The next morning, Twain searches for and finds his pipe, while discovering that Ballou and Ollendorf have also reverted to their vices of gambling and drinking.

Here, the kind of physical risk that Twain undertakes shows nature

"The South Pass" in *Roughing It*. Illustration by Roswell Morse Shurtleff.

at her most indifferent and destructive moments. Nature cares not about the morality of humans, for the vices these travelers share do not ensnare them nor do they, once dropped, save them. If anything, nature appears benign, while lethal. One could almost use this as evidence that Twain uses a theme that later Naturalists proclaimed, that nature is "flatly indifferent," as Stephen Crane would write in "The Open Boat."

Twain does admit that nature can also be soothing. During his sojourn at Lake Tahoe, Twain's mood is calm and enthusiastic. Just as Huck enjoys floating down the river, so too does Twain enjoy "drifting around in the boat" (174). Twain writes that he and his friend Johnny (John D. Kinney) "lolled on the sand in camp, and smoked pipes and read some old well-worn novels" (175). Lake Tahoe, "a noble sheet of blue water lifted six thousand three hundred feet above the level of the sea, and walled in by a rim of snow-clad mountain peaks that towered aloft full three thousand feet higher still," impresses Twain as "the fairest picture the whole earth affords" (169).

Twain accidentally sets fire to this pristine wilderness, and the pair of adventurers find themselves on the beach, watching a "tossing, blinding tempest of flame" (176). Twain's impression of this disaster, aside from being "homeless wanderers," suggests an awe at nature's beauty in destroying the wilderness: "As far as the eye could reach the lofty mountain-fronts were webbed as it were with a tangled net-work of red lava streams. Away across the water the crags and domes were lit with a ruddy glare, and the firmament above was a reflected hell" (176). He continues: "Every feature of the spectacle was repeated in the glowing mirror of the lake! Both pictures were sublime, both were beautiful; but that in the lake had a bewildering richness about it that enchanted the eye and held it with the stronger fascination" (176). The similarities to Hawaiian volcanoes, "lava streams," "reflected hell," suggest a common thread here: nature's healing powers for the soul in terms of beauty and enchantment also bring the threat of conflagration and destruction. Indeed, Twain's identity as an observer can be lost within this nature: "We sat absorbed and motionless through four long hours. We never thought of supper, and never felt fatigue" (176–77). Nature even becomes an experience that cannot be expressed adequately: "We made many trips to the lake after that, and had many a hair-breadth escape and blood-curdling adventure which will never be recorded in any history" (177). One can only imagine that these adventures help form Twain's sense of nature's beauty and power. He might also realize that he has the power to change nature radically, in this case with fire.

While Twain and his companions rest at Carson after the snowstorm escapade, he claims that he is witness to the "great land-slide case of Hyde vs. Morgan" (240), an apparent hoax though not a historical one (concocted by Twain). In Chapter 34, one Dick Hyde hires General Buncombe to sue Tom Morgan; it seems that Morgan's ranch has buried Hyde's ranch when a land-slide moves Morgan's property directly on top of Hyde's. Morgan refuses to move; a mock trial ensues, but Buncombe is not aware of the joke. Ex-governor Roop makes his decision, despite all contrary evidence and argument, that "the plaintiff, Richard Hyde, has been deprived of his ranch by the visitation of God! And from this decision there is no appeal" (246–47). It takes Buncombe two months to understand that "he had been played upon with a joke" (247). Nature, in this pretense, is God's will; the hoax depends on Buncombe's gullibility and the guile of others. Also, Hyde's identity can be lost or submerged by Morgan's. The one ranch can assimilate the other. Nature, here, even if fictionalized, can alter the notion of property; as a hoax, it is also clear that the inhabitants of Carson can bend nature to man's will.

The earlier hoax that Bemis tells his fellow passengers in Chapter 7 represents the kind of self-betrayal that Twain feels in the snowstorm episode, as well as the projection of a created identity. Bemis is chased by a buffalo, and takes to a tree. The longer tale is told after "twenty-four hours," enough time to invent details (61). Given as a tall-tale sketch, the bull and the horse achieve larger-than-life status as the one chases the other; Bemis climbs a tree, the buffalo soon follows. Fellow passengers doubt that a buffalo can climb a tree, and Bemis replies, "Because you never saw a thing done, is that any reason why it can't be done?" (65). Bemis arranges a noose from his lariat, waits for the buffalo, drops the noose over the buffalo's neck, and shoots the buffalo in the face; the buffalo dangles twenty feet from the ground, "going out of one convulsion into another faster than you could count!" (66). The travelers protest; when asked for proof, Bemis asks if they saw him bring back his lariat or horse, and if they saw the buffalo again. They say "no" to each, and Bemis responds, "Well, then, what more do you want?" (66). Twain writes, "I made up my mind that if this man was not a liar he only missed it by the skin of his teeth" (66).

Bemis acquires, if anything, the reputation of being a skilful liar rather than the one of being a coward. He creates his identity, using as a projection of it his masterful handling of the buffalo. The snowstorm

4. Roughing It

episode, in contrast, shows Twain without that sense of fictive control. As a traveler, Twain seems to resolve that he maintain the appearance of being an observer. He does that at his own expense, as in Chapter 28, when he believes he has found gold only to have it be mica. Twain remarks that he will "still go on underrating men of gold and glorifying men of mica" (208). Many of the mining incidents undercut Twain's own ego; mining is hard work, with little to show for it: "We were stark mad with excitement ... but our credit was not good at the grocer's" (213).

Twain does claim to have been a millionaire for ten days, along with his partner Calvin H. Higbie, to whom *Roughing It* is dedicated, in Chapters 40 and 41. Higbie discovers a "blind lead" that cuts diagonally across an established vein, the Wide West, which allows them to locate a separate claim. Their fortune is made, assuming that they attempt to work the claim within ten days, the law at the time. They bring in a third partner, a foreman of the Wide West company. All three are called away, Twain to take care of an ailing Captain Nye, Higbie to help another prospector, and the foreman to take care of urgent business in California, so the ten days elapse with no work done on the claim. The foreman alone is able to be part of the group of men taking over the now-vacant claim. Twain writes that this may seem "a wild fancy sketch," but that "many witnesses" and "official records of Esmeralda District" back up his story (291). There is, of course, no historical evidence to this. In this sketch, then, the tall tale is evident, and Twain's objectivity as traveler and observer is established on the same plane as Bemis the buffalo hunter.

Twain, as many have observed, had a lifelong desire to be wealthy, a capitalist. He sought out the company of industrialists; he married into a respectable family; he wished to belong to an American, civilized culture. The preface to *Roughing It*, as noted, indicates a focus on the mining industry of Nevada, a land of easy riches and quick success. Twain does not make his fortune as a prospector, but does, with only a few chapters devoted to his Nevada experiences, show his need or quest for fortune, and his failure in this line of work. He turns this lapse into useful fiction, one used to bolster his deflated ego. As an internal, mental text of his travels, however, *Roughing It* serves to sketch out a number of Twain's paths as a writer. He does takes risks in *Roughing It* concerning his career choices; he does develop a sense of the river, learning to pilot his way, discovering that one of his talents is writing. Chapter 42 of *Roughing It* begins with a list of his "various vocations," among them a "grocery clerk," a blacksmith, a "bookseller's clerk," a drug store clerk," a tolerable printer," a riverboat pilot, a "private secretary," "a silver miner," and a "silver mill operative" (292–93). He decides, after one last attempt at mining, to try his hand at journalism, as the city editor of the Virginia *Territorial Enterprise*. Twain, because he does not wish to "become dependent upon somebody for my bread," is "scared into being a city editor," despite his lack of experience (295). As Twain notes, "necessity is the mother of 'taking chances'" (295). Once again, risk forms one of the structural themes of *Roughing It*.

As usual, Twain's first task becomes an occasion for fictionalizing the reality that he sees. The chief editor tells him to "get the absolute facts" (296). "Otherwise," he continues, "people will not put confidence in your news" (296). This is, of course, familiar advice to the riverboat cub pilot. In his "first day's experience as a reporter," Twain discovers that "nobody knew anything," with his notebook "still barren" (296). His editor suggests a story about hay wagons. Twain finds "one wretched old hay wagon dragging in from the country," makes it "sixteen" wagons, "brought it into town from sixteen different directions," and "made sixteen separate items out of it" (296–97). Later, he writes about "some emigrant wagons" which had met trouble in "hostile Indian country" (297). He finds one wagon master going to California who "would not be in the city next day to make trouble," and so he adds "his list of names and added his party to the killed and wounded" (298). Twain writes, "I put this wagon through an Indian fight that to this day has no parallel in history" (298). Twain has found his true vocation, not as objective journalist, but as writer of fiction: "I felt that I could take my pen and murder all the immigrants on the Plains if need be and the interests of the paper demanded it" (298).

Chapter 20 proves a focus for *Roughing It* in the same way, that of showing the reader how fiction creates reality while also demonstrating how elusive truth is. The famous ride of Horace Greeley to make "an engagement to lecture at Placerville" is told by four narrators in the same words by each. The fifth narrator — a "poor wanderer" (154) near death on the road — attempting to retell the anecdote is warned by Twain not to repeat the story, "that tiresome old anecdote" (155), and dies in "our arms" (155). The other four narrators, a stagecoach driver, a man from Denver, a cavalry sergeant, and a Mormon preacher, represent different segments and levels of society. Twain claims that he heard the same story about Hank Monk driving so hard he jostles Horace Greeley so much that Greeley "shot his head clean through the roof of the stage" (153), in a "period of six years," some "four hundred and eighty-one or eighty-two times" (155). The story has "come to me in all the multitude of tongues that Babel bequeathed to earth" (155). Indeed, "I never have smelt any anecdote as often as I have smelt that one ... Bayard Taylor has written about this hoary anecdote; Richardson has published it; so have Jones, Smith, Johnson, Ross Browne ... and I have heard that it is in the Talmud. I have seen it in print in nine different foreign languages; I have been told that it is employed in the inquisition in Rome; and I now learn with regret that it is going to be set to music. I do not think that such things are right" (156). Twain concludes the chapter by wondering if stagecoach drivers "bequeathed that bald-headed anecdote to their successors, the railroad brakemen and conductors" and also wonders if "these latter still persecute the helpless passenger with it" (156).

Twain provides an endnote that claims that the Horace Greeley ride "never occurred" (156), and asks "If it were a good anecdote, that seeming demerit would be its chiefest virtue, for creative power belongs to greatness, but what ought to be done to a man who would wantonly contrive so flat a one as this? If I were to suggest what ought to be done to him I should be call extravagant — but what does the thirteenth chapter of Daniel say? Aha!" (156). Of course, the incident did occur, on July 30, 1859.[34] Also, there is no Chapter 13 in most versions of the Bible, though one exists in the Catholic version. As in the Bemis tall tale, truth proves to be malleable. And that seems to be the point to *Roughing It* in large measure, that truth can become myth or can become a larger-than-life falsehood that resembles some kind of truth. Indeed, even truth can be claimed to be a lie, and as long as it seems plausible that way, it will be a lie. That explains the dedication to Calvin Higbie, the Washoe Zephyr wind, Jim Blaine's grandfather's old ram story, the snowstorm adventure, and the Buncombe hoax (and, of course, a good deal of the book). While *Innocents Abroad* also deals with the elusiveness of truth, *Roughing It* revels in it. *Roughing It* becomes a myth-maker of the American West, creating for its writer a new writer, Mark Twain, and helping to fashion new values for the traveler, someone who can now go West, and, with some frontier spirit, vanquish the nostalgia for the East, and become someone brand new, an individualist, tough and ornery, who can profit from the virgin territory.

5

A Tramp Abroad: *Travel Experiment and Narrative Lapse*

When people do not respect us we are sharply offended; yet deep down in his private heart no man much respects himself.
— Pudd'nhead Wilson's New Calendar.

A Tramp Abroad is a record of Twain's trip to Europe from April 1878 to August 1879, although it actually seems to relate to the first third of his travels there, which includes the time spent in southwestern Germany, Switzerland, eastern France, and northern Italy. Twain made the trip in order to write the book, having signed a contract with Frank Bliss to publish it; he later switched publishers to his father, Elisha Bliss. His first impressions about being in Germany are favorable and he had high hopes for the book. For example, he writes on June 2, 1878, to his old friend, David Gray, a Buffalo newspaper editor, that he and his family "are delightfully located for the summer," and their "balconies are just the thing to take supper in — or read or smoke or write" (*MEPUL*; original at Franklin D. Roosevelt Library, Hyde Park, N.Y.). He wishes that Gray were there to join him daily walks: "What times we should have." He writes to Gray that he has "begun writing a book about Germany, in the sort of narrative form which I used in Innocents, Roughing It & Bermuda stuff. I think I shall enjoy the work when I get fairly into the swing of it." Twain relates that he has been translating "pretty & ingenious tales ... written ostensibly for the young," with "some touches in them of a delicacy which requires mature perception."

5. A Tramp Abroad

He had considerable difficulty with writing the manuscript, however, fearing that he could not write enough and soon discovering that he needed a structure or a focus to control the text. He writes to his presumed publisher, Frank Bliss, on August 20, 1878, that "I find it is no sort of use to try to write while one is traveling," but that, thanks to his friend Joseph Twichell, he has "invented a new & better plan for the book. Therefore I shall tear up a great deal of my present batch of MS, & start fresh" (*MEML*; also *MPub*, 109). This new plan involved a journey with the pretense of being a walking or hiking tour, but instead using every other form of transportation. During the composition of the manuscript, however, as he writes to Mary Fairbanks in a letter of March 6, 1879, he found himself working even harder to find focus: "I've been having a dismal time for months over this confounded book, working hard every time I got a chance & tearing up a lot of the MS next time I came to read it over" (*MTF*, 225). He reports to Joseph Twichell on January 23, 1879, that he has "torn up 400 pages of MS, but I've still got about 900 which need no tearing," and thinks himself "half finished" (*MPub*, 110). His March 6 letter to Fairbanks indicates that he miscalculated the length of the manuscript, and at that point was only one-third complete.

Near the end of writing the manuscript, he found that he had written too much, even for the subscription trade, so he cut material. A number of deleted chapters appear in *The Stolen White Elephant, Etc.* (1882), *Life on the Mississippi* (1883), and *Letters from the Earth* (1962).

This record of his trip lacks the autobiographical pretense that other travel writings contain; rather, it fictionalizes the journey so much so that the narrator seems to be a bachelor who wishes to learn German, and to study art. Twain invents an "agent," Mr. Harris, as a companion for the trip, as well. Some details, however, suggest that Twain as a persona is on the journey; he mentions silver mining (Chapter 42), printing (Chapter 23), being on a steamboat (Chapter 10), and traveling with the "Innocents Abroad" (Chapter 47, 553). That he went to Germany with his wife and daughters, Livy's friend Clara Spaulding, a German nursemaid, a butler, and traveled through the Alps with Joseph Twichell all seems forgotten in the text. His letter to William Dean Howells on January 30, 1879, which complains about how much he hates travel and how difficult the writing has become, summarizes some of the progress that he has made: "I have exposed the German language in two or three chapters ... I mean to describe a German newspaper.... In my book I allow it to appear ... that I am over

A TRAMP ABROAD;

ILLUSTRATED BY W. FR. BROWN, TRUE WILLIAMS, B. DAY AND OTHER ARTISTS—WITH ALSO THREE OR FOUR PICTURES MADE BY THE AUTHOR OF THIS BOOK, WITHOUT OUTSIDE HELP;

IN ALL

THREE HUNDRED AND TWENTY-EIGHT ILLUSTRATIONS.

BY

MARK TWAIN,

(SAMUEL L. CLEMENS.)

(SOLD BY SUBSCRIPTION ONLY.)

HARTFORD, CONN.:
AMERICAN PUBLISHING COMPANY.
CHATTO & WINDUS, LONDON.
1880.

Title page of *A Tramp Abroad*

here to make the tour of Europe *on foot*. I am in pedestrian costume ... but mount the first conveyance that offers.... My second object here is to become a German scholar; my third, to study Art, & learn to paint. I have a notion to put a few hideous pen & ink sketches of my own in my book ... I employ an agent on a salary, & he does the real work when any is to be done ... & in yesterday's chapter we have started back to Heidelberg on a raft, & are having a good time ... I shall pick up useful passengers here & there to tell me the legends of the ruined castles ... I have invented quite a nice little legend for Dilsberg Castle ... I want to make a book which people will *read*,—& I shall make it profitable reading in spots — spots merely *because* there's not much material for a larger amount" (*MTHL*, 120–21). This summary to Howells of his work so far aptly depicts narrative technique, content, and intent; he even mentions his artwork, a natural extension of one of the premises of the book, that he learn to paint. Twain makes it clear that much of his work is supposed to be fictional, instructional, and entertaining.

This travel book has been criticized as uneven, lacking in coherence and in enthusiasm for its material. As noted earlier, however, *A Tramp Abroad* served Twain as a "nuclear" work for *The Prince and the Pauper* and *Huckleberry Finn*, most likely as a notebook of ideas for these novels, ideas tested and perhaps discarded. As noted, Twain's revision process left much material out of the final text. Some critics have suggested that the manuscript should have been edited even further, resulting in abridged versions in modern times. Of all the travel books, this one does seem notable for its flights of greatness and its moments of tedium. Structurally it is weak, dependent as it is on the bachelor narrator and a hired "agent" as a dubious guide and companion, on the recurrent motif of recording German legends and lore (with many tales about lovers who destroy each other), on the occasional description of foreign customs (such as dueling), on the general principle of unfulfilled goals (such as using the train instead of hiking), on infrequent attacks on European pretension, on the lapses of the narrator and his companions to learn art or German, and on fellow Americans who seem gullible or manipulative. The structure lacks one clear focus; it does not have the innocent Easterner learning the ways of the West, nor does it have the innocent American taking apart European traditions. It does seem to be a hodgepodge of material that relates to a central failure to recognize reality, thereby making it even less effective as a traditional travel narrative, which at the least allows a narrator to observe from a sophisticated stance the customs of savages. Some of that may well be there, but not as a dominant influence. This text does appear to be an attempt to capitalize on his earlier travel works, which were profitable, but Twain struggled with the material that he fashioned from an assortment of episodic moments. One could claim that perhaps Twain was attempting to find yet another way to transcend the typical travel book by way of parody, and if this is parody then the text stumbles. However, as a notebook of ideas for other projects, such as *The Prince and the Pauper* and *Huckleberry Finn*, this text seems like a goldmine of possibilities.

For example, Twain uses general observations about England from his journey in *The Prince and the Pauper*, information he added to his research for the novel. This novel, with its odyssey of two youths in different but parallel paths, seems a precursor in many ways to *Huckleberry Finn*, and could rightfully be termed a warm-up novel to the greater one of the two. *A Tramp Abroad*, with the raft trip to Heidelberg, tests the notion of a journey to view societies along the river, just as *Huckleberry Finn* allows Huck and Jim to observe life along the Mississippi. Encounters with young American boys in *A Tramp Abroad* (Chapters 27 and 38) may well be initial explorations of the vernacular voices in *Huckleberry Finn* or even in the later novel, *A Connecticut Yankee in King Arthur's Court*, where the inane early Clarence and Sandy seem the extended versions of these conversations. A conversation that the narrator in *A Tramp Abroad* has with a young American woman seems an exercise in the art of lying, an art practiced usefully by Tom and Huck. One of the discarded chapters for *A Tramp Abroad* contains a discussion of the art of French lying, where "lying with no intent to deceive, is the highest & purest form of lying" (*MELM*; formerly Box 6, # 55). Lying serves characters in Twain's fiction quite well when they practice to make life better for others; the Duke and the King finally meet their just desserts when they practice the noble art of lying in order to bilk people. Lying successfully for awhile, Tom also finds his falsehoods unlayered until his identity is unraveled in *Pudd'nhead Wilson*.

Certainly, *A Tramp Abroad* contains much to recommend it: the tale of Baker's blue jay, the raft trip to Heidelberg, the ascent of the Riffelberg, the man who put up at Gadsby's, the essay/appendix "The Awful German Language." These artful passages show the skill Twain has in capturing moments which reveal comically thwarted expectations. These anecdotes show lapses of reality, the burlesque existence matched with the practical, reflecting the folly and pretense of controlling reality. One cannot, Twain seems to suggest, hope to make wishes come true just by wishing; nor can one hope to succeed without being grounded in some kind of reality, even if one must create a verbal reality. While it may be fashionable to ascribe to Twain post-modernist tendencies — I could claim that Twain uses language in this travel book to dissolve identities and realities — Twain may well be using humor as an escape from travel conventions which he does not wish to use in this text. He is using "stretchers" to explode notions of his being the instructor or the traveler noting customs of the savages of Europe. While some of the text does record local customs, such as dueling in Germany and France, legends and tales, and hotel protocol, the dominant thrust — the narrator learning German and art, not succeeding very well, and hiking, while avoiding walking — remains the American unwilling or unable to experience Europe. It's as if, having provided sufficient criticism of Europe in *Innocents Abroad*, Twain could not resort to extended social commentary in *A Tramp Abroad*. Hence, he uses this excursion to develop primarily American themes, to practice the art of the tall tale, and to tread water until the themes presented here find imaginative release in *Huckleberry Finn*.

Education or training is a core of travel literature; the tourist expects to learn something about mores or customs of the country. The text does have several early chapters on German students working hard at their studies, but the main focus seems to be about their dueling adventures. Twain astutely seems to stereotype the German culture of violence without pain and knowledge without compassion. Knowledge in *A Tramp Abroad* is important, though Twain explores the methods of acquiring knowledge with a number of experimental narrative structures. One way is the accumulation of native folklore or tales, many of which turn out to be disastrous relationships between men and women, and this accumulation suggests that Twain is forming a way of using American folklore as a way to understand knowledge itself, a topic that he more fully understands and discusses in *Life on the Mississippi*. By recording these folktales, Twain is showing how short anecdotes capture the sense of a culture. In Germany it appears Twain finds men and women ill at ease with each other and unable to comprehend each other.

Twain moves rather quickly in *A Tramp Abroad* to an American folktale that he creates, just after one initial attempt at editing a German story, that of the Knave of Bergen. Chapter 2 and 3 relate the tale of Baker's blue jay. The narrator imagines that he can hear ravens talking about him, and then recalls a California miner, Jim Baker, who has learned the language of animals. Baker tells the story of a blue jay who finds a hole in an abandoned cabin, and begins packing it with acorns, determined to fill the hole. The blue jay becomes increasingly frustrated with the task, until joined by many more blue jays, "five thousand of them" (41). These birds discuss the problem of being unable to fill the apparent vacuum until one spots the open door and announces, "hang'd if this fool hasn't been trying to fill up a house with acorns" (41). Even the first blue jay realizes the joke and all laugh, "and guffawed over that thing like human beings" (41). As Baker relates it, "It ain't any use to tell me a blue-jay hasn't got a sense of humor, because I know better. And memory, too" (41). The birds visit the site for the next three years. Only an owl "that come from Nova Scotia to visit the Yo Semite" (42) does not recognize the joke, "but then he was a good deal disappointed about Yo Semite, too" (42). The illustration of an effete, top-hatted gentleman on page 42 striking the pose of an owl (with spectacles resembling an owlish glare) seems to suggest the lack of humor the man has.

This tall tale uses the refreshing vernacular of the American West not otherwise apparent in *A Tramp Abroad*, aside from other American tourists, and suggests the overall nature of the text: Twain's attempt to fill in the gaps of his understanding while being unable to do so. No matter how hard he tries, he cannot quite find the bottom of this bottomless hole that is his book. While there are interesting themes and observations to find here, all of the material could well be discussed as "acorns" which find no bottom and little meaning. He can only patch his observations together with a drudgery of spirit, for the book became a torture to write and to revise; but he can also use this text to practice writing humorous sketches, which may, perhaps, allow him the energy to return to better projects, such as the two novels he was then working on fitfully. The acorns represent minutiae of information, data bit by bit, dropped into the empty recesses of knowledge, knowledge without understanding, information with no framework for memory. He was stalled on writing *Huckleberry Finn*, and perhaps needed to start thinking about his American tramp by thinking about California. By placing this story in America, Twain removes himself from the European environment that he finds hard to write about.

Even in this scattered book one can find a notebook about travel that still relates fairly well to the major themes Twain revisits in his travel works.

First, as mentioned earlier, the device of using a narrator and a companion seeking knowledge seems a mirror of Orion and his brother in *Roughing It*, of Mr. Brown and the narrator in the letters from Hawaii and in the earlier *Alta* letters. Second, the theme of nostalgia for America is apparent in all of his travel works, including this one. Twain clearly misses American food prepared at home. Third, the question of stable identities exists in *A Tramp Abroad*, even in the German tales that Twain repeats, as in the legend of "The Cave of the Specter" (Chapter 15), which relates how Sir Wendel Lobenfeld shoots his crossbow at Lady Gertrude, his beloved, in a case of mistaken identity. Finally, the rafting excursion to Heidelberg seems a shadowy reflection of *Roughing It*'s Lake Tahoe visit, of *Life on the Mississippi*'s river trip, and even *Huckleberry Finn*'s rafting down the river, which reflects in general the American pretense of finding peace and tranquility in nature, of finding a timeless realm which carries no risks and no threats. It is an authentic nature, a sight/site that allows a civilized traveler to commune with natural landscapes, gives peace and harmony, and provides a romanticized vision of a world no longer connected to the evils of society and the rudeness of ordinary time.

The raft trip to Heidelberg, in particular, allows the travelers to avoid using the carriage, but to observe people along the river: "Men and women and cattle were at work in the dewy fields" (128). The trip is idyllic: "We went slipping silently along, between the green and fragrant banks, with a sense of pleasure and contentment that grew, and grew, all the time" (126). As in *Huckleberry Finn*, where the journey allows satiric glances at the villages on the shoreline, Twain uses this opportunity to relate how only the women work, the men able to gossip with the raft's crew, and to describe how hard women work: "The women do all kinds of work on the continent ... she does not have to work more than eighteen or twenty hours a day, and she can always get down on her knees and scrub the floors of halls and closets when she is tired and needs a rest" (128). The cynicism here is not the kind one sees in *Huckleberry Finn*, but does seem a harbinger of things in the novel. Certainly, the indolent life on board the raft is clearly related to *Huckleberry Finn*, as well as *Roughing It*'s Lake Tahoe trip. When natural disaster strikes in Chapter 17, the sea "running inches high" (156) — the raft springs a leak, and a storm brews — the travelers are saved by a man tying a rope from the raft to a tree, a melodrama of some proportion made comical by the alarm of the crew and the simplicity of the solution; *Roughing It* contains a poem, "The Aged Pilot"

(369–75), which makes the point more amply. Twain seems to be practicing familiar themes, particularly humor that pokes fun at melodramatic absurdities.

One of the odd tramps made by the narrator is in Chapter 13, when the narrator gets lost in a hotel room at night, circling one chair for 43 miles. He is unwilling to wake Harris when he cannot get to sleep; he intends to go outside, but, in attempting to dress in the dark, begins to lose his way. His freshly wound pedometer records that he has been truly lost for a very long time, and he eventually wakes up others by his random acts of violence with furniture in the room. The narrator even loses track of time in the darkness. This is grand humor, a foreshadowing of the riverboat pilot's skill at mastering the shape of the river without really seeing it in the dark of night. It is absurd humor, making fun of the narrator's inability to cope with change. It also suggests the very real difficulty of Twain's writing, a discovery process that seems to go nowhere at times. The text is bound together loosely by the supposed walking tour Harris and the narrator are conducting, and by the loose task these two are managing, that of collecting folktales and customs; this simple anecdote amplifies the difficulty that Twain has in finding a way to give meaning to that walking tour, by simply walking in circles in the dark.

The absurd sense of humor grows with the ascent of the Riffelberg, which involves a massive expeditionary force of 154 people, as well as a great deal of equipment, and creates a procession 3,122 feet long (420). This extended tale contains numerous dilemmas for the travelers, including getting lost, and getting over several large boulders (eventually they dynamite them out of the way, though one of them inconveniently has a chalet on its top). They do make it to the top, but find getting down a problem. After suggesting that they use umbrellas to descend — no one volunteers — the narrator decides that they ought to ride the glacier back to Zermatt, a feat that will take the men about 500 years, given the glacier's slow movement. The raw humor of this sketch does seem haphazard, although clearly borrowing from the tradition of the tall-tale and the burlesque: here, the men, by their very numbers and excess of effort, are similar to larger-than-life heroes of the frontier American West; the events and situations they encounter are often as unusual as those found in Old Southwestern humor. Because the ascent occurs in Europe, one might then also assume that this tall-tale inverts the American tradition of frontier writing, for the two travelers, the narrator and Mr. Harris, are riding on the coattails of their

European guides (152 of them), importing, as it does, not the vernacular strengths of these people, but the very weakness that excess provides. In other words, the narrator may control what these guides do, but they are stupid for doing so. (Of course, one may then say that they are simply following orders to make more money from their equally stupid American travelers.) This is delicious writing in the vein of *Roughing It*, mocking those tourists in Europe who overindulge in creature comforts, expecting that the sights will be authentic experiences while insisting that these be familiar and without discomfort, an organized and picturesque moment. Twain seems always aware, as are we, because of his letters and notes, that travel can be rather inconvenient, referring, for example, to a "carbuncle" that plagues him at the beginning of *Following the Equator*; Twain was not in the best of health at the beginning, nor during, this later tramp around the world.

The sketch lacks some focus; the narrator interrupts the tale at one point to relate the conversation of a "grandson" and Mr. Harris (441–44), the object being to capture the language of a naive and pretentious American youth and fop, reminding the reader that "he and the innocent chatterbox whom I met on the Swiss lake are the most unique and interesting specimens of Young America I came across during my foreign tramping" (444). Chapter 27 relates the meeting of the narrator with the earlier youth of America, someone who moves from one subject to another without apparent guile or purpose. Both characters might well have served Twain as examples for Huck's various performances when evading the truth. The narrator rarely answers a question of the "grandson" the same way. Here, aside from the usual condescending look at pretension, the ascent of the Riffelberg drifts from the story line. As a burlesque, perhaps, the story may need an interruption, but the point for it isn't clear. The conversation could reflect on the narrator's self-deprecating humor; much of it discusses how the youth intends to "flit" about Europe (442), and how he lacks plans for his travels: "I don't map out any plans" (443). The contrast between this overly organized ascent of the Riffelberg and the poorly organized travel plans of the youth may well emphasize the nature of the burlesque. It's as if Twain means to use this notebook's invented story, based on his and Twichell's ascent, which apparently took only four hours, as a comment on the very subject of traveling. With his own entourage of family and friends, Twain might well be envisioning himself as the rootless youth, hoping that he could also "flit" from place to place. It may thus be true that Twain, rather than ridiculing the average group of tourists in Europe who expect planned comfort and organization, may be referring to the large group of people who were with him on this European vacation; he was no longer a bachelor, able to go where he pleased. Whatever the reason, this Riffelberg ascent parodies and mocks a number of adventurers, including Edward Whymper and Bayard Taylor, by making their conquests seem minuscule compared to his mountain climb.

The man who put up at Gadsby's, as a sketch, reportedly details the disintegration of one man's fortunes while waiting for a claim against the federal government to be settled. Twain watches some fishermen waiting patiently for fish to bite, and recalls walking through a snowstorm in Washington, D.C., in 1867 with his old friend John Henry Riley (a fellow correspondent, then working for the San Francisco *Alta California*); a man named Lykins stops them and says that he is looking for Riley, because he needs Riley to facilitate a position of postmaster of San Francisco for him. Lykins is in a rush to complete the appointment, but Riley tells him a cautionary tale about the man who put up at Gadsby's, a hotel in Washington some thirty years earlier. A man from Tennessee, with a black coachman, a four-horse carriage, and "an elegant dog," arrives at Gadsby's, in a rush to collect on a claim "against the government," and says that he can't wait for breakfast, but must "fetch the money, and then get right along back to Tennessee, for he was in considerable of a hurry" (266). He returns that same night, apparently without the claim settled, and orders a room. In successive months and years, while still waiting, the man from Tennessee sells off the carriage, trading down for second-hand models and smaller vehicles, eventually selling off these as well, and sells the horses, the black coachman, and the dog. There are eleven illustrations peppering the text with the successive losses of transportation and companions. Riley pauses, Lykins still impatient for the end of the story, and says that the man from Tennessee has been waiting for thirty years now for his claim to be settled. Lykins still does not get the point, that impatience will lead nowhere in Washington: "Well, where's the point of it?" (270). Riley advises him to "put up at Gadsby's" (271), and walks away. Lykins, of course, "never got that post-office" (271). Twain returns at the end of the sketch to present times, remarking that the fishermen of Lucerne should "put up at Gadsby's," for "it is likely that a fish has not been caught on the lake pier for forty years" (271). Still, "the patient fisher watches his cork there all the day long, just the same, and seems to enjoy it" (271). Time itself collapses in the endless moments of waiting for the fish to bite or the claim to be awarded. This is not as rich a story as "Baker's Blue Jay Yarn" or Horace Greeley's infamous stagecoach ride in *Roughing It*—where timelessness exists in varying stages—but the same point is made. Congress can take an awful long time to do anything; sometimes the wait is as timeless as the fishing off the lake pier.

    This tale reflects one of the basic themes of *A Tramp Abroad*, that of thwarted expectations, but it also seems to suggest that hope never ends for those who are patient enough. Of course, the end is never realized, but the charm may simply lie in being a patient fisherman, enjoying the vista and the experience. The previous chapter (25) introduces a similar tale, that of the narrator's conversation with a young American woman who he and Harris see in the dining room at the Schweitzerhof Hotel in Lucerne. Harris and the narrator disagree on her age, so the narrator says that he will speak to her. She greets him with great enthusiasm, claims that she knows the narrator well, asks if he remembers "when the sea washed the forward boats away" (248), and "how frightened poor Mary was" (249). Embarrassed, and numb with "a stupefying surprise" (248) for "my memory was a blank" (249), the narrator attempts to go along with the conversation as the woman discusses details of their supposed friends and acquaintances. She talks familiarly about family, children's names, and other things until it is painfully clear that the narrator cannot remember her at all; she laughs at his "blushes" and says "I have enjoyed this talk over old times, but you have not. I saw very soon that you were only pretending to know me, and so as I had wasted a compliment on you in the beginning, I made up my mind to punish you ... Mary and the storm, and sweeping away of the forward boats, were facts—all the rest was fiction" (253). The narrator returns to Harris, who is astonished that the conversation with a stranger has taken a half an hour. Determined not to show that he has been duped by the young American woman, the narrator then proceeds to volunteer increasingly dubious information about their conversation (details invented, of course), which puzzles Harris greatly: "I had been well scorched by the young woman, but no matter, I took it out of Harris. One should always 'get even' in some way, else the sore place will go on hurting" (257). The narrator cannot get even with the young American woman, but evades the humiliation by attempting the same fictional pose with Harris. As in the sketch for the man who put up at Gadsby's, one must be patient, but here, the patience rests in creating a reality out of a web of convoluted lies. Truth depends largely on the person telling it, and sometimes the art of lying is a verbal strategy best practiced until gotten right. *Huckleberry Finn* and *Tom Sawyer* are rife with this art, sometimes used successfully, particularly at the end of *Huckleberry Finn*, when Huck discovers he has a falsehood, the name Tom Sawyer, which will allow him an identity on the Phelps farm. *A Tramp Abroad*, particularly in the scene with the young American woman, serves as a background for learning how to lie without losing one's identity, which the narrator comes close to doing, for he seems fairly puzzled about the young woman's source of knowledge and begins to doubt his sanity or at least his memory. Again there are better anecdotes about memory in other travel works that Twain wrote, but perhaps this too was a practice session for *Huckleberry Finn*'s sets of falsehoods and establishing a better reason for the art of lying than just social embarrassment.

The opening chapter forms a foundation for *A Tramp Abroad*'s discussions about identity by offering a folktale that Twain found in F. J. Kiefer's *The Legends of the Rhine from Basle to Rotterdam*, translated by L.W. Garnham, entitled "The Knave of Bergen." An executioner attends a royal masquerade ball masked as a knight, dances with the queen of the festival (the Empress), and wins her admiration, as she dances with him a number of times. At the end of the evening, after all of the other dancers are unmasked, the mysterious knight refuses, until the queen commands him to reveal himself. Upon being revealed as a commoner, the King (or Emperor) is incensed at the insult to the crown and orders him put to death. The executioner throws himself at the feet of the Emperor and suggests that he be knighted at that moment in order to preserve the honor of the Queen. The Emperor is surprised at the audacity of the executioner, but relents, and knights him, calling him the Knave of Bergen, who then dances one more dance with the Queen. This clearly is a tale about a secret identity, and, unmasked, about the common individual becoming a new, and ennobled, identity. The Knave comes close to the ultimate loss of identity but manages to create a new one.

By slipping around the question of who the narrator is — Twain is sometimes a bachelor, and occasionally Mark Twain and sometimes married — and blurring the edges of who Harris might be — Joe Twichell did not hike around Europe as the text suggests — Twain is creating a confusion of identities. This confusion exists with the genre of this travel book as well, because it simply can't stand still in Europe, wandering off to

America with the story about Gadsby's hotel (or, in a bit of a stretch, the "Professor's Yarn," which he removed from *A Tramp Abroad*, and later used in *Life on the Mississippi*).

"The Awful German Language," as one of the appendices to *A Tramp Abroad*, reminds the reader of one of the announced reasons for taking the trip to Europe: the narrator and Mr. Harris will learn, among other things, the German language (17). The narrator discovers that it is a "perplexing language," "so slip-shod and systemless, and so slippery and elusive to the grasp," and "there are more exceptions to the rule than instances of it" (601). Twain describes the word "Regen" (rain) in the various cases and genders that it might take in context with other words, deciphering the possibilities that he might use for "the bird is waiting in the blacksmith shop on account of the rain," and declares to his teacher that the bird is staying in the blacksmith shop "wegen (on account of) den Regen" (602). This answer apparently is incorrect, since "wegen" always takes the genitive case, thus "wegen des Regens" (602). After that example, the narrator discusses the construction of compound words, use of parenthetical asides, and placement of verbs, which force the reader to wait until the end of the sentence, to "find out for the first time what the man has been talking about" (603). The narrator provides additional examples of perplexity, including separable verbs (with English translations, to make his point), and personal pronouns. He is annoyed at the "poverty of a language which has to make one word do the work of six" (605), when he describes the word "sie." As the narrator says, "think of the exasperation of never knowing which of these meanings the speaker is trying to convey" (605).

As Twain deconstructs language here — and it seems useful to refer to him directly, not as the narrator, for Twain's letters to others refer to his frustration with the German language — he seems to represent the unreliable and empty gaps in language. What he also does is locate this language in an unstable universe, where identity and gender are at question: "The reader will see that in Germany a man may think he is a man, but when he comes to look into the matter closely, he is bound to have his doubts; he finds that in sober truth he is a most ridiculous mixture; and if he ends by trying to comfort himself with the thought that he can at least depend on a third of this mess as being manly and masculine, the humiliating second thought will quickly remind him that in this respect he is no better off than any woman or cow in the land" (607–08). Identity, as one of Twain's concerns, is defined here as an act of humiliation, removing even sexual identity, as the "man" finds himself without reference points about gender.

One of Twain's discarded anecdotes about language for *Following the Equator* demonstrates the importance of knowing the right word in a foreign tongue. Twain writes that he has a "foreign neighbor here in this quiet corner of London" who "boldly talks the English language just as if he were acquainted with it" (*MELM*; formerly DV330). This gets him in trouble when he interviews "a fine strapping grenadier of an Irishwoman" for a position of servant in his household. She does not know if he wants a maid or a cook but hopes that he will need a cook. She asks: "What kind of servant is it you want, sir?" The man forgets the word "maid" but he remembers "a word which meant the same thing & would answer." He replies: "I want a virgin." She responds: "You want a what?" And he continues: "A virgin. Are you a virgin? You do not look like a virgin." Twain notes that "he is better this morning, but it is thought that he will not get well."

Twain does seem to admire the flexibility of "Schlag" or "Zug," words which can have many meanings: "you can hang any word you please to its tail and make it mean anything you want to" (610). He also admires the straightforward rules of pronunciation and particularly the "singularly and powerfully effective" words which "describe lowly, peaceful and affectionate home life; those which deal with love, in any and all forms, from mere kindly feeling and honest good will toward the passing stranger, clear up to courtship; those which deal with out-door Nature, in its softest and loveliest aspects ... in a word, those which deal with any and all forms of rest, repose, and peace; those also which deal with the creatures and marvels of fairyland; and lastly and chiefly, in those words which express pathos" (615). Twain later suggests changes to the language, after "nine full weeks" of studying it (616).

This appendix reflects not just humor — as dissection of the German language, it deflates at the same time it describes — but the unstable realities that language can present. Questions of identity and gender dot the landscape of Twain's discourse. His focus on German words which convey thoughts of home, love, nature, and tranquility suggests a state of mind that Twain would seek throughout his travels, as well as in his fiction. Humor in this case as a social satire or as parody may be pointing out Twain's avoidance of darker themes, those unsettling ones of identity and reality. The appendix also may be reflecting Twain's uneasiness at traveling at all, since the words he finds so compellingly effective are ones that apply to stable rootedness. Of course, there is enough evidence to indicate that Twain hated traveling at the same time that he enjoyed it, a contradiction without apparent resolution. Still, thoughts of Elmira (Quarry Farm, and perhaps the study that Susan Langdon Crane had made for him) and family may have been present while pondering the complexities of the German language, as much as dominant American virtues, which home, love, nature, and tranquility represent in part. As is the usual case with Twain's seeming affection for one or another cultural trait, even this attention to the home can be undercut: in an discarded chapter on Munich, Twain describes the houses of Germany as "prison-like," and because of their thick walls and overall appearance, "a Bavarian's house is his Bastile" (*MELM*; formerly Box 6, # 51).

This may well reflect the uncertainty about writing *A Tramp Abroad*. Twain enjoys traveling yet finds it disabling, because any home becomes a trap of comfort, while a road trip represents a freedom from domesticity. His focus on language, the way to express feelings, as an uncertain way of actually being able to express those feelings, becomes a focus on the uncertainties of life. These German homes make the families inside prisoners. Twain's extrapolations from reading Hypolite Taine's method of analyzing cultures may play a role here, though it is not clear that Twain had read Taine at this point. Nevertheless, Twain reads closely the language of the people he visits, while carefully describing the houses that people inhabit, looking for ways to generalize the character of these natives in terms of the kind of shelter that they prefer to build. One can overgeneralize about the discarded chapter on *A Tramp Abroad*, and claim that the remark "a Bavarian's house is his Bastile" has a political edge to it; the Bastille is an iconic call to arms for the French Revolution. This then suggests that the German culture and German people are ready for a revolution of their own — but that seems a bit of a stretch. Twain had a large retinue with him on this particular journey to Europe, his wife and daughters, a nursemaid named Rosina Hay, Livy's friend Clara Spaulding, and eventually Joseph Twichell for a short month, family and friends who seem missing from the travel book itself, if noticeably present on the long tramp in Europe. The German folktales tend to have the common theme of lovers divided or lost loves. Perhaps these two things — absent family and unhappy love — suggest something else is going on, that perhaps the journey itself has lost its appeal to Twain. In *Life on the Mississippi* Twain writes that "when one makes his first voyage in a ship, it is an experience which multitudinously bristles with striking novelties; novelties which are in such sharp contrast with all this person's former experiences that they take a seemingly deathless grip upon his imagination and memory. By tongue or pen he can make a landsman live that strange and stirring voyage over with him; make him see it all and feel it all. But if he wait? If he make ten voyages in succession — what then? Why, the thing has lost color, snap, surprise; and has become commonplace. The man would have nothing to tell that would quicken a landsman's pulse" (379). Somehow an excursion to Europe has become commonplace for Twain. Given his struggle with the text, it seems the correct conclusion.

The tourist will find little instruction in this book on food, transportation, lodging, sights, and the exchange value of money, the usual details one needs from a travel writer. One will find that European food is awful in hotels; Twain yearns for American food. Actually there is quite a lot about food, but the European fare suffers badly with the detailed lists that Twain prepares, lists of pure, unadulterated American food, even providing odd recipes that make food quite unappetizing (the one for German coffee, which somehow includes the remains of a cow, is rather amazing). The sights that must be seen are sometimes drudgery to be seen. Twain does admit that his opinions about art have changed: "The Old Masters were still unpleasing to me, but they were truly divine contrasted with the copies. The copy is to the original as the pallid, smart, inane new waxwork group is to the vigorous, earnest, dignified group of living men and women whom it professes to duplicate. There is a mellow richness, a subdued color, in the old pictures, which is to the eye what muffled and mellowed sound is to the ear" (379). He still considers art to be good art as long as it is faithful to reality. There are moments of satire and sarcasm that seem familiar to the reader of *Innocents Abroad*; one of the discarded chapters, thrown away in desperation to make something out of the material, "The French and the Comanches," included in *Letters from the Earth*, has that kind of attack, particularly against the morality of the French, suggesting that American missionaries ought to try to reform the French. The sights are exaggerated; the transportation system seems mostly rail travel, despite the avowed intention to walk much of the way.

There is a resistance to this text, certainly. Twain tried to make it work, even though he had no guiding principle. He had done the European tour alone with the Pilgrims in *Innocents Abroad*; he had managed to survive the Western frontier alone in *Roughing It*. It appears that not being alone, for this third travel book, disabled the writer in some way. This was a book project before he made the trip, perhaps the one journey made specifically toward that end. One could claim that this text is an experiment in the travel genre in that it tries to parody the work he had done in *Innocents Abroad* by showing how the American is incapable of traveling outside of his comfort zone, that he requires isolation from home and family in order to appreciate the journey. The text bears this out to some degree, with the focus on the emptiness of useful narrative structures; there seems to be so much baggage on the trip that he could not read the signs of the river on his journey. Twain includes the music to Lorelei (music notes and lyrics), pictures that he drew, curious dialogue markers between the narrator and Harris, lists of equipment for the Riffelberg climb, bizarre recipes for absurd dishes, crude maps of different routes, and a hand-written description of Old Blue China (evidently a cat and a mouse at play). These are not useful things to have for a tourist's instruction — the bad art of Twain is self-indulgent humor at best — and these graphic aids seem to be a way to break the text by experimenting with ways to make the text more than just words on a page.

The focus on occasional German folktales is interesting, however, because these seem to be Twain's way of comparing European ways of expressing cultural traits with American modes of expressing anecdotal truths about the human experience. The American story seems so appealing compared to the European, and that may be the point. But trying out this kind of literary analysis by virtue of comparison tends to undercut the notion of what this book was meant to be, a description of Twain's excursion abroad. Again, he had done that, so this new attempt turned not to be as fresh as he wanted. Twain combines the two ways of telling a story in his own sketch on German manure, the story of Huss and his daughter, in Chapter 22, which he calls "Skeleton for Black Forest Novel." Huss will not allow his daughter to marry a Hans Schmidt, because he does not have a manure pile; he lets Paul Hoch, with a sufficient manure pile, have her hand in marriage, until it is discovered at the wedding that Paul has been stealing from Huss's pile. Meanwhile, Hans has discovered an enormous manure pile in the woods, and is thus married immediately to Huss's daughter, Gretchen. This may well be a way of Twain sketching out his frustration with the very text he is creating.

6

Life on the Mississippi: *Travel as a Form of Knowledge*

> *Wrinkles should merely indicate where smiles have been.*
> —Pudd'nhead Wilson's New Calendar.

Life on the Mississippi began as a serial publication in the *Atlantic Monthly*, at the urging of William Dean Howells and Joseph Twichell, in 1875, of seven installments now called "Old Times on the Mississippi." This series covers Twain's early years as a cub pilot on the river. Twain used the series, with little revision, for chapters 4 through 17. He had intended to write a longer book about changes occurring on the river and in society along the river, but other projects intervened for seven years. At some point, he had almost persuaded Howells to join him on the excursion. On April 10, 1882, Twain signed a subscription book contract with James R. Osgood to produce the Mississippi book; Twain traveled with Osgood and a stenographer, Roswell H. Phelps, to St. Louis, where they went downriver to New Orleans, returned to St. Louis, and then continued north to Minnesota. By late May, Twain began to piece together his book for Osgood.

Because he chose to use the early series, "Old Times on the Mississippi," as part of the shape of the new book, Twain's intention to describe contemporary life on the river had to shift in narrative tone and technique. Parts of the book have the pretense of the cub pilot learning the ways of the river; in other parts the authorial voice of the seasoned traveler recognizes the changes in society along the river. As a result, the book has an uneven focus at times. Also, because the subscription trade demanded a lengthy book to sell well, Twain found himself padding the text with appendices, most of it appropriated from other writers, with material from *A Tramp Abroad* and *Huckleberry Finn*, and with other sources. After all that extra baggage, Twain eventually found that the manuscript was too long, so he asked Osgood and his editors to trim the text, which they did. Still, the resulting revisions, and the uneven nature of the narrative voice, do not change some of the observations that the travel writer makes about American life and about his own insights. Twain held this travel work in high regard, intending late in life to revise it extensively, and considered it his best work.

Life on the Mississippi develops a number of strategies for Twain's method in writing travel literature, the key one being the proper use of memory. Mr. Brown's use of memory, apparently a photographic one, is a misfortune because it is chaotic and unfocused. Twain writes, "His memory was born in him, I think, not built" (156). "He could *not* forget anything," Twain continues, "the most trivial details remained as distinct and luminous in his head, after they had lain there for years, as the most memorable events" (157). "Such a memory as that is a great misfortune," Twain remarks, for "its possessor cannot distinguish an interesting circumstance from an uninteresting one" (158). Twain describes how such a person would "clog his narrative with tiresome details and make himself an insufferable bore" (158). His description of how this person would tell a narrative about a dog reflects the narrative technique used for Jim Blaine's story about his grandfather's old ram in Chapter 53 of *Roughing It*. Twain talks about this tale in his Autobiographical Dictations on October 13, 1906, in much the same way: "The idea of the tale is to exhibit certain bad effects of a good memory; the sort of memory which is too good; which remembers everything and forgets nothing; which has no sense of proportion, and can't tell an important event from an unimportant one, but preserves them all, states them all, and thus retards the progress of a narrative, at the same time making a tangled, inextricable confusion of it and intolerably wearisome to the listener" (*MELM*). Twain concludes in *Life on the Mississippi* that "a pilot must have a memory; but there are two higher qualities which he must also have. He must have good and quick judgment and decision, and a cool, calm courage that no peril can shake" (158–59). A good memory, then, is one that is built up, layer by layer, over time, until the "shape of the river" becomes a clearly focused map of how to navigate the river.

Life on the Mississippi

BY

MARK TWAIN

AUTHOR OF "THE INNOCENTS ABROAD," "ROUGHING IT,"
"THE PRINCE AND THE PAUPER," ETC.

WITH MORE THAN 300 ILLUSTRATIONS

Mississippi Steamboat of Fifty Years Ago.

[SOLD BY SUBSCRIPTION ONLY.]

BOSTON
JAMES R. OSGOOD AND COMPANY
1883

Title page of *Life on the Mississippi*

This memory also becomes a map of how to navigate the imagination, as long as the mind with a good memory knows how to express the facts that are contained, because a memory without a sense of direction or focus lacks a real purpose. The memory needs to be a confident mastery of facts, felt intuitively with observational skills that are clearly meaningful. Twain's judgment and courage, his "two higher qualities," occasionally fail him in his later writing, however, as many have noted, when despair about the human condition would thwart positive thinking.

Hence, the importance of the sphinx passage from *Innocents Abroad*: "It was MEMORY — RETROSPECTION — wrought into visible, tangible form" (Chapter 58). If memory can successfully recall the details, then the whole shape and meaning of a place or incident can be fathomed or understood. Some critics, notably John R. Brazil, have suggested that Twain felt himself distanced from the romantic memory of the past, that he invalidates the pilot's notion of memory with a cynical view of its imperfections, but the pilot's understanding of the river, along with the importance of a focused memory, kept Twain's faith in his own ability to reconstruct the past — the art of retrospection — alive, well into *Following the Equator*. It is a curious memory to be sure, for Twain's memory often failed him, particularly when beginning his autobiography. However, with works like *Roughing It*, Twain needed to use his memory, because he lacked letters, journals, or notes to guide him in that project. While his travel works can be termed accurate accounts of the era or place, they are accurate only up to the point where Twain wishes to make a point, whether that point be social criticism, self-deprecating analysis, or humorous reflection. Generally speaking, Twain sought to capture time with the art of memory, the art of "RETROSPECTION" that he brings to a text. This is a shaped memory, something that requires that he give this memory a structure to be able to see the shape rather than just the facts. A memory without a shape just spills the facts; a memory with a shape can tell a story, one that has a point, a meaning that synthesizes these facts.

Throughout *Life on the Mississippi*, Twain seeks to delay time, to make it pause long enough to make some sense of it, even as he realizes that death will end all speculation. He writes of his days as a pilot that "time drifted smoothly and prosperously on, and I supposed — and hoped — that I was going to follow the river the rest of my days, and die at the wheel when my mission was ended. But by and by the war came, commerce was suspended, my occupation was gone" (246). Historical time interrupts the expectation that time will cease, that he will always be a pilot, until the end of his physical time. And the river will always be there: "The loneliness of this solemn, stupendous flood is impressive and depressing ... and so the day goes, the night comes, and again the day — and still the same, night after night and day after day — majestic, unchanging sameness of serenity, repose, tranquility, lethargy, vacancy — symbol of eternity, realization of the heaven pictured by priest and prophet, and longed for by the good and thoughtless" (292). This stable moment in time, an eternal River, is lonesome, alienating and disinterested in the affairs of mankind, indifferent to all, again a moment of death and blankness, a loss of all thought. The similarity to the Sphinx in *Innocents Abroad* is clear. Both are frozen moments in time.[35] In his notebook for January 1897 through July 1899, Twain writes that "when my physical body dies, my dream body will doubtless continue its excursions & activities without change, forever" (*MELM*; formerly Notebook 40 [32]). This seems a fond and foolish notion, perhaps, but it is a necessary belief in order to carry on, to find solace in the dream world that will somehow defeat time. Dreams, for Twain, are always timeless and sometimes without spatial orientation.

In his Autobiographic Dictation of October 14, 1906, Twain discusses his growing awareness that facts can sometimes betray the imagination. He says that reciting from a text in front of an audience makes the reader "an artificiality, not a reality," and that it would be better that the teller of the tale, "without the book," "absorb the character and presently become the man himself." To do so involves creating a persona of artfulness without artificiality, "those studied fictions which seem to be the impulse of the moment, and which are so effective: such as, for instance, fictitious hesitancies for the right word; fictitious unconscious pauses; fictitious unconscious side remarks; fictitious unconscious embarrassments; fictitious unconscious emphases placed upon the wrong word, with a deep intention back of it — these and all the other artful fictive shades which give to a recited tale the captivating naturalness of an impromptu narration" (*MELM*). Twain continues in this passage to discuss the effective use of the narrative "pause," how to use it and when to use it. Throughout it becomes clear that the memory must guide the speaker, just as the stable, unmoving moment in time guides the observer, both becoming one kind of artifice that Twain recognizes as "fictitious unconscious" parts of a whole, a paradox of time which has stopped for one timeless moment, interrupted by a significant "pause," which itself is a timeless moment. All, it seems, is fiction, whether it be the timeless River or Sphinx.

Throughout *Life on the Mississippi* the evident nostalgia for the river long gone pervades Twain's discussion of it. In particular, the monopoly enjoyed by the Pilots' Benevolent Association for a few short years before the Civil War occupies Chapter 15. Twain's lifetime fascination with American capitalism also becomes apparent here. As Twain remarks, this union of pilots "was perhaps the compactest, the completest, and the strongest commercial organization ever formed among men" (176). A dozen of the best pilots form the equivalent of a union, with a pension plan a major draw for "useless, helpless pilots" (179) and their widows and children, require a minimum salary of two hundred and fifty dollars a month, and are promptly fired. In time, however, the tide turns; association pilots are needed in a time of great demand; they refuse to work alongside non-association pilots. Association pilots establish a system of data collection, so that pilots can learn from each other conveniently; non-association pilots cannot use this system. After awhile, insurance companies begin to appreciate that "accidents seemed to keep entirely away from the association men" (186). Eventually the association pilots win the commercial war; all pilots join in time, including apprentice pilots. "The organization seemed indestructible" (189), writes Twain. They even go "into the insurance business" (189). In the end, however, the association collapses. Twain sketches out how the railroad and the Civil War decrease trade on the river, until "behold, in the twinkling of an eye, as it were, the association and the noble science of piloting were things of the dead and pathetic past" (192). The collapse of the financial empire that Hank Morgan creates in *A Connecticut Yankee in King Arthur's Court*, leading to the interdict and the demise of the technological world of the Yankee, is foreshadowed by this nostalgic regret for the abrupt disappearance of the association and "the noble science of piloting." Morgan's lament is the greater: "Yes, I seemed to have flown back out of that age into this of ours, and then forward to it again, and was set down, a stranger and forlorn in that strange England, with an abyss of thirteen centuries yawing between me and you! Between me and my home and my friends! Between me and all that is dear to me, all that could make life worth the living!" (*A Connecticut Yankee*, 493). In both cases, nostalgia breeds the hope that dreams will make the pain bearable, even as Twain recognizes that it is all a "pathetic past," unrecoverable time, nostalgia itself pathetic.

When Twain visits his boyhood home and village, all seems changed. The town has grown: "It is no longer a village; it is a city, with a Mayor, and a council, and water-works, and probably a debt" (545). Twain recalls the past when "in my time the town had no specialty, and no commercial grandeur" (546), but "now a huge commerce in lumber has grown up, and a large miscellaneous commerce is one of the results" (546). Twain's memory of the place remains the same at first: "The only notion of the town that remained in my mind was the memory of it as I had known it when I first quitted it twenty-nine years ago" (524). He thus ignores the "new houses" because "they did not affect the older picture in my mind, for through their solid bricks and mortar I saw the vanished houses, which had formerly stood there, with perfect distinctness" (524). And so Twain "passed through the vacant streets, still seeing the town as it was, and not as it is, and recognizing and metaphorically shaking hands with a hundred familiar objects which no longer exist" (524). He then withdraws into the past: "the things about me and before me made me feel like a boy again — convinced me that I was a boy again, and that I had simply been dreaming an unusually long dream" (524). This is an imaginative nostalgic moment, one that becomes a timeless dream, similar to the final dream of Hank Morgan in *Connecticut Yankee*. And then he returns to the present, albeit with regret: "My reflections spoiled all that; for they forced me to say, 'I see fifty old houses down yonder, into each of which I could enter and find either a man or a woman who was a baby or unborn when I noticed those houses last, or a grandmother who was a plump young bride at that time" (524). He still finds the river vantage point from Holiday's Hill "very beautiful," and "it had this advantage over all the other friends whom I was about to greet again: it had suffered no change; it was as young and fresh and comely and gracious as ever it had been; whereas, the faces of the others would be old, and scarred with the campaigns of life, and marked with their griefs and defeats, and would give me no upliftings of spirit" (525). Only by living in the past with his memory, even if that nostalgia is a reminder of the loss, can Twain see the charm of what life had been in his youth; when faced with the real time that he shares with those who have also faced time in their own ways, all largely unknown and inexpressible lives and experiences, he finds it difficult to understand that present moment of time, preferring instead the memory.

Twain relates a chance meeting with "an old gentleman" who he does not know, but who had lived in Hannibal for "twenty-eight years" (525), and asks about his friends. A number of them have "gone to the dogs" (526), or been "defeated" by life, one dying in Mexico "without a friend to attend the funeral" (526). Twain mentions "one of my early sweethearts" (526), and is told how she has been "married three times" (527), buried "two husbands, divorced from the third, and I hear she is getting ready to marry an old fellow out in Colorado somewhere. She's got children scattered around here and there, most everywheres" (527). One "chucklehead" becomes the "first lawyer in the State of Missouri" (527), and succeeds in life because he had gone to St. Louis, a place where fools are not recognized: "if you send a d__d fool to St. Louis, and you don't tell them he's a d__d fool, *they'll* never find it out" (527). This is a useful acquaintance, for Twain is more likely to find out the truth rather than be offered sugar-coated platitudes. It would be best perhaps if Twain finds out that all of his childhood friends have succeeded in life, because the past would then be that pleasant time-free landscape where nothing bad happens, but this new friend is like every other Mr. Brown that Twain invents, someone who tells the unvarnished truth with the plain language that Twain prefers to use.

While some have not done well, Twain finds it comforting that "a dozen or so of the lot" have been "prosperous — live here yet — town littered with their children" (528). He inquires about himself, not having revealed his own name to begin with, and the fellow responds: "Oh, he succeeded well enough — another case of d__d fool. If they'd sent him to St. Louis, he'd have succeeded sooner" (529). It becomes clear to Twain from this inhabitant of Hannibal that a person's life seems indifferently dependent on skill or intelligence or moral character. In Chapter 54, in fact, Twain remembers two children who drowned, one a sinner and another a model boy. Twain recalls that he found "Dutchy," the good boy, on the bottom of a deep hole in a creek, surely a traumatic event. On the occasion of both deaths, a mighty thunderstorm erupted; in the case of Lem Hackett (Clint Levering), the storm seems "the right and proper thing to do" (531), while in the case of "Dutchy," the storm seems "some mistake" (536). Twain, as a boy, is troubled by the indifference of Heaven: "All heart and hope went out of me" (537). Twain recalls that "it would be vain for me to turn over a new leaf, for I must infallibly fall hopelessly short of that boy" (537), and feels that nature seems indifferent to who perishes and who does not. Later, Twain visits a number of Sunday schools and finds that the children there provoke a "yearning wistfulness," for they represent "boys and girls some of whom I had loved to love, and some of whom I had loved to hate, but all of whom were dear to me for the one reason or the other, so many years gone by — and, Lord, where be they now!" (538). Rather than see these children as individuals with new lives ahead of them, Twain slips rhetorically into a vision of the past, again the nostalgia betraying a wistfulness that seems almost despair. Coaxed into a speech in front of these very real children, Twain continues his wistful admiration of these children. He completes the chapter with a remark or two about "the Model Boy," one who was, in his time, "perfect in manners, perfect in dress, perfect in conduct, perfect in filial piety, perfect in exterior godliness," but at core, a "prig" (539). Twain is perplexed to find to his disappointment that this Model Boy has succeeded in life (539). Again, Twain needs to resort to his memory and his reconstruction of it in order to accept these changes to his town and to his past: "I woke up every morning with the impression that I was a boy — for in my dreams the faces were all young again, and looked as they had looked in the old times; but I went to bed a hundred years old, every night — for meantime I had been seeing those faces as they are now" (540). This, too, represents a timeless moment, each morning a nostalgic recovery of the past, one that retreats into an aged and weary vision of the present. This is remarkable writing. Twain's trip to the past, to see how the Great River has changed over the years, has become a burden of identity, for clearly he would rather be back in the days of the early Hannibal. Readers would likely sympathize, more so the Southern readers who would be remembering what it was like, through the perspectives of idyllic distortion, before the Civil War.

While in Hannibal yet, Twain remembers a carpenter, "a mighty liar," who claims to have murdered sixty people, all named Lynch (541). He is "the Mysterious Avenger" (544), doomed by his vow of revenge against Archibald Lynch, who had killed his bride at his wedding. Twain, as a boy, spends the summer with the carpenter, enthralled at the detailed descriptions of each of the sixty murders. At last, after another Lynch in town confronts the carpenter, the truth is out: "He was a hero to me no longer, but only a poor, foolish, exposed humbug" (545). Twain is "ashamed" (545), and realizes the "heavy loss" in his life, for the teller of the tall-tale has been "the greatest hero I had ever known" (545). The artfulness of this carpenter is still recalled fondly, "for some of his imaginary murders were so vividly and dramatically described that I remember all their details yet"

(545). Here, Twain suggests through this anecdote that lying, once exposed, becomes an embarrassment, while being a creative liar, such as this carpenter, can create reality. This is just one of the many times that Twain uses a story, fabricated or not, to show the power of telling a story, and displaying the anxiety that comes with realizing that anecdotes, tall tales, and fiction must of necessity be based on fact but are mostly untrue.

Twain, in Chapter 56, demonstrates that ability to construct a reality from useful lies. Someone remembers incorrectly that Jimmy Finn, the town drunkard, "was burned to death in the calaboose" (548). Twain writes, "Observe, now, how history becomes defiled, through lapse of time and the help of the bad memories of men" (548). He corrects that history, claiming that "a poor stranger, a harmless, whisky-sodden tramp" had asked a "troop of bad little boys" (548) for a match for his pipe. Only Twain, as a boy, supplies the matches. Later, the tramp is arrested and jailed; he sets his straw bed on fire, and dies a horrible death behind bars. Twain feels enormously guilty for having supplied the matches: "the impressions of that time are burned into my memory" (549). As a "boy of ten years," Twain feels he "was carrying a pretty weighty cargo" of guilt (550). He talks in his sleep, his younger brother Henry overhearing him mutter details about the death of the tramp. Twain, not knowing how much Henry has overheard, attempts to "probe him with a supposititious case" (551), a case about a drunk who borrows a pistol. He asks a series of "suppose" questions about a loaded gun: "Suppose you forgot to tell him to be careful with it, because it was loaded, and he went off and shot himself with that pistol" (551). Henry believes that it might well be murder, "but I don't quite know" (551). Now more nervous than ever about his guilt, Twain gingerly discusses the tramp burned to death in jail. Henry gives a "heavy verdict": "If the man was drunk, and the boy knew it, the boy murdered that man" (552). Twain shuddered, but Henry changes the outcome of the story by guessing that Ben Coontz was the real boy who lent the matches. Twain now relaxes, "my burden being shifted to other shoulders, my terrors soon faded away" (553). Memory can be a fickle thing, then, allowing one to reconstruct it when necessary. Of course, there is nothing to verify this story. Ben Coon, if related imaginatively to Ben Coontz, was a bartender in Tyron's Hotel in Angel's Camp, California; Twain met him in January 1865; Coon apparently told him a tale about a man named Coleman who had a prize jumping frog; Twain appropriated Coon's story (and manner of delivering it, for Coon was not aware of its humor) into the "Jumping Frog Story." Here, Ben Coontz takes the blame, allowing Twain to reflect on how telling the truth depends on how others perceive the truth or misinterpret it. It is somehow convenient that Twain tells this story about the matches with his brother Henry as the victim of the elaborate test, because Henry is the one person Twain trusts most, and the one person unable to dispute the story as it is told.

A related anecdote occurs in Chapter 52, with the story about a supposed letter that an ex-convict, "Jack Hunt," wrote to a prisoner, "Charlie Williams," a letter that turns out to be a "pure swindle" (518). Twain reprints the letter in this chapter, and relates at length the circumstances for it. The letter pretends to give details about Hunt's life outside prison, and his conversion to Christianity and a life of moral virtue. The letter wins sympathy from all who read it, including those who hear it during church sermons. Twain, as the narrator, intends to write an article about the poor Williams languishing in prison and about the Hunt letter, until Charles Dudley Warner questions the authenticity of the letter. Upon investigation, the chaplain of the prison where Williams resides writes to one of the sympathetic listeners of one of the church sermons, a Mr. Page, and claims that Williams is a "dissolute, cunning prodigal" (521), establishing the letter as a fraud written by Williams in order to gain support for his release from prison. All support vanishes. Many had been swindled by the letter; now, many seek to forget it: "As a rule, the town was on a spacious grin for a while, but there were places in it where the grin did not appear, and where it was dangerous to refer to the ex-convict's letter" (521). Here, again, truth depends on those who claim to be telling it. Apparently, there is no basis to this anecdote at all, Twain having concocted it. This story, once more a lie told as a truth, itself a lie, seems a multi-faceted one: simultaneously it declares that truth is fictive, that society can believe in falsehood, that moral uncertainty (or deception) can be successful and that identity can always be questioned.

A discarded chapter from *A Tramp Abroad*, inserted into *Life on the Mississippi* as "The Professor's Yarn" (Chapter 36), is a short story illustrating the effectiveness of a confidence man and professional gambler, a sketch that also outlines how deception can succeed. John Backus, presumed to be a cattleman, attempts to con the professor in this sketch with a surveying scheme, something the then "young land-surveyor"—not yet a college professor, another reminder that identity can change—resists. Backus apparently falls into a group of gamblers, and the professor feels concerned that Backus will lose his ten thousand dollars. In the end, Backus gambles heavily, seems about to lose all of his money, and then wins the entire pot from the others in the game. He turns out to be a professional gambler, adept at lying. The sketch seems not to have a place in *Life on the Mississippi*, something Twain admits freely — "I insert it in this place merely because it is a good story, not because it belongs here — for it doesn't" (386). But everything has its place, apparently, for this sketch becomes another reverberation of the identity and falsehood discussion that Twain seems to be carrying on with the tourists reading this text.

Even the question of Twain's identity, as many have noted, as Twain suggested in Chapter 50, is a falsehood that Twain created. Twain claims that the name "Mark Twain" was appropriated from Captain Isaiah Sellers, who had used that pen name in articles for the New Orleans *Picayune* (498). Twain's pretense suggests that he used a parody of Sellers' work in the New Orleans *True Delta*, borrowing the pen name, which sent "a pang deep into a good man's heart" (497). Twain recognizes that now "there is no suffering comparable with that which a private person feels when he is for the first time pilloried in print" (497). Upon Sellers' death, Twain claims that "I was a fresh, new journalist, and needed a *nom de guerre*; so I confiscated the ancient mariner's discarded one, and have done my best to make it remain what it was in his hands — a sign and symbol and warrant that whatever is found in its company may be gambled on as being the petrified truth. How I've succeeded, it would not be modest in me to say" (498). Sellers never used the name, of course, another lie Twain invented. It is more likely that a bartender in Nevada would chalk up a young Clemens' bar tab with an automatic "mark twain" on some kind of chalkboard, since Clemens preferred two drinks upon arriving, a tally of drinks common to Nevada custom of the day. It could well be that Ben Coon, as a former steamboat pilot on the Illinois River, and a bartender in California in 1865, when Twain met him, may have helped Clemens realize his new identity. Of course, the genteel reader of the nineteenth century would like it more if "Mark Twain" simply meant two fathoms, or safe water for passage on a typical steamboat. That's the way the name is usually discussed in literature classes when it comes to talking about the name Samuel Clemens chose to use. Twain always did prefer Scotch whiskey, two at a time.

This travel work experiments with the notion of knowledge, framing the other work that Twain is challenged by, namely *Huckleberry Finn*, a work he has yet to complete, but a work that will drive Twain toward a different understanding of what knowledge is and can become. The early chapters of *Life on the Mississippi* demonstrate the book learning and book knowledge of the historian, a kind of traditional travel material suitable for the reader who wants dry facts about the history of the great river, particularly its early explorers. Throughout the text, this level of historical knowledge pours from Twain's pen, facts about the cities and towns along the river, numbers of people, amount of goods shipped, but these facts, though they demonstrate useful information about the river, do not show how knowledge ought to be used. The way knowledge ought to be used is part of the cub pilot's training, a knowledge that becomes intuitive, almost instinctual and unconscious.

The new river that Twain explores has changed so much so that modern technology "has knocked the romance out of piloting" (300). Lamps have been installed along the river; snag-boats clear the river from hazards Twain once had to memorize. The knowledge required in 1882 to be a riverboat pilot now lies in charts devised by Horace Bixby and George Ritchie, and not in the memory banks of the pilot. Uncle Mumford's monologue in Chapter 28 acts as a resistance to the assumption that the river can be tamed this way: "But this ain't that kind of a river. They have started in here with big confidence, and the best intentions in the world; but they are going to get left ... they wanted the water to go one way, the water wanted to go another. So they put up a stone wall. But what does the river care for a stone wall? When it got ready, it just bulged through it" (303). Uncle Mumford is a composite character, modeled on the second mate of the *Gold Dust*, one of the steamboats Twain traveled on in 1882, and is similar to Mr. Brown in the *Letters from Hawaii*, someone who is a traveling companion speaking Twain's thoughts. In this case, however, Twain sides with those intending to improve the river with a levee system, though he confesses he does not know which of the competing five theories about the legitimacy of the levee system is the best. Twain admits that the profit motive should prevail: "When a river in good condition can enable one to save $162,000 and a whole summer's time, on a single cargo, the wisdom of taking measures to keep the river in good condition is made plain to even the uncommercial mind" (310). This is a wistful optimism surely, for Twain throughout *Life on the Mississippi* is flabbergasted by the disappearance of notable landmarks. The whole town of Napoleon is gone:

6. Life on the Mississippi 111

> Yes, it was an astonishing thing to see the Mississippi rolling between unpeopled shores and straight over the spot where I used to see a big self-complacent town twenty years ago. Town that was county-seat of a great and important county; town with a big United States marine hospital; town of innumerable fights — an inquest every day; town where I had used to know the prettiest girl, and the most accomplished, in the whole Mississippi valley; town where we were handed the first printed news of the "Pennsylvania's" mournful disaster a quarter of a century ago; a town no more — swallowed up, vanished, gone to feed the fishes; nothing left but a fragment of a shanty and a crumbling brick chimney! [363].

Napoleon's loss reminds Twain of his loss of his brother Henry and, possibly, the memory of an old infatuation with Laura Wright. A good deal of the knowledge Twain has stored up over the years has now become useless. Twain, perhaps in exasperation, starts cataloguing some of the changes along the river, such as the growth of Greenville, Mississippi, and an economic discussion of the cotton industry.

It is as if Twain needed to write out these facts in order to burn this system of knowledge out of his system, before he can tackle the larger project of Huck Finn's evolution, before he can deal with that question of what constitutes a truly useful level of knowledge. Twain shows that he can successfully master the kind of knowledge to be had from books about the river; he describes and can list the features of contemporary commerce along the river. This forms a foundational level of knowledge that he must have. But that level of knowledge will not suffice for an understanding of human life, a level of knowledge not quite entertained by this travel work as Twain begins his journey in 1882. The material appropriated from "Old Times on the Mississippi" certainly deals with that, but the trip that Twain takes in 1882 does not reflect much of that knowledge. There are modest attempts to find some individuals with that deeper knowledge, notably Horace Bixby and Captain Sellers, but not much is said about how their knowledge of the river (or of life) has become an instinctual form of knowledge. Captain Sellers seems to have been swallowed by the facts of the river, apparently able to recite arcane facts about the river with a prodigious memory; Horace Bixby has mapped it so thoroughly that few need to know the shape of the river any longer. No, that knowledge seems to dwell in the past, the past that Twain yearns to understand for himself as he continues to St. Paul; he can only find fragments of that knowledge by asking a stranger in Hannibal about his old friends and acquaintances. That stranger can only offer terse and pithy comments.

The knowledge that Twain rejects fully is anything remotely connected to Sir Walter Scott, a knowledge based on, according to Twain, castles, ogres, and knights, a knowledge framed with chivalric ideals, an idealism that perverts the soul, a romanticism ill-suited to the culture of the South even while it reflects its character. Twain goes so far as to blame Scott for the Civil War, claiming that the false ideals of Scott have permeated the South, that the culture of the South, resting on the romanticism that Scott represents, becomes an enemy to the people who believe in those ideals. Scott's influence is so great that the "South has not yet recovered from the debilitating influence of his books. Admiration of his fantastic heroes and their grotesque 'chivalry' doings and romantic juvenilities still survives here, in an atmosphere in which is already perceptible the wholesome and practical nineteenth-century smell of cotton-factories and locomotives; and traces of its inflated language and other windy humbuggeries survive along with it" (416–17).

This attack on Sir Walter Scott almost engulfs the text. Twain uses it as a way to explain the corruption of the South before the Civil War and the decay of Southern culture, still dependent on that form of knowledge, after the great War between the States. This is, of course, a bit much. But this simplification, similar to Twain's attack against James Fenimore Cooper's style, allows Twain to reflect on the changes that have occurred along the river since the Civil War. Most of these changes have been economic rather than social for, as Twain notes, the citizens of the South have found it impossible to forget the war and must relive it every day: "The case is very different in the South. There, every man you meet was in the war; and every lady you meet saw the war. The war is the great chief topic of conversation" (454).

In the same way, the South has not forgotten the ideals that Sir Walter Scott's works represent. As Twain describes the banks of the Mississippi, primarily the inhabitants, he dwells on the paltry lives and souls of these people, who are infested with the Scott disease. This helps the reader understand one of the narrative planks of the text, that of the constant reminder of death and destruction. Twain's visit to the Mississippi coincided with one of its great floods, the aftermath still apparent. This natural disaster would, of course, remind one of the death scenes that occur. However, that alone does not seem to explain the general pattern of death and cemeteries that are strewn throughout. An anecdote about a revengeful German, having lost his wife and daughter to murderous thieves, who

6. Life on the Mississippi 113

spends 18 years watching over dead bodies housed in a kind of mausoleum of the not-yet-dead is a typical tale of death and woe. The inhabitants of this mausoleum have little bells that they can ring in case they come back to life, warning this caretaker that he must rescue them. This German finds the last thief in this horrible room alive, having rung his bell, and then proceeds to let him die all over again as an act of revenge. A long chapter on cemeteries in New Orleans also reminds the reader of Twain's seeming obsession with death. Though the choice of the title for this text was not his first, preferring to use some variant of the word "abroad," Twain's emphasis on death seems curious, "life" being so often absent.

Twain, as an example of this obsession, writes of Vicksburg's siege during the Civil War. The tourist might well be interested in the basics of travel along the river, such as food, transportation, sights, and exchange values for currency, but reads instead of the hardships of the inhabitants of that Southern city during the war. Food costs dearly in that lesson of history: "flour two hundred dollars a barrel, sugar thirty, corn ten dollars a bushel, bacon five dollars a pound, rum a hundred dollars a gallon; other things in proportion" (376). These are outrageous rates of exchange, even for our own times. Mule meat is one of the staples at the end of the siege. No transportation exists: "The river lay vacant and undisturbed; no rush and turmoil around the railway station, no struggling over bewildered swarms of passengers by noisy mobs of hackmen" (376). Lodging, safe lodging, consists of the caves burrowed into the hillsides of Vicksburg. Sights are grim at best, stupefying in silence:

> silence so dead that the measured tramp of a sentinel can be heard a seemingly impossible distance; out of hearing of this lonely sound, perhaps the stillness is absolute: all in a moment come ground-shaking thunder-crashes of artillery, the sky is cobwebbed with the crisscrossing red lines streaming from soaring bombshells, and a rain of iron fragments descends upon the city, descends upon the empty streets — streets which are not empty a moment later, but mottled with dim figures of frantic women and children scurrying from home and bed toward the cave dungeons [376–7].

In time, the inhabitants of Vicksburg become used to the chaos and destruction.

In a remarkable paragraph in this chapter on Vicksburg, Twain writes of the way that the journey on a ship is similar to the experiences of inhabitants of this besieged city:

> Those are the materials furnished by history. From them might not almost anybody reproduce for himself the life of that time in Vicksburg? Could you, who

did not experience it, come nearer to reproducing it to the imagination of another nonparticipant than could a Vicksburger who did experience it? It seems impossible; and yet there are reasons why it might not really be. When one makes his first voyage in a ship, it is an experience which multitudinously bristles with striking novelties; novelties which are in such sharp contrast with all this person's former experiences that they take a seemingly deathless grip upon his imagination and memory. By tongue or pen he can make a landsman live that strange and stirring voyage over with him; make him see it all and feel it all. But if he wait? If he make ten voyages in succession — what then? Why, the thing has lost color, snap, surprise; and has become commonplace. The man would have nothing to tell that would quicken a landsman's pulse [379].

This seems to suggest that the travel guide will also lose the ability to describe the interesting sites and sights that the tourist ought to view. The experience needs to depend not on memory to be recorded but on the immediacy of impact, something that Twain will deny elsewhere. Memory has to be prodigious in its grasp for the riverboat pilot and the travel guide to succeed in guiding their passengers along the river of life, but here Twain suggests the opposite, that an overused memory becomes a dull mirror of reality. Twain then paraphrases an account of someone who survived this ordeal in Vicksburg, an account moving and desperate in its description of the horrors of war. Twain writes that this man had a diary for only six days, each succeeding day with fewer and fewer entries, until the "seventh day, diary abandoned; life in terrific Vicksburg having now become commonplace and matter of course" (383). The tourist might be interested in Vicksburg, writes Twain, because it "is full of variety, full of incident, full of the picturesque. Vicksburg held out longer than any other important river town, and saw warfare in all its phases, both land and water — the siege, the mine, the assault, the repulse, the bombardment, sickness, captivity, famine" (383). The tourist, however, will find the national cemetery here to be suitable for this bit of history:

> The grounds are nobly situated; being very high and commanding a wide prospect of land and river. They are tastefully laid out in broad terraces, with winding roads and paths; and there is profuse adornment in the way of semitropical shrubs and flowers; and in one part is a piece of native wild-wood, left just as it grew, and, therefore, perfect in its charm. Everything about this cemetery suggests the hand of the national government. The government's work is always conspicuous for excellence, solidity, thoroughness, neatness. The government does its work well in the first place, and then takes care of it [384].

Tourists, according to travel theorists, always appreciate a sight that has been transformed into something beautiful and organized, something that captures the picturesque without being grim (a cemetery that seems natural); this is a "staged authenticity," a created landscape that is a falsehood of sorts, a comforting reality rather than something actually real. It is a curious thing, perhaps, that the "national government" is in charge of the Vicksburg memorial, that it is organized and a suitable monument, because the South was poorly treated during the Reconstruction. This is probably an ironic statement, if not satiric.

Clearly *Life on the Mississippi* is a record of the destruction of the South, even if it promises to be a remembrance of the life that Twain once had on the banks of the river. This travel text looks forward to the writing of the novel of life, that record of Huck Finn's journey toward self-awareness, an allegory of why the Civil War had to be fought. The Sir Walter Scott disease that inflicts pain and suffering on the people of the South needs to be burned out of the system by the act of viewing the dead, of seeing the cemetery aspects of life on this journey toward one's youth. Twain makes this journey, of course, to profit from the text, a kind of natural progression from *A Tramp Abroad* and its European experience to the American landscape; once there, he realizes that the immediate past is a lost moment, because of the Civil War. He needs to dwell on death in order to find life, a life he will find by moving backward in time, before the culture of romance brings forth the Civil War. Twain is also oscillating from the experience of writing *The Prince and the Pauper*, itself a progression from *Tom Sawyer*, as a way of dealing with the question of conscience and identity — a major theme for *Huckleberry Finn* — and as a way of writing something suitably couched in the language of "literature." This oscillation is one of time and location, moving the novel to England and to a different time, where an imagined prince is learning how to be a better person and ruler; *Huckleberry Finn* transcends the necessity of using elevated language and finds a suitable way to be nostalgic about a way of life yet critical of the morals of its time, and still have its main character learn how to be a better person and a voice of American optimism.

7

Following the Equator: *Travel as Nostalgia, Loss, and Recovery*

> *Don't part with your illusions. When they are gone you may still exist but you have ceased to live.*
> —Pudd'nhead Wilson's New Calendar.

> *Often, the surest way to convey misinformation is to tell the strict truth.*
> —Pudd'nhead Wilson's New Calendar.

Following the Equator (1897) records Twain's last major voyage, literally around the world (1895–96), and metaphorically within himself. His late writings, as many have noted, show experiments in conquering his doubts about humanity and the nature of the self. This final trip around the world, as a work of travel literature, is the last major public notebook that captures Twain's state of mind during the journey and after the trip. Writing during a period of great stress—Susy's death, his near bankruptcy—Twain muddled through, disguising his grief and anxiety with humor and insight. As a traveler, Twain seems able to reflect on questions of identity, civilization, race, and travel, particularly time travel.

This text is all the more remarkable for that American perspective, for it was the only text "written wholly in England."[36] While at a distance from America, Twain could better distance himself from his financial and personal disasters. He writes to Orion Clemens from London on March 28, 1897, "We are all in pretty fair condition, as to health, & none of us in fear that the debts will not be paid" (*MEML*). Twain also writes, "We intend that there shall be no slip-shod work in the book if we can help it." Although it was written under stress, Twain intended to do as good a job as possible; he describes the editing process in detail in a letter to Frank Bliss on March 19, 1897, remarking that he wants to bring this book up to same level as *Innocents Abroad* (*MEPUL*); he also writes to Henry Huttleston Rogers on the same date that "I am trying my very best to make a good book of it" (*MTHHR*, 267). Twain later claims in a letter to Wayne MacVeagh on August 22, 1897 that he focused on this last travel book in isolation from other projects: "It was the only book I have ever confined myself to from title-page to Finis without the relief of shifting to other work meantime; & I would rather go hang myself than do the like again" (*MEML*). Twain, as Dennis Welland indicates, took great pains to make sure the text reflected his work; in letters to Chatto and Windus, his English publisher, Twain complained about numerous faults that the printers seemed to be producing; for example, in a letter dated July 22, 1897, he writes: "They don't pay strict enough attention to my punctuation. Their commas are too handy; I hate commas" (*MEML*). For all the attention that he did pay to the accurate transcription of his last travel book, it seems historically unsettling that Frank Bliss would tamper so much with the text, making the English edition (*More Tramps Abroad*) more faithful to Twain's manuscript.

Susan Gillman in "Mark Twain's Travels in the Racial Occult: *Following the Equator* and the Dream Tales" writes that Twain's travel book and a number of dream tales, which includes *The Mysterious Stranger*, "invoke and adapt the notions of spirit communication and disembodied space-and-time travel ... as a means of revisiting the old terrain of U.S. slavery and linking it to the newer global imperialism, the worldwide nationalism, nativism, and racism of the late 1890s" (194). Gillman writes that when Twain goes to Ceylon "we have clearly arrived at the very center of the voyage, Twain's own paradoxical heart of darkness, where this remote orientalized land of dream and romance merges, both pleasurably and disturbingly, with memories of Twain's boyhood in the antebellum South" (202). However, Twain's "heart of darkness" becomes a testament of faith that the racial differences will, with an effort of memory, disappear within the context of a timeless moment.

While the text mirrors doubt and despair, as a result of personal tragedy, it also becomes a document of faith in oneself. He needed to write the book on a number of levels: he had to lecture to earn money to pay his debts; he had to fulfill his contract with publishers (American and British); and, perhaps most importantly, he had to complete the cycle of travel writing that he had started some thirty years earlier. Susy's death delayed the start of writing the manuscript and made the task all the more difficult. Twain's struggle with the text has been well documented.[37] Twain writes in a letter to William Dean Howells (April 2–13, 1899) that "I wrote my last travel-book in hell," while attempting to make the trip seem "an excursion through heaven.... How I did loathe that journey around the world!—except the sea-part & India." However, in a letter to Joseph Twichell (*MEPUL*; January 19, 1897; original at Yale University, Beinecke Rare Book and Manuscript Library, New Haven, Conn.), Twain remarks that Susy's death makes him a "pauper," and that he writes to save himself: "I work all the days, and trouble vanishes away when I use that magic. This book will not long stand between it and me now ... I have many unwritten books to fly to for my preservation." The final text elicits praise from readers such as James Whitcomb Riley, who writes Twain on February 25, 1898, that "I have been glorying in your last book—and if you've ever done anything better, stronger, or of wholesomer *uplift*, I can't recall it" (*MEML*). This last travel book is a testament to Twain's ability to write himself out of the despair that seems to be engulfing him; he was ill during the trip, virtually bankrupt, striving mightily to pay back his creditors, and Susy's death at the end of it made it difficult to plunge ahead into the writing of the text. The "sea-part" refers to the sense of timelessness he was able to find on board, adrift on the ocean with no lecturing responsibilities; the "India" part of his journey becomes a reconstruction of the culture of death in that country, along with the Taj Mahal memorial that will somehow give him a sense of respite from the memory of Susy, and the sense of unutterable loss that he feels with her death.

Many have thought this a lesser text somehow in relation to the first two travel works, *Innocents Abroad* and *Roughing It*; Twain padded liberally, even lifting quotations from about thirty other authors, in order to meet the demands of the subscription book trade. For someone so fixed on the positive aspects of a good memory, it is odd to realize that Twain's memory could be so corrupt; he relied, for example, on Orion's notes to flesh out portions of *Roughing It*. Of course he padded all of his earlier travel works; *Following the Equator*, however, seems to lack the energy and rationale that some of this excess in earlier works provides. If anything, Twain did more research for *Following the Equator* than the other travel works; however, the purpose of these added quotations and facts from a number of sources seems less clear. He could not rely, of course, on personal observation, because he was not in any one country long enough. He needed to understand the Thuggee religion, for example, and, without personal experience, other texts were necessary. He also thought that to understand India, one needed some sense of the history of colonial rule by England, thus the inclusion of historical materials written by several sources, both English and Indian. But the padding seems excessive, unless one argues that some of this padding is necessary to emphasize by repetition the existence of death in Indian culture, the very real threat of Thug assassins and the very real threat of Indian revolt.

The opening chapters in *Life on the Mississippi*, for example, which discuss the history of the Mississippi River and the development of America, give the facts necessary to establish the very notion of history as a changing, evolving document, one which parallels the cub pilot's growing knowledge of the river as a book to learn each day. "The Awful German Language," as an appendix to *A Tramp Abroad*, also so-called padding, works to round out one of the premises of the travel work, the pretense of learning the German language as a goal for the narrator and his companion. No, the real padding of *Following the Equator* lies in the additional material that centers mostly in chapters on South Africa written in haste to make the book a sizable one. It is true that these padded chapters do have a number of points to make, however; Twain had planned to save material on South Africa for a separate book. These added chapters reflect on the Boer conflicts, the Jameson Raid, and Cecil Rhodes, but he lacked any direct experience, the politics were unfamiliar to him, and Twain's words seem hollow at times, even if he directly interviewed a few individuals (prisoners whom he met briefly, for example). This South African padding presents Twain's annoyance at the lack of moral progress in humanity, particularly those who would enslave others physically, mentally, or emotionally. The haste in writing probably short-circuits some of the anger that Twain felt in South Africa, for he saw in that country aspects of the human condition that were unwelcome reminders of the conflict in American society relating to racial assumptions and prejudices. Some of this so-called padding is literary in nature, material inserted to provide a continuity between some of his earlier work and this travel text.

The maxims at the beginning of chapters in *Following the Equator* are, in fact, from "Pudd'nhead Wilson's *New* Calendar," a device used in the

FOLLOWING THE EQUATOR

A JOURNEY AROUND THE WORLD

BY

MARK TWAIN

SAMUEL L. CLEMENS

HARTFORD   NEW YORK
AMERICAN PUBLISHING CO.   DOUBLEDAY & McCLURE CO.
MDCCCXCVII

Title page of *Following the Equator*

7. Following the Equator

novel as having originated from "Pudd'nhead Wilson's Calendar." Readers have long noted that while some of the maxims suit the contents of chapters in the novel, others do not and some do not follow Wilson's characterization. In the travel book, the maxims seem to have the same structural intent, if any, that of occasionally summing up or clarifying the content of the chapter that follows. As preface, Wilson's calendar items are described this way: "These wisdoms are for the luring of youth toward high moral altitudes. The author did not gather them from practice, but from observation. To be good is noble; but to show others how to be good is nobler and no trouble." Also, the travel book is inscribed to "my young friend Harry Rogers, with recognition of what he is, and apprehension what he may become unless he form himself a little more closely upon the model of The Author." The inscription playfully admonishes the son of Henry Huttleston Rogers to mirror Twain's example, presumed to be the moral one, as the preface for the maxims suggests. This, then, amplifies the traditional and conventional role of traveler, that of instructor, who will guide the moral progress of the reader. This use of the opening proverbs thus connects this travel text to the grim earlier work of fiction, which might well remind Harry Rogers that he must attend to his education, lest he fall into the trap that the impostor Tom finds himself unable to extricate himself from, the clutches of Roxy and the corruption of his own soul. The nature vs. nurture debate is here also,

Twain in his Oxford robe (courtesy of the Mark Twain Project Bancroft Library University of California, Berkeley).

and young Rogers needs to be reminded that he should have a sense of humor, perhaps, about who to model himself upon, his father, the successful financier, or the humorist, the bankrupt Twain.

Some of the maxims, as suggested, lack clear connection to the content of the chapter they lead. For example, in Chapter 8, the maxim reads, "It could probably be shown by facts and figures that there is no distinctly native American criminal class except Congress." The chapter itself relates most directly to a naturalist on board ship who regales Twain with oddities of nature, including the Great Moa and the Ornithorhyncus, the latter a duckbill platypus, to which the naturalist pens a poem, an act of "unconscious" plagiarism of the "Sweet Singer of Michigan," Julia Moore (107), someone he admires though he can laugh at her sentimental poetry. All of this resembles one of the tasks that a travel writer does, that of writing about nature's diversity, but the connection to the maxim remains unclear. It is difficult to see the connection between the American Congress as a set of criminals and the native odd animals of Australia. Buried in the chapter is one reference to an Australian "sundowner," a man who is "merely the Australian equivalent of our word, tramp. He is a loafer, a hard drinker, and a sponge" (101). The English edition, *More Tramps Abroad*, probably is closer to Twain's punning skills, as he seemed rather fond of the connective tissue that the word "Abroad" might supply; he liked the title "Abroad on the Great River," and "Abroad on the Mississippi," but his publisher chose *Life on the Mississippi* for that earlier travel work; Twain did find it handy for the even earlier text *A Tramp Abroad*, for Twain considered it humorous for that text if he could be a kind of transient loafer in that work. Or, of course, if the maxim can hold true somehow, then members of Congress are tramps as well, criminals in some extreme way for not doing their jobs. In terms of referring to the naturalist's science of observation, the maxim fits, if obliquely. The chapter also opens with a brief story about two natives found lost at sea, unable to speak a known language, "who cannot name their lost home, wandering Children of Nowhere" (100). Twain changes topics abruptly: "Indeed, the Island Wilderness is the very home of romance and dreams and mystery" (100). These islands allow men who have fought and failed in the struggle for life in the great world; and for men who have been hunted out of the great world for crime... love an easy and comfortable career of trading and money-getting, mixed with plenty of loose matrimony by purchase, divorce without trial or expense, and limitless spreeing thrown in to make life ideally

Be good + you will be lonesome.

Mark Twain

Frontispiece photograph in *Following the Equator* of Twain enjoying the ocean. Taken by Walter G. Chase, a fellow passenger on the *Warrimoo*, en route to Australia (courtesy of the Mark Twain Project Bancroft Library University of California, Berkeley).

perfect" (100). Could this be the reference to Congress members, individuals who reflect the outcasts in this island wilderness? As a reference point, the connection is slight, the challenge to make the opening maxim or proverb connect with the several and sundry points contained in the chapter, perhaps a deliberate challenge for the reader to make some sense of the ironic statement in Pudd'nhead Wilson's Calendar framework device, if there is any.

Other maxims more clearly reflect the text, such as the one to the first chapter, which reflects the flexibility of moral character. Chapter two, which contains a lengthy story without an ending that the reader is invited to complete, begins with "When in doubt, tell the truth" (35), a calendar item that makes a good deal of sense. Huck Finn's first response when faced with the Phelps family is similar, until he is rescued by their own assumptions as to who he is.

More importantly, this chapter also relates several incidents about the importance of a good memory, briefly mentioning "Blind Tom, the negro pianist ... it was said that he could accurately play any piece of music, howsoever long and difficult, after hearing it once" (36), and describing at length a "memory-expert" entertaining the Viceroy of India. Given from the perspective of a "gentleman who had served on the staff of the Viceroy of India" (36), Twain's anecdote relates that this "high-caste Brahmin" (36) could be given words from various languages out of syntactic order and numbers from different mathematical problems, "all in disorder," and, after thinking, "repeated all the sentences, placing the words in their proper order, and untangled the disordered arithmetical problems and gave accurate answers to them all" (37).

Twain then describes in the same chapter General Grant's "fine memory" as an anecdote of his past; Twain meets a friend, a "Senator from Nevada" who invites him to see President Grant, then in his first term. Twain and the senator find themselves alone with Grant, a close situation which finds Twain unable to function: "I had never confronted a great man before, and was in miserable state of funk and inefficiency" (38). After a perfunctory handshake, there is an "awkward pause, a dreary pause, a horrible pause," after which Twain can only say "Mr. President, I — I am embarrassed. Are you?" (38). Ten years pass; the next time Twain meets Grant, Grant greets him with "Mr. Clemens, I am not embarrassed. Are you?" (41). The moment of truth, as the maxim promises — "When in doubt, tell the truth" — finds Twain telling the truth in his moment of self-doubt. At this point, Chapter Two invites the reader to respect the importance of a good memory, the delight in having one.

Twain then remarks that Grant's funeral, an occasion of "dirges and the boom of artillery," make "millions of America" think of "the man who restored the Union and the flag, and gave to democratic government a new lease of life, and, as we may hope and do believe, a permanent place among the beneficent institutions of men" (41). Grant's "fine memory" becomes the occasion to remember how Grant was able to save the nation, as well as create a "permanent place" for democracy in America, a timeless moment of duration, an enduring monument to his achievements. That would or should be enough, for Twain has meandered seemingly into reflecting on the essence of a memory that can be timeless in the society that spawned the great General Grant. He does not end there, for the Grant anecdote is historical, and Twain seems to need another way to emphasize the narrative structure of memory.

The endless story that follows, which concerns a story a passenger had begun to read but "was interrupted before the end was reached" (42), amplifies this sense of timelessness, for the end can never be told properly anyway. The passengers invent endings, but all are found wanting. A John Brown loses his hat in a creek; he strips off his clothes to swim and fetch it; the horse and buggy carrying his clothes ride off, with Brown trying to catch up; he finally does, but can only dress himself with a shirt, coat, and tie, and must grab a lap robe to cover himself when he thinks he hears someone approaching; a number of women greet him on the road, including Brown's beloved, a Mary Taylor; the women wish to ride the buggy home, but find themselves perplexed by how to accomplish that, since the buggy will not hold all of them; Brown finds himself in danger throughout the conversation, particularly when their plans involve him moving or removing the lap robe; finally, Mary steps into the buggy and reaches for the robe, at which point the passenger relating the story says he was interrupted. None of the passengers can solve the endless story, so "it is the reader's privilege to determine for himself how the thing came out" (47). The opening maxim for this chapter, "when in doubt, tell the truth" (35), offers little direct help in finding an ending to the tale, unless one assumes that Brown should just confess that he is naked, embarrassing himself and the women, just as Twain finds himself embarrassed in front of President Grant. The maxim does bear fruit, but the main focus still remains that of the endless moment, the frozen scene where "Mary was still reaching for the lap-robe" (47), a story without an ending.

This rich chapter thus ends on the note of an interrupted memory, and invites the reader to supply a suitable ending, something the great writer Twain (and other passengers) seem unable to supply. This is a challenge, of course. Twain's humor is delicious with this deliberate hoax, as good or better than the Morgan/Hyde landslide case in *Roughing It*, and there really is no ending. Perhaps the best the reader can hope for is a succession of dreams, different endings leading to various embarrassments, like Horace Greeley's head bouncing through the roof of the stagecoach on his famous ride or like his infamous letter on turnips in *Roughing It*, the latter anecdote reminding us that interpretation can lead any number of ways, all depending on the reader's set of cultural lenses. The lap robe story is denser, more detailed, and certainly more organized than the traditional slow-cooked and oral narrative story that Twain claims is the height of humor in his sketch "How to Tell a Story" (1895):

> The humorous story is American, the comic story is English, the witty story is French. The humorous story depends for its effect upon the manner of the telling; the comic story and the witty story upon the matter.
> The humorous story may be spun out to great length, and may wander around as much as it pleases, and arrive nowhere in particular; but the comic and witty stories must be brief and end with a point. The humorous story bubbles gently along, the others burst.[38]

This sexually charged lap robe story almost depends on the circuitous nature that Twain writes about as American verbal storytelling, but the suspense at each step of the way, each maneuver of John Brown designed to save face becoming ensnarled in imminent disaster, drives this story to the verge of witticism without end, a hoax without an end, a punch line that the reader hopes to find. The Golden Arm story that he relates in "How to Tell a Story" has such a final lemon squeezer, something to "burst" in the eye of the listener, but the lap robe is left intentionally blank. The whole chapter revolves around memory, a good and prodigious one being the best, but suddenly that is gone, inviting the reader to invent the memory, to bring the ending to a close by virtue of one's own experiences rather than depending on Twain's. This chapter will "burst" over time throughout *Following the Equator*, because the reader is reminded on occasion that the memory is suspect unless fortified by the knowledge that the traveler is accumulating by the act of traveling, that the travel experience itself will provide the answer, not the travel guide. Truth, if that is what the traveler seeks, will not be in the mere facts of existence, but in how one contrives to skirt around the edges of the truth, making of that experiential moment something greater than truth, hopefully some moment of optimism and humor.

Several letters to and from Twain relating to one incident recorded in *Following the Equator* concerning prisoners in jail in South Africa demonstrates how Twain manipulates the relative nature of truth and the nature of captivity and loss of freedom. These prisoners need something other than the memory of where they are, and Twain strives to provide that for them. Twain's notes about a letter to his wife, but not sent to her, and the actual letter sent to her seem betray a seeming blindness to the circumstances of those prisoners. Perhaps Twain perhaps felt (in this series of letters, several to his wife, one to Henry Rogers, and in notes never published) that Livy does not need to know the kind of cruel humor he is capable of and he needs to disguise his observations about the Reform prisoners in South Africa, those individuals held responsible for the Jameson raid. In a letter dated May 23–24, 1896, Twain writes to Livy that he "went to the jail with the Chapins & Mrs. Hammond & Smythe. About 50 political prisoners there ... I made a sitting-talk of some length.... The prisoners are a fine body of men; almost all them educated gentlemen — possibly all. They look healthy & well-kept" (*MEML*). This is bland observation. In a notes for the letter he did not send, Twain writes "made a talk (or speech — sitting —) to the prisoners; explained to them why they were better off in jail than they would be any where else; that they would eventually have gotten into jail anyhow, by the look of their countenances; that if they got out they would get in again; that it would be better all around if they remained quietly where they are & made the best of it; that after a few months they would prefer the jail & its luxurious indolence to the sordid struggle for bread outside; & that I would go & see Pres. Kruger & do everything I could, short of bribery, to double their jail-terms. They are a mightly fine body of men; & apparently all educated gentlemen" (*MELM*; formerly Notebook 30, TS, 11–12). Do they understand the humor? Twain writes to Henry Huttleston Rogers on May 26, 1896, that "I have seen the prisoners, and made them a nonsensical speech. They are trying to be cheerful, but I suppose that by and by their captivity will begin to tell heavily upon them" (*MTHHR*, 215). Some clearly do understand that humor can be uplifting. In a monologue delivered dockside to reporters on October 15, 1900, Twain recalls that "some of the prisoners didn't seem to take much to the joke, while others seemed much amused"

(*MTS*, Fatout, 343). Apparently President Kruger, having heard about Twain's talk to the prisoners, "ordered more stringent restrictions for the prisoners, but when Mark Twain interceded for them and explained the joke, the severity was eased" (*MTS*, Fatout, 344). Twain did not care for the kind of political leaders who led many of the countries he passed through, and South Africa, with its muddled politics, was not an exception.

Twain uses little from his visit with the Reform prisoners in his travel book, except a paragraph which describes how the "confinement told upon their bodies and their spirits; still, they were superior men, and they made the best that was to be made of the circumstances" (*Following the Equator*, 698). That seems uncharacteristic of Twain, since he often reveals doubts about mankind's ability to progress, and he does not use the easy joke about doubling prison terms. This is a pity, in some ways, for Twain's skills at satire are proven, and this story outside of the text has the legs to stand on its own. It is a sign of the haste of composition of this part of the text—that things begin to fall apart narratively—with less of the humor that is possible. Twain's increasing anger about political repression spills into the text. Much of this last decade of the century is a turning point for Twain, as he begins to grow increasingly bitter about mankind's inability to connect moral progress with technological progress, particularly when wars are fought in order to establish empires and colonies, colonies that subjugate others into virtual slavery.

It is difficult to find wholesome a story about a black prisoner in South Africa which reflects the cruelty of civilization:

> The guards put a big black in the stocks for dashing his soup on the ground; they stretched his legs painfully wide apart, and set him with his back down hill; he could not endure it, and put back his hands upon the slope for a support. The guard ordered him to withdraw the support—and kicked him in the back. "Then," said Mr. B., "the powerful black wrenched the stocks asunder and went for the guard; a Reform prisoner pulled him off and thrashed the guard himself" [*Following the Equator*, 698].

(Mr. B. is apparently a Mr. Brown, someone he saw in the prison in Pretoria.) Twain, in one of his notebook entries on South Africa, emphasizes the contrast between the civilized white man and the native black man, the white cruel and the black naturally civilized:

> The black savage whom the Boer has driven out was brimming over with good nature and comradeship and friendliness ... he was a savage, and all his customs were savage; but he had a sunny spirit, and at bottom a good disposition. He

was replaced by the Boer, a white savage, who is dirty; houses himself like a cow; is indolent; worships a fetich; is grim, serious, solemn, and is always diligently fitting himself for heaven, probably suspecting that they couldn't stand him in the other place" [*MELM*].

This is a common theme in *Following the Equator*, that the civilized, European, and white ethnicities have become anti–Christian and barbaric in their dealings with the native populations of the countries that they rape and pillage. The white has become a savage, more savage than the traditional "savages" of the world, supposedly uncivilized and uneducated, and justifiably ruled by the superior white savage.

Twain's notion of "savage" lacks consistency, however. He uses the term to describe the Maori as a "superior breed of savages" (*Following the Equator*, 318). He writes further that "I do not call to mind any savage race that built such good houses, or such strong and ingenious and scientific fortresses, or gave so much attention to agriculture, or had military arts and devices which so nearly approached the white man's" (318–19). Twain claims that "these, taken together with their high abilities in boat-building, and their tastes and capacities in the ornamental arts, modify their savagery to a semi-civilization" (319). Twain later writes, "All the savage lands in the world are going to be brought under subjection to the Christian governments of Europe. I am not sorry, but glad. This coming fate might have been a calamity to those savage peoples two hundred years ago; but now it will in some cases be a benefaction. The sooner the seizure is consummated, the better for the savages" (625). Much earlier in the text Twain writes of the Hawaiian culture, particularly Kamehameha, "a remarkable man for a savage" (48). This Hawaiian king "started the march of civilization" (51). Further, "savages are eager to learn from the white man any new way to kill each other, but it is not their habit to seize with avidity and apply with energy the larger and nobler ideas which he offers them ... the details of Kamehameha's history show that he was always hospitably ready to examine the white man's ideas" (51).

"Savage," as a pejorative term, depends on the semblance of civilization that a race can have; the less that race resembles a European, the more savage it becomes. Hence, the Boer guard can indeed become a "savage," while the black prisoner inverts the meaning of the term, becoming more civilized in his nobility. And, in turn, "we white people are merely modified Thugs; Thugs fretting under the restraints of a not very thick skin of civilization," Twain writes about the Thuggee in India, another inversion of the traditional order of things. Twain remarks that "we have reached a little altitude where we may look down upon the Indian Thugs with a complacent shudder; and we may even hope for a day, many centuries hence, when our posterity will look down upon us in the same way" (437). This is a larger issue that relates to individual identity, for Twain is now considering cultural identity, the formation of a national stereotype — just as the American is a rapacious individual in collision with the various ethnic and racial groups Twain describes in *Innocents Abroad*— the foundation of a shift in cultural perspective that makes one culture arise, the other fall, both cultures equally lacking in social consciousness of compassion and sanity.

Civilization, as a term for Twain, also lacks some constant to measure it against. He remarks in a discarded chapter on France in *A Tramp Abroad* that concealing lack of morals, in this case the presence of a "harem" in every French household, "is a great point in favor of French civilization." Having a mistress is apparently acceptable in a number of civilizations, but the French seek to hide the truth that "a Frenchman's home is where another man's wife is," and "one observes nothing comparable to this reserve & modesty among any other of the partly-civilized nations." Twain claims that the "practice of sending our American youth to Paris to

"A Railway Station" in *Following the Equator*. Illustration by Frederick Dielman.

finish their education & acquire a French polish, cannot be too highly commended. They can learn a multitude of things in Paris which they could not learn so thoroughly anywhere else except in Dahomey." He writes that some "have argued that the atmosphere of French civilization rots the soul," and says that "rash generalizations like that are unjust." He goes on to write that "one should say it rots the soul more than does the atmosphere of the higher civilizations, such as those of England, America & Germany." It is up to the "upper civilizations," particularly to the "credit of America" to send "teachers to her — lay missionaries in the fair fields of civilization, who could confer upon her that enlightenment which has done so much for ourselves" (*MELM*; formerly Box 6, # 55). He claims that the introduction of soap has begun this mission of enlightening the savages of France. In another set of notes for *A Tramp Abroad*, Twain remarks that civilization, particularly a democratic one, lacks real freedoms, since it is ruled by "a King just as other absolute monarchies are. His name is The Majority." He writes that "ten millions of voters are compacted together in him," a majority who have "dull brains, limited means & ignorance." This king, the voters as a body, "*always* represents the mass of the Ignorance & Incapacity of his land" (*MELM*; formerly Box 6, # 70). Even civilization has its faults, except as it might have virtues of industry and progress, particularly good transportation systems. Twain remarks in another set of manuscript pages that "the pavements & sidewalks are kept in good repair, & are daily & effectively cleansed" (*MELM*; formerly Box 6, # 62). Thus it can be said that civilization can be as savage as any other primitive society; Twain writes in *Following the Equator* that "there are many humorous things in the world; among them the white man's notion that he is less savage than the other savages" (213). This nihilist view is in keeping with Twain's disenchantment with the possibility of progress in mankind's search for meaning and peace. No civilization, it appears, is really civilized. *Following the Equator*, particularly when Twain writes of South Africa, seems a grim indictment of the insanity of civilization, but the roots of this sarcasm are deep in his writings, running from *Innocents Abroad* through *A Tramp Abroad*.

Twain's balance of satire extends to religion as well:

> There is probably not one person whose reverence rises higher than respect for his own sacred things; and therefore, it is not a thing to boast about and be proud of, since the most degraded savage has that — and, like the best of us, has nothing higher. To speak plainly, we despise all reverences and all objects of

reverence which are outside the pale of our own list of sacred things. And yet, with strange inconsistency, we are shocked when other people despise and defile the things which are holy to us [514–5].

Following the Equator begins with a remarkable chapter which addresses the questions of identity — who are we? how does society accept or deny or form our identities? how do we accept ourselves? — which Twain's other travel writings touched on as well. Daniel Beard, Twain's favorite illustrator in *Connecticut Yankee,* provides the first amplification of the identity problem that Twain constructs for himself: the steamer chair that Twain sits on, after contemplating a "holiday" at sea, collapses, which "brought us to shame before all the passengers" (26). Beard's illustration adds the caption that "even the gulls smiled." This noted author, almost at peace with the world and himself, is upended by shoddy workmanship; the first joke is at Twain's expense. His public identity collapses underneath him. *Following the Equator* ends symmetrically on the same note of self-deprecation: the last paragraph discusses how "privately proud" Twain is after the "circumnavigation of this great globe in that little time," until a "vanity-snubbing astronomical" report on a "great body of light" tells of a trip that meteor or comet took "which would enable it to do all that I had done in *a minute and a half*" (712). Just as the first chapter demonstrates, the narrator, even at the end of the book, realizes in the final sentence that "human pride is not worth while; there is always something lying in wait to take the wind out of it" (712). Other individuals in Chapter 1 who reflect the problems of identity include the captain, who "with his gentle nature, his polish, his sweetness, his moral and verbal purity, seemed pathetically out of place in his rude and autocratic vocation. It seemed another instance of the irony of fate" (28). Not only does he not seem to belong to the society of the ship, but he lacks the luck necessary to survive — almost another "Dutchy" from *Life on the Mississippi,* moral to the core, but unlucky in life. The captain "was going home under a cloud" (28), having run the ship aground while approaching Vancouver, evidently expecting to lose his job in Sydney, for "this was his first voyage as captain" (28), presumed to be his last command. The purser "was a sick man," prone to "ghastly sieges of pain in his heart," which "lasted many hours" (28), who "was full of life and cheer and activity the next day as if nothing had happened" (29). One could say that Twain feels especial sympathy for this purser, given the grief Twain went through before beginning to write this book. These officers seem to have split identities, polar selves, just as Twain contemplates the pages he has yet to go in this last travel book, still grieving over Susy's death in America, while he lives in England.

Others on board the ship also reflect identities which lack substance or which have been dismissed by society. "The brightest passenger in the ship, and most interesting and felicitous talker" is a "young Canadian" unable to resist the whiskey bottle (29), a "remittance man," someone who, like the captain, is on his last metaphorical voyage, a "ne'er-do-weel," a relative who cannot be reformed by his family, "sent abroad to get him out of the way" (33). Another "remittance-man," an Englishman, first sent to Canada, now to Australia, manages to run afoul of the law in Australia, and tries to "proclaim himself an earl in the police court ... and fail to prove it" (34).

This first chapter also includes a lengthy discussion of the moral center or lack of it that helps form an identity. The Canadian's lack of resistance to alcohol prompts a discussion on how the desire to drink is the enemy, not the drinking itself: "When the desire intrudes, it should be at once banished out of the mind" (29). Twain discusses the vice of smoking, and how he manages to "quit any of my nineteen injurious habits at any time, and without discomfort or inconvenience" (30) by denying the desire. Twain includes a brief discussion with his doctor about a case of lumbago, which had confined him to bed. The doctor says that Twain must moderate his smoking, his consumption of coffee, tea, incompatible foods, and "two hot Scotches every night" (30–31). Twain says that he lacks "the will-power. I can cut them off entirely, but I can't merely moderate them" (31). Twain follows his own advice, and after "forty-eight hours the lumbago was discouraged and left me" (31). He recommends this medical advice to a lady who had "reached a point where medicines no longer had any helpful effect upon her" (31). Twain tells her to "stop swearing and drinking, and smoking and eating for four days" (31), but she did not have these vices, for "she had neglected her habits.... She had nothing to fall back on" (32). As a result, "she was a sinking vessel, with no freight in her to throw overboard and lighten ship withal. Why, even one or two little bad habits could have saved her, but she was just a moral pauper" (32). Twain refers to his youth in a humorous passage on how he tried to limit himself to just one cigar a day; eventually, he has his cigars made for him on an increasing scale, until he "could have used it as a crutch" (33). Here, Twain suggests playfully that moral strength comes from character that contains some element of corruption. The maxim from *Pudd'nhead Wilson's New Calendar* which begins the chapter says it best: "A man may have no bad habits and have worse" (25).

Chapter 4 relates how following the equator can lead to an unintentional corruption of identity, since time on the ocean can change depending on where the ship is in relation to the meridian. Early in the chapter Twain writes of a Waterbury watch that he wins in a tournament of horse-billiards. In Pretoria, South Africa, where the "parliamentary clock had a peculiarity," for "on the half-hour it strikes the succeeding hour, then strikes the hour again at the proper time," Twain begins to doubt the watch; it does not keep pace with the Pretoria clock; he finally beats "her brains out against the bedstead" (73). He attempts to stop time, because he cannot adjust to a difference in time, that between his watch and the clock. As the ship crosses the International Date Line, Twain loses a day, "never to be found again" (75). Twain claims that "we shall be a day behindhand all through eternity" (75); "while we were crossing the 180th meridian it was Sunday in the stern of the ship where my family were, and Tuesday in the bow where I was" (75). He says further, "the day they were living in stretched behind them half way round the globe, across the Pacific Ocean and America and Europe; the day I was living in stretched in front of me around the other half to meet it" (75). A child is born in steerage, but there is "no way to tell which day it was born on" (76). Twain writes, "The child will never know its own birthday.... This will breed vacillation and uncertainty in its opinions about religion, and politics, and business, and sweethearts, and everything, and will undermine its principles, and rot them away, and make the poor thing characterless, and its success in life impossible" (76). The "poor thing" will lack an identity, being lost in time.

The last chapter, aside from ending on a note of humbleness, also refers to a story about a Dr. James Barry, a "wild young fellow," who was "guilty of various kinds of misbehavior" (711), but who was a sterling physician and capable fellow. At his death, "it was then discovered that he was *a woman*" (712). She "had disgraced herself with her people; so she chose to change her name and her sex and take a new start in the world" (712). This is a case of the "remittance-man" from the first chapter, but carried to a different level. This individual can be banished from society, losing one identity, and yet create a new identity which succeeds. It is also a case of switched gender roles, similar to Roxy's and Tom's in *Pudd'nhead*

7. Following the Equator

Twain at a Norwegian shanty, Great Falls, Montana, 31 July 1895 (courtesy of the Mark Twain Project Bancroft Library University of California, Berkeley).

Wilson, which he published a few years earlier. Twain writes in one of his discarded notes for *Following the Equator*, "Take off your mask & let us see your real self" (*MELM*; formerly DV330). Even at Barry's death, it remains unclear that the real self emerges, since all society has left is the image that she created, a fictitious self with the real one denied public access.

It then becomes no surprise that the question of identity applies to some of the natives that Twain encounters, particularly the Indian servant that he names "Satan" (366), changing the name and the identity because the native pronunciation proves too much for Twain. Also, the fear of a fellow traveler becomes apparent in Twain's lengthy discussion of the Thuggee religion, because that fellow traveler could be a Thug assassin (429). Twain finds it difficult in his travels to find a secure identity for the natives that he sees. He writes that in India "you soon find your long-ago dreams of India rising in a sort of vague and luscious moonlight above the horizon-rim of your opaque consciousness, and softly lighting up a thousand forgotten details which were parts of a vision that had once been vivid to you when you were a boy, and steeped your spirit in tales of the East" (357). He finds that India "is a country that runs richly to name. The great god Vishnu has 108—108 special ones—108 peculiarly holy ones—names just for Sunday use only. I learned the whole of Vishnu's 108 by heart once, but they wouldn't stay; I don't remember any of then now but John W" (357). The memory falters with the romanticized picture of India, with the profusion of unusual and unpronounceable names. India becomes a dream world, one where identities are lost and Twain, as a narrator, feels threatened by the loss of his own real self.

Central too is the question of the savage native being assimilated into civilization. Whether it be the Kanaka selling himself into slavery to owners of Queensland sugar plantations in Australia (81–86), the Australian aborigine tribes nearing extinction (208–09), the Maori warriors in New Zealand who "fell fighting with the whites and against their own people in the Maori war" (322–23), or more generally, the Indian natives under the rule of the British, Twain observes the slave-like condition which these natives have had to accept. In some countries that he visits, the natives demonstrate their intelligence and courage, the white culture that has absorbed them its cruelty. Twain writes, "In many countries we have chained the savage and starved him to death ... in many countries we have burned the savage at the stake ... in many countries we have taken the savage's land from him, and made him our slave, and lashed him every day, and broken his pride, and made death his only friend" (212). This is the ultimate tragedy of civilization, for it takes all cultural contexts away from the native populations that are under the domination of empire-building white cultures. This is a sad dissolution of cultural identity.

"The great bulk of the savages must go," writes Twain (690), when he considers the plight of the natives in South Africa. "The humanest way of diminishing the black population should be adopted, not the old cruel ways of the past" (690), Twain seems to claim, the "old ways" being treachery and theft, the methods of Cecil Rhodes "and his gang" (691). "This is slavery," Twain continues, "and is several times worse than was the American slavery which used to pain England so much" (691). Twain uses satire effectively, claiming that "we humanely reduce an overplus of dogs by swift chloroform; the Boer humanely reduced an overplus of blacks by swift suffocation; the nameless but right-hearted Australian pioneer humanely reduced his overplus of aboriginal neighbors by a sweetened swift death concealed in a poisoned pudding" (691). Twain claims that he "would rather suffer either of these deaths thirty times over in thirty successive days than linger out one of the Rhodesian twenty-year deaths, with its daily burden of insult, humiliation, and forced labor for a man whose entire race the victim hates" (691). A page or two later, Twain remarks on the "tamed blacks" of South Africa, who are, except for the "dowdy clothes of our Christian civilization," "remarkably handsome" (692). "These fiendish clothes, together with the proper lounging gait, good-natured face, happy air, and easy laugh, made them precise counterparts of our American blacks" (692), Twain reflects. Indeed, on seeing "a score of colored women" dressed in the latest European fashions, walking across a town square in King William's Town, Twain finds himself "among old, old friends; friends of fifty years, and I stopped and cordially greeted them" (693). Twain does not understand "a word they said," but he thinks he is back in America: "I was astonished; I was not dreaming that they would answer in anything but American" (693). Their voices "were familiar to me — sweet and musical, just like those of the slave women of my early days" (693). He has moved into the timeless realm where the American abomination of slavery still rules and history remains unchanged. He needs to be in that dream world, for in dreams lie the reality that he can control.

In his discussion of a spiritual self, one which exists outside the physical being, particularly in his entries for January 7, 1897 (*MELM*; formerly Notebook 42), Twain writes of his memory of "The Recent Carnival of Crime in Connecticut," that he had attempted to "account for our seeming *duality*—the presence in us of *another.*" He writes that this attempt made use of a conscience, a separate being from ourselves; he adds that he has read Robert Louis Stevenson's tale of Dr. Jekyll and Mr. Hyde, and that "was nearer the thing," "the dual persons in our body — quite distinct in nature & character & presumably each with *a conscience of its own.*" Twain proceeds to reject this notion of two selves who do not know each other, replacing it with one of his own, a "*spiritualized self* which can *detach itself*" from the physical body, with both selves retaining a memory (albeit sometimes dimly remembered) of the other's activities. The physical self is hampered by its limitations of time-bound constraints — "waking, I move slowly" — but the spiritual self finds few constraints: "In my dreams my unhampered spiritualized body flies to the ends of the earth in the millionth of a second."

Just as he had imagined the women in King William's Town as having emerged from his past in *Following the Equator,* Twain later imagines in this notebook entry that he was "in the presence of a Negro wench" so "vivid" to him that he can see clearly her "round black face, shiny black eyes, thick lips, very white regular teeth showing through her smile" (*MELM*; formerly Notebook 42). She "was about 22, and plump — not fleshy, not fat, merely rounded and plump; and good natured and not at all bad looking." In this dream Twain is offered a "mushy apple pie — hot," as well as "a disgusting proposition to me." Twain finds the proposition "disgusting," but it does not "surprise" him "for I was young (I was never old in a dream yet) and it seemed quite natural that it should come from her." Twain remarks that "it was not a dream — it all happened. I was actually there in person — in my spiritualized condition." Justin Kaplan and Susan Gillman have discussed this notebook passage amply; here it seems useful to note that Twain's dream, laden with sexuality, allows him to imagine the sexual encounter without violating any social taboo. Also, this timeless moment reflects Twain's recognition that he is among "old friends," even if he is among other races. As a traveler in time and in space, Twain finds himself as part of a larger fabric of life, just as he had imagined the colors of Ceylon, or even, in a satiric vein, as he had pictured the varieties of skin colors which separate white men from other races: the "whites look bleached-out, unwholesome, and sometimes frankly ghastly" [381].

This South African episode, where Twain believes he has gone back to Missouri in time, happens to him again in India when he sees a "burly German" hit a native servant, reminding him of his past in America where slavery exists yet in his mind. Twain remarks, "The native took it with meekness, saying nothing, and not showing in his face or manner any resentment. I had not seen the like of this for fifty years. It carried me back to my boyhood, and flashed upon me the forgotten fact that this was the usual way of explaining one's desires to a slave" (351). Twain then recalls how his father occasionally hits "our harmless slave boy, Lewis, for trifling little blunders" (352). He also remembers seeing "a man fling a lump of iron-ore at a slave-man in anger ... I knew the man had a right to kill his slave if he wanted to, and yet it seemed a pitiful thing and somehow wrong, though why wrong I was not deep enough to explain it if I had been asked to do it. Nobody in the village approved of that murder, but of course no one said much about it" (352). In this memory Twain finds himself in a kaleidoscope of time:

It is curious—the space-annihilating power of thought. For just one second, all that goes to make the *me* in me was in a Missourian village, on the other side of the globe, vividly seeing again these forgotten pictures of fifty years ago, and wholly unconscious of all things but just those; and in the next second I was back in Bombay, and that kneeling native's smitten cheek was not done tingling yet! Back to boyhood—fifty years; back to age again, another fifty; and a flight equal to the circumference of the globe—all in two seconds by the watch!" [352].

In fact, Twain becomes overwhelmingly nostalgic for a lost sense of place or time. He shows nostalgia for home or place; he despairs that the American will not evolve in moral character; he maintains a false illusion that his identity could be stable; he finds a lack of harmony among different cultures; he examines acts of self-deception or moral uncertainty; he reviews strategies of moral withdrawal; he ponders the fleeting notion of "truth." He also demonstrates how he can invent memories of the past in order to negate awkward points in time. He becomes increasingly aware of how false it is to believe in technological progress, which ought to lead to moral enlightenment. In response to these nostalgic moments, he creates a timeless world as an act of faith in order to remove himself from the inevitable despair that arises from too closely lapsing into nostalgia. Twain particularly enjoys India:

> When I think of Bombay now, at this distance of time, I seem to have a kaleidoscope at my eye; and I hear the clash of the glass bits as the splendid figures change, and fall apart, and flash into new forms, figure after figure, and with the birth of each new form I feel my skin crinkle and my nerve-web tingle with a new thrill of wonder and delight. These remembered pictures float past me in a sequence of contracts; following the same order always, and always whirling by and disappearing with the swiftness of a dream, leaving me with the sense that the actuality was the experience of an hour, at most, whereas it really covered days, I think [358].

This kaleidoscope of memory occurs later in the context of an American ice storm which he compares to the Taj Mahal: "By all my senses, all my faculties, I know that the ice storm is Nature's supremest achievement in the domain of the superb and the beautiful; and by my reason, at least, I know that the Taj is man's ice storm" (580). Memories merge: "If I thought of the ice storm, the Taj rose before me divinely beautiful; if I thought of the Taj, with its encrustings and inlayings of jewels, the vision of the ice storm rose. And so, to me all these years, the Taj has had no rival among the temples and palaces of men, none that even remotely approached it—it was man's architectural ice storm" (578). This is the pivotal image in Francis Madigan's discussion of Twain's method of acceptance of Susy's death, that nature's beauty and man-made artifice can serve to soothe the pain of loss. The dream encompasses this vision and makes it whole and sound. The ice storm, a potentially destructive event, and the Taj Mahal, a memorial to a wife's death, become life-giving, a tranquility of artistic achievement and stability in one moment of time, the one a natural storm, freezing the moment, the other a man's creation, remembering his lost beloved with a solid structure of his timeless love.

He writes of Baroda, India, that "I wonder how old the town is. There are patches of building — massive structures, monuments, apparently — that are so battered and worn, and seemingly so tired and so burdened with weight of age, and so dulled and stupefied with trying to remember things they forgot before history began, that they give one the feeling that they must have been a part of original Creation" (408). Even a governmental report by a Major Sleeman in 1839 about the Thuggee

> reads with the same freshness and charm that attach to the news in the morning paper ... now you hope, now you despair, now you hope again; and at last everything comes out right, and you feel a great wave of personal satisfaction go weltering through you, and without thinking you put out your hand to path Mithoo on the back, when — puff! the whole thing has vanished away, there is nothing there; Mithoo and all the crowd have been dust and ashes and forgotten, oh, so many, many, *many* lagging years! [433–34].

Twain finds later that a Hindu servant, who is squatting while waiting for his master to return, seems motionless in time: "At the end of an hour he had not changed his attitude in the least degree ... I quitted this vicinity, then, and left him to punish himself as much as he might want to. But up to that time the man had not changed his attitude a hair. He will always remain with me, I suppose; his figure never grows vague in my memory" (468). India stays with him, for the images there are timeless and comforting in the dream self that can yet visit that country with his memory.

Twain's early intentions with *Following the Equator* seems genuinely to write a "lazy man's book": "While I am not going to write a guide book, yet if it can help people to enjoy the same journey, why I shall think it something of a success" (Portland *Oregonian*, August 11, 1895). Twain also says in this Portland interview that an author,

> even when he is making no attempt to draw his character from life, when he is striving to create something different, even then, however ideal his drawing, he is yet unconsciously drawing from memory. It is like a star so far away that

7. Following the Equator   141

the eye cannot discover it through the most powerful telescope, yet if a camera is placed in proper position under that telescope and left for a few hours, a photograph of the star will be the result. So, it's the same way with the mind, a character one has known some time in life may have become so deeply buried within the recollection the lens of the first effort will not bring it to view. But by continued application the author will find, when he is done, that he has etched a likeness of some one he has known before.

Following the Equator turns out not to be the product of a lazy man, for this text becomes a challenge to write, and a challenge to understand. The memory that Twain talks about in his interview before he begins his journey becomes quite important while he struggles with the text in England. He focuses his telescope of memory on the question of what makes cultures different, on what civilization has wrought, and of the multiple ways an identity can be formed or appreciated. He finds himself alone in England, apart from his family for awhile, with Susy gone forever. That makes the writing difficult and the moments of epiphany, the moments of acceptance and transcendence more difficult to trace. It is a struggle to find himself as much as a struggle to make the travel book enjoyable for the reader. The ice storm/Taj Mahal image does seem to be one of the more striking ways to find solace; the obliteration of time when he finds himself back in Missouri is another moment of acceptance. At some point the text does drift away from these epiphanies, but Twain finds himself almost out of bankruptcy at the end of this long trip and difficult book. He has found some measure of peace with the memory's focused image, that of himself in harmony with the community that he returns to, readers who can appreciate the occasional witticism and humor and the social commentary that they need to read in order to become better inhabitants of this small planet. Twain finds himself at rest with the people of the world.

Throughout Twain's travel writings one can find a common thread, one that suggests Twain felt nostalgic about the disappearing frontier in the American landscape, felt uneasy about the assimilation of native cultures by Western civilization, felt adrift on the question of what an identity is, especially his own, and felt it necessary to look for a stable set of moral beliefs that would guide him and civilization in general. His travel writings take place in a realm of timelessness, one that Twain attempts to create yet fails to maintain, an attempt to defeat time within historical time. He realizes that within this imaginative recovery of the past, the present intrudes, and that the future will bring inevitable death. In *Following the Equator*, Twain's attempt to find solace in the bitter conflict

"Hello, Mark" in *Following the Equator*. Illustration by C. H. Warren.

and colonization of other races results in a realization that the boundaries among these races will continue to exist, that the white man will continue to exploit, and that only through the act of memory, which creates a timeless moment, can he eliminate the boundaries between himself and others. Only in this way can he join the world as a fellow citizen and only in this way can readers join him in the exercise of their own memories as they travel in spirit through this last major travel work.

8

Mark Twain's Travel: Looking for an Identity in Fiction

> *It is by the goodness of God that in our country we have those three unspeakably precious things: freedom of speech, freedom of conscience, and prudence never to practice either of them.*
> —Pudd'nhead Wilson's New Calendar.

Mark Twain wrote five travel books to make money, and to establish his career as a writer, but he also used the theme of traveling throughout his fiction. The major structures of time, identity, nostalgia, and memory exist in Twain's travel works as unifying principles, principles common to his major fiction and to his travel writing. These structures do evolve, some maturing within the fiction to transcendent principles that may guide the reader in ways that the travel works do not.

The tourist figure is used directly in early fiction. Seemingly lost in the cave with Becky Thatcher, Tom Sawyer creates in the cave a timeless world where his identity seems to depend on the human contact with Becky, the scrap of candle, and his kite string. *The Adventures of Tom Sawyer* depends on history as much as *Innocents Abroad*, though the novel seems to glorify the passage of time, while the travel work pities and parodies it. Injun Joe is trapped by the good intentions of Judge Thatcher, who has the cave sealed. Injun Joe is a character designed for the tourists of Europe, as he remains trapped at the cave's entrance:

> The poor unfortunate had starved to death. In one place near at hand, a stalagmite had been slowly growing up from the ground for ages, built by the water-drip from a stalactite overhead. The captive had broken off the stalagmite, and upon the stump had placed a stone, wherein he had scooped a shallow

hollow to catch the precious drop that fell once every three minutes with the dreary regularity of a clock tick — a dessert spoonful once in four and twenty hours. That drop was falling when the Pyramids were new; when Troy fell; when the foundations of Rome were laid; when Christ was crucified; when the Conqueror created the British empire; when Columbus sailed; when the massacre at Lexington was "news." It is falling now; it will still be falling when all these things shall have sunk down the afternoon of history, and the twilight of tradition, and been swallowed up in the thick night of oblivion. Has everything a purpose and a mission? Did this drop fall patiently during five thousand years to be ready for this flitting human insect's need? and has it another important object to accomplish ten thousand years to come? No matter. It is many and many a year since the hapless half-breed scooped out the stone to catch the priceless drops, but to this day the tourist stares longest at that pathetic stone and that slow-dropping water when he comes to see the wonders of McDougal's cave. Injun Joe's cup stands first in the list of the cavern's marvels; even "Aladdin's Palace" cannot rival it [254].

This passage clearly parallels Twain's mummified Sphinx prose in Egypt. The purple prose manages to elevate a murderer to the status of a tourist site, his cup as interesting as the Holy Grail or a nail from Christ's cross. Twain's reference to a "tourist" visiting the cave also marks Injun Joe's passage as mythical and timeless, a highlight of a traveler's adventure to Tom's fictive world. Injun Joe's memorial, his cup, seemingly is as monumental as any sight/site that Twain parodied in *Innocents Abroad*. Here, of course, the site/sight is purely American, if a bit threatening to the contemporary reader, Injun Joe representing the mixture of races, the "hapless half-breed," the stranger who threatens the community and who must somehow be expelled from society. This stranger has little to offer the community; his tale is only cautionary.

Two works incubated with *A Tramp Abroad*. Twain worked on *The Adventures of Huckleberry Finn* and *The Prince and the Pauper* at nearly the same time, although *Huckleberry Finn* took longer to complete. Identity plays a major role in these two novels; the threat of death, which plays a relatively minor role in *A Tramp Abroad*, becomes a larger issue in the two novels. *Life on the Mississippi*, of course, prepares the reader for the focus on death and decay, the importance of knowledge and memory, and the nostalgia found in going home but not to the same time.

Jim, in *The Adventures of Huckleberry Finn*, first does not reveal the identity of the dead man in the floating house because he does not need to reveal the death of Huckleberry's father. Huck's dead father would compromise Jim's position, since Huck would then be forced to acknowledge or accept this loss of his own identity as a son — perhaps making Huck realize what he is doing by helping to free Jim. Any recognition of the community that he has left behind, even by finding a release from his abusive father, might remind Huck that he is engaged in an illegal activity, and endanger Jim's flight toward freedom. Huck's dead father, a hapless relic on a wrecked house, threatens Jim's existence. If Huck had paused to reflect on the memorial moment that this discovery might have entailed — reflecting on his father's death, observing it in some way — he would have become a "tourist" in time, recognizing his connection to the past, perhaps reaffirming the necessity of dealing with Jim as an escaped slave. He is reminded enough in the novel of his obligations to society, resulting in the realization that he will go to hell for having saved Jim. All Jim knows is that anyone from Huck's community might well force the issue too soon. As two travelers on the river, forming new memories and a new bond of friendship — which Jim relies on for his safety and his eventual freedom — Huck must learn from the experience of the trip what it means to be human, what it means for Jim to be set free. He needs not to be a son to his father, inheriting the foul ideas of Pap, but needs to be his own man, someone with an identity that he creates and is content to express.

Twain creates this journey with a number of communities gone wrong, showing Huck what follies exist on shore, and by extrapolation, the folly of the community which formed Huck and his father. By exposing Huck to a variety of experiences that demonstrate the folly of Southern life and civilization, Twain can develop Huck's character as an evolving conscience of Southern culture, particularly as a corrupt and decaying influence. The Shepherdson/Grangerford feud, which Huck is forced to observe, leads to certain death because of the false sense of duty and obligation to the family — in much the same way that Huck must learn to reject the false opinions of his bigoted father. His father has a twisted perspective of education and family:

> Well, I'll learn her how to meddle. And looky here — you drop that school, you hear? I'll learn people to bring up a boy to put on airs over his own father and let on to be better'n what he is. You lemme catch you fooling around that school again, you hear? Your mother couldn't read, and she couldn't write, nuther, before she died. None of the family couldn't before they died. I can't; and here you're a-swelling yourself up like this. I ain't the man to stand it — you hear? [24].

Education teaches not just reading but, in a perfect world, the ability to think. Being able to read — and to write, which Huck apparently learns to do quite well — makes the world a place something one can understand with moral purpose. In Pap's version of the family, the child can never be better than the father, nor can any child go beyond what father is. Huck's version includes the safety of others who would help him, members of society who see that Pap is all wrong as a father. Worse yet, the society that would reject Huck's father finds itself bound to its own laws. The laws of this Southern culture (though they follow legal principles generally accepted even today) are bound by tradition. Society is unwilling or unable to evolve, to allow moral conscience the ability to evolve as Huck learns to evolve. The laws do not respect the civilized notions of Judge Thatcher and the Widow Douglas:

> The judge and the widow went to law to get the court to take me away from him and let one of them be my guardian; but it was a new judge that had just come, and he didn't know the old man; so he said courts mustn't interfere and separate families if they could help it; said he'd druther not take a child away from its father. So Judge Thatcher and the widow had to quit on the business [26].

Because that legal challenge does not work, Judge Thatcher tries a new approach, that of re-educating Pap, to reform him of his abusive ways. Education and civilization should change the man, as if new clothes alone will harness the savage:

> When he got out the new judge said he was a-going to make a man of him. So he took him to his own house, and dressed him up clean and nice, and had him to breakfast and dinner and supper with the family, and was just old pie to him, so to speak. And after supper he talked to him about temperance and such things till the old man cried, and said he'd been a fool, and fooled away his life; but now he was a-going to turn over a new leaf and be a man nobody wouldn't be ashamed of, and he hoped the judge would help him and not look down on him. The judge said he could hug him for them words; so he cried, and his wife she cried again; pap said he'd been a man that had always been misunderstood before, and the judge said he believed it. The old man said that what a man wanted that was down was sympathy, and the judge said it was so; so they cried again. And when it was bedtime the old man rose up and held out his hand, and says: "Look at it, gentlemen and ladies all; take a-hold of it; shake it. There's a hand that was the hand of a hog; but it ain't so no more; it's the hand of a man that's started in on a new life, and'll die before he'll go back. You mark them words — don't forget I said them. It's a clean hand now; shake it — don't be afeard." [26–27].

Pap does go back on his word, a number of times. The melodramatic speech of Pap is worthless. All of the tears are for effect, an artifice, an act of lying that is selfish. Pap cannot be retrained; he wants Huck for his money so that he can get drunk. Pap enslaves Huck, a clear parallel to Jim's status:

> He kept me with him all the time, and I never got a chance to run off. We lived in that old cabin, and he always locked the door and put the key under his head nights. He had a gun which he had stole, I reckon, and we fished and hunted, and that was what we lived on. Every little while he locked me in and went down to the store, three miles, to the ferry, and traded fish and game for whisky, and fetched it home and got drunk and had a good time, and licked me. The widow she found out where I was by and by, and she sent a man over to try to get hold of me; but pap drove him off with the gun, and it warn't long after that till I was used to being where I was, and liked it — all but the cowhide part [29–30].

Huck's existence is a parody of the slave's presumed life, a stereotypical assumption of how the slave might appreciate being a slave. This idyllic life, except for the "cowhide part," represents the supposed freedom from civilization that Huck appears to want. However, this life also mirrors the mythical contented slave's life:

> It was kind of lazy and jolly, laying off comfortable all day, smoking and fishing, and no books nor study. Two months or more run along, and my clothes got to be all rags and dirt, and I didn't see how I'd ever got to like it so well at the widow's, where you had to wash, and eat on a plate, and comb up, and go to bed and get up regular, and be forever bothering over a book, and have old Miss Watson pecking at you all the time. I didn't want to go back no more. I had stopped cussing, because the widow didn't like it; but now I took to it again because pap hadn't no objections. It was pretty good times up in the woods there, take it all around [30].

This kind of life depends on Huck reverting to a kind of wild child state, one that lacks discipline, order, and, particularly, civilized manners, the virtues of civilization. Huck no longer needs education, particularly anything learned from a book. His education, in terms of the novel, will come from the journey itself, for he will be educated by various types of people who he will find along the river. Some of these, like the Duke and the King, represent the morality of Pap; others will impress Huck with the nobleness of an individual, like Jim. Huck determines at last that he must run off and save himself from Pap's abuse, but not before he hears one more time the madness of Pap's bigotry and prejudice:

> Oh, yes, this is a wonderful govment, wonderful. Why, looky here. There was a free nigger there from Ohio — a mulatter, most as white as a white man. He had the whitest shirt on you ever see, too, and the shiniest hat; and there ain't a man in that town that's got as fine clothes as what he had; and he had a gold watch and chain, and a silver-headed cane — the awfulest old gray-headed nabob

in the state. And what do you think? They said he was a p'fessor in a college, and could talk all kinds of languages, and knowed everything. And that ain't the wust. They said he could vote when he was at home. Well, that let me out. Thinks I, what is the country a'coming to? It was 'lection day, and I was just about to go and vote myself if I warn't too drunk to get there; but when they told me there was a state in this country where they'd let that nigger vote, I drawed out. I says I'll never vote ag'in. Them's the very words I said; they all heard me; and the country may rot for all me — I'll never vote ag'in as long as I live. And to see the cool way of that nigger — why, he wouldn't 'a' give me the road if I hadn't shoved him out o' the way [33–34].

Huck will contemplate his own soul later, exclaiming that he will go to hell if that means helping Jim go free. Pap does not have the capacity to change, to accept a freed slave's right to vote, and prefers to abstain from voting. Pap does not see that education has changed the slave to someone who is a full citizen with an occupation that makes him a completely respectable member of society. Education is one of the main themes of this novel; Huck needs to be given the lessons of life along the river so that he can do the right thing with Jim; education does not require a school but does require an openness to accept new ideas. Pap wants to remain ignorant. This drunken speech reflects the attitudes of the times before the Civil War; Twain's words capture the sense of the gulf that still exists in his own time, particularly after the disaster of Reconstruction. Pap's demise may be Twain's way to express the wish that the South will eventually recognize the abomination of slavery and its racially hateful attitudes. When Jim finds him, murdered and alone, Pap is symbolically hidden by Jim. Jim's power is now dominant. He is a slave on his way to freedom, a freedom to find his potential just as the educated "mulatter" found employment in a college as a professor, more competent to vote than Pap. Pap, in his last drunken frenzy with Huck, exclaims:

"Tramp — tramp — tramp; that's the dead; tramp — tramp — tramp; they're coming after me, but I won't go. Oh, they're here! don't touch me — don't! hands off — they're cold; let go. Oh, let a poor devil alone!"
... By and by he rolled out and jumped up on his feet looking wild and he see me and went for me. He chased me round and round the place with a clasp-knife, calling me the Angel of Death, and saying he would kill me, and then I couldn't come for him no more. I begged, and told him I was only Huck; but he laughed *such* a screechy laugh, and roared and cussed, and kept on chasing me up [36].

Pap, in his delirium, recognizes that Huck is no longer Huck but his death, perhaps the death of his own ideas and the absence of his own identity with the emerging new American consciousness, where slavery is gone. It is difficult for Huck to forget what his father stands for and what he represents, a perversion of the Southern individual. Huck maintains his faulty conscience until he realizes Jim's humanity and the faults of society. At first, he is assaulted by his own memory of Pap's philosophy toward laws and slaves:

> Jim said it made him all over trembly and feverish to be so close to freedom. Well, I can tell you it made me all over trembly and feverish, too, to hear him, because I begun to get it through my head that he was most free — and who was to blame for it? Why, me. I couldn't get that out of my conscience, no how nor no way. It got to troubling me so I couldn't rest; I couldn't stay still in one place. It hadn't ever come home to me before, what this thing was that I was doing. But now it did; and it stayed with me, and scorched me more and more. I tried to make out to myself that I warn't to blame, because I didn't run Jim off from his rightful owner; but it warn't no use, conscience up and says, every time, "But you knowed he was running for his freedom, and you could 'a' paddled ashore and told somebody." ... I got to feeling so mean and so miserable I most wished I was dead. I fidgeted up and down the raft, abusing myself to myself, and Jim was fidgeting up and down past me [123–24].

Huck decides, temporarily, to give up the struggle, to give in to his father's training, and betray Jim; Jim wisely reminds Huck of his elemental human side, and how memory needs to tapped in order to see the friendship that the two share:

> "Pooty soon I'll be a-shout'n' for joy, en I'll say, it's all on accounts o' Huck; I's a free man, en I couldn't ever ben free ef it hadn' ben for Huck; Huck done it. Jim won't ever forgit you, Huck; you's de bes' fren' Jim's ever had; en you's de only fren' ole Jim's got now" [125].

Huck rows off, with Jim's words reverberating in his mind, and sees an opportunity to rid himself of the guilt; he sees two men in a boat in search of escaped slaves, but then invents a glorious lie about his family and winds up with forty dollars from the men, who are eager to avoid the smallpox they assume is on board Huck's raft. This is a key point in the novel, when Huck learns that Providence (or God) can help him when he masters the art of deception, of learning to control how others perceive his identity:

> Then I thought a minute, and says to myself, hold on; s'pose you'd 'a' done right and give Jim up, would you felt better than what you do now? No, says I, I'd feel bad — I'd feel just the same way I do now. Well, then says I, what's the use you learning to do right when it's troublesome to do right and ain't no trouble to do wrong, and the wages is just the same? I was stuck. I couldn't

answer that. So I reckoned I wouldn't bother no more about it, but after this always do whichever come handiest at the time [127].

This handy philosophy lets Huck reformulate his life a number of times. He needs to lie to the Grangerfords, creating an identity that would let him reunite with Jim. This adventure, which sidelines him from the journey on the river, exposes Huck to the hypocrisy of Southern nobility:

> Col. Grangerford was a gentleman, you see. He was a gentleman all over; and so was his family. He was well born, as the saying is, and that's worth as much in a man as it is in a horse, so the Widow Douglas said, and nobody ever denied that she was of the first aristocracy in our town; and pap he always said it, too, though he warn't no more quality than a mudcat himself.
> ... The old gentleman owned a lot of farms and over a hundred niggers. Sometimes a stack of people would come there, horseback, from ten or fifteen miles around, and stay five or six days, and have such junketings round about and on the river, and dances and picnics in the woods daytimes, and balls at the house nights. These people was mostly kinfolks of the family. The men brought their guns with them. It was a handsome lot of quality, I tell you [142–44].

These Southern gentlemen seemingly kill each other for the sport of the feud, having long forgotten the reasons for hating each other. The family is wealthy, owning many slaves, indulging in picnics and balls, seemingly enjoying the festivities of life, but also obsessed with killing the Shepherdsons. Buck Grangerford notes that both families are heroic in their clashes, claiming that neither family breeds cowards. Buck later dies in the feud, and Huck learns to grieve for someone his own age, someone entrapped in a false sense of history and honor:

> The boys jumped for the river — both of them hurt — and as they swum down the current the men run along the bank shooting at them and singing out, "Kill them, kill them!" It made me so sick I most fell out of the tree. I ain't a-going to tell all that happened — it would make me sick again if I was to do that. I wished I hadn't ever come ashore that night to see such things. I ain't ever going to get shut of them — lots of times I dream about them. ... I got down out of the tree. I crept along down the river-bank a piece, and found the two bodies laying in the edge of the water, and tugged at them till I got them ashore; then I covered up their faces, and got away as quick as I could. I cried a little when I was covering up Buck's face, for he was mighty good to me [153–54].

Death becomes personal for Huck, who seemingly has not recognized until then the death and corruption in the family, despite the chalk fruit on their dining room table and Emmeline's obsessively nihilist obituary poems and dark paintings about death. Jim and Huck reunite after this latest battle of the Shepherdson and Grangerford families. For a brief while Huck remembers the pleasure of the journey, becoming nostalgic for the life on the raft, nostalgic for a life without the death he has just witnessed:

> I never felt easy till the raft was two mile below there and out in the middle of the Mississippi. Then we hung up our signal lantern, and judged that we was free and safe once more. I hadn't had a bite to eat since yesterday, so Jim he got out some corn-dodgers and buttermilk, and pork and cabbage and greens — there ain't nothing in the world so good when it's cooked right — and whilst I eat my supper we talked and had a good time. I was powerful glad to get away from the feuds, and so was Jim to get away from the swamp. We said there warn't no home like a raft, after all. Other places do seem so cramped up and smothery, but a raft don't. You feel mighty free and easy and comfortable on a raft [154–55].

The raft represents the nostalgic moment of freedom from society, from the civilization that would ensnare both of them, for Huck a choice between his deformed upbringing and his evolving conscience, and for Jim a choice between his continued slavery and his opportunity to be free. Travel literature ought to address the food one eats, after all, and this amply makes the sense of freedom something one should hunger for and enjoy. The raft, as a transportation system for the tourist, seems an idyllic way to travel. The raft gives these travelers the timeless moment of certainty of a temporary vacation. The raft also provides a way to observe the faulty society along the river, giving them useful observations that might guide them once they return to the civilization they have left — once the journey is complete, once Jim and Huck end their adventures. Huck can report back to society the lessons he has learned with the book that he writes, completing the hero's quest for meaning, giving the journey along the river the significance it deserves, showing this society that it lacks the capacity to change its corrupt ways, except for some of the individuals who seem to have transcended some of immoral codes of that society, such as Mary Jane Wilks and Aunt Sally Phelps, who are so good-hearted and compassionate that they eclipse the evil that others demonstrate.

The home invasion of this idyllic raft by the Duke and the King shatters the illusion that any vacation will last forever. The Duke and the King are, however, instrumental in providing to Huck a clear example of the corruption of con men, of the nefarious ends of falsehoods, falsehoods and lies that lack any higher purpose. Huck learns the art of lying from these scoundrels, learns to appreciate the power of manipulative language, and learns to fabricate a kind of truthfulness from the fictive worlds of the

Duke and the King. Huck is able to turn the lies of the Duke and the King into a saving grace by salvaging the inheritance of the Wilks family—indeed, the Duke and the King have added an extra four hundred and fifteen dollars to make up a presumed deficit. Twain gave a lecture in 1882 to a meeting of the Historical and Antiquarian Club of Hartford, the essay published as "The Decay of the Art of Lying," that helps define this art of lying:

> Lying is universal—we all do it; we all must do it. Therefore, the wise thing is for us diligently to train ourselves to lie thoughtfully, judiciously; to lie with a good object, and not an evil one; to lie for others' advantage, and not our own; to lie healingly, charitably, humanely, not cruelly, hurtfully, maliciously; to lie gracefully and graciously, not awkwardly and clumsily; to lie firmly, frankly, squarely, with head erect, not haltingly, tortuously, with pusillanimous mien, as being ashamed of our high calling.

Huckleberry Finn demonstrates the art of lying as a form of survival and as a form of identity formation. Huck rejects the falsehoods of Tom Sawyer early on when he realizes that Tom's gang had no real substance. He finds "an old tin lamp" and proceeds to rub it futilely for the genie's arrival: "So then I judged that all that stuff was only just one of Tom Sawyer's lies. I reckoned he believed in the A-rabs and the elephants, but as for me I think different. It had all the marks of a Sunday school" (17). Religion is a dubious avenue for knowledge, as is the romance of traditional literature. Throughout *Huckleberry Finn* the romance of Tom's world, the literature of Sir Walter Scott as many critics have noticed, is rejected in favor of the real world of the river. However, Huck finds it essential to learn the real art of lying as the novel proceeds. One of his early lessons in lying comes from Judith Loftus, who unlayers Huck's set of lies when he attempts to pass himself off as a girl: "Why, I spotted you for a boy when you was threading the needle; and I contrived the other things just to make certain. Now trot along to your uncle, Sarah Mary Williams George Elexander Peters, and if you get into trouble you send word to Mrs. Judith Loftus, which is me, and I'll do what I can to get you out of it" (75). Huck had earlier deceived his drunken father, Pap, with an elaborate plan at Pap's cabin to escape his abusive clutches with a scene of murder and mayhem: "I did wish Tom Sawyer was there, I knowed he would take an interest in this kind of business, and throw in the fancy touches" (41). But that level of deception does not work for Judith Loftus: "Don't forget and tell me it's Elexander before you go, and then get out by saying it's George-Elexander when I catch you. And don't go about women in that old calico. You do a girl tolerable poor, but you might fool men, maybe" (74). She continues the lesson by telling him how to thread a needle, how to throw a lump of lead at a rat, and how to catch something in a lap like a girl. Huck learns other lessons of lying from the Duke and the King and from other situations. He also learns how damaging lies are to others when the lies are malicious, learning how to apologize to Jim for having lied about their temporary separation on the raft. Jim says, "En all you wuz thinkin 'bout wuz how you could make a fool uv ole Jim wid a lie. Dat truck dah is *trash*; en trash is what people is dat puts dirt on de head er dey fren's en makes 'em ashamed" (105). Huck apologizes: "It was fifteen minutes before I could work myself up to go and humble myself to a nigger — but I done it, and I warn't ever sorry for it afterwards, neither. I didn't do him no more mean tricks, and I wouldn't done that one if I'd knowed it would make him feel that way" (105).

Huck, at the end of the novel, participates in a charade of escape that belittles Jim, so this moment of apology does not last. In fact, soon after this apology, Huck frets about his help to a slave who says that "he would steal his children — children that belonged to a man I didn't even know; a man that hadn't ever done me no harm" (124). As Huck relates, "My conscience got to stirring me up hotter than ever, until at last I says to it, 'Let up on me — it ain't too late, yet — I'll paddle ashore at the first light, and tell'" (124). Truth, here, means enslaving and returning Jim to his master. It also proves a release for Huck: "I felt easy, and happy, and light as a feather, right off. All my troubles was gone" (124). Huck's deformed conscience rights itself when he paddles off to tell someone, meeting two men in a skiff. He allows them to think that he has left on the raft his father, who has smallpox. Huck ponders the art of lying at this point:

> I knowed very well I had done wrong, and I see it warn't no use for me to try to learn to do right; a body that don't get started right when he's little, ain't got no show — when the pinch comes there ain't nothing to back him up and keep him to his work, and so he gets beat. Then I thought a minute, and says to myself, hold on — spose you'd a done right and give Jim up; would you felt better than what you do now? No, says I, I'd feel bad — I'd feel just the same way I do now. Well, then, says I, what's the use you learning to do right, when it's troublesome to do right and ain't no trouble to do wrong, and the wages is just the same? I was stuck. I couldn't answer that. So I reckoned I wouldn't bother no more about it, but after this always to whichever come handiest at the time [127].

Related strongly to the notion of Providence, loosely defined as the laws of the natural world, lying becomes a useful art.

Huck continues to invent identities, such as George Jackson for the Grangerford family, and adopts identities posed for him by the Duke and King. Huck finds himself interrogated by one of the Wilks' daughters, the "hare-lip" Joanna, who exclaims, "Honest injun, now hain't you been telling me a lot of lies?" (224). Mary Jane and Susan, the other daughters, force Joanna to apologize to Huck for having accused him of lying: "She done it so beautiful it was good to hear; and I wished I could tell her a thousand lies, so she could do it again" (225). This apology leads to Huck's attempt to set things right: "My mind's made up; I'll hive that money for them or bust" (225). Huck uses lies to defeat the Duke and the King's plans, but these are straightforward lies designed to make things right, two wrongs in this case making all things right. But lying becomes an elegant form of truth when Huck finally arrives at the Phelps farm.

When Huck finally returns to civilization that resembles family and home, a family that does not have the Grangerford decay or the Wilks tragedy, he finds himself at the Phelps farm. Huck feels nostalgia for this place, because this plantation reminds him of the home that he started from:

> When I got there it was still and Sunday-like, and hot and sunshiny; the hands was gone to the fields; and there was them kind of faint dronings of bugs and flies in the air that makes it seem so lonesome and like everybody's dead and gone; and if a breeze fans along and quivers the leaves it makes you feel mournful, because you feel like it's spirits whispering — spirits that's been dead ever so many years — and you always think they're talking about you. As a general thing it makes a body wish he was dead, too, and done with it all [276].

This is nostalgia for a past long gone, a death of the self, a cemetery where the travelers have returned for their final rest. The journey is finished. The spinning-wheel of fate, although here a real sound for Huck, reminds him of the fabric of life being woven together:

> When I got a little ways I heard the dim hum of a spinning-wheel wailing along up and sinking along down again; and then I knowed for certain I wished I was dead — for that is the lonesomest sound in the whole world [277].

At this final stop on his journey, Huck, now temporarily separated from Jim, must depend on the lessons that he has learned from his observations of life along the river, particularly the art of lying:

> I went right along, not fixing up any particular plan, but just trusting to Providence to put the right words in my mouth when the time come; for I'd noticed

that Providence always did put the right words in my mouth if I left it alone [277].

Huck presents one of his grandest lies, one that allows him the freedom to tell the truth (about Tom Sawyer's life and family), a lie that gives him a secure identity:

> Well, I see I was up a stump — and up it good. Providence had stood by me this fur all right, but I was hard and tight aground now. I see it warn't a bit of use to try to go ahead — I'd got to throw up my hand. So I says to myself, here's another place where I got to resk the truth. I opened my mouth to begin; but she grabbed me and hustled me in behind the bed, and says:
> .... "It's Tom Sawyer!"
> By jings, I most slumped through the floor! But there warn't no time to swap knives; the old man grabbed me by the hand and shook, and kept on shaking; and all the time how the woman did dance around and laugh and cry; and then how they both did fire off questions about Sid, and Mary, and the rest of the tribe.
> But if they was joyful, it warn't nothing to what I was; for it was like being born again, I was so glad to find out who I was. Well, they froze to me for two hours; and at last, when my chin was so tired it couldn't hardly go any more, I had told them more about my family — I mean the Sawyer family — than ever happened to any six Sawyer families. And I explained all about how we blowed out a cylinder-head at the mouth of White River, and it took us three days to fix it. Which was all right, and worked first-rate; because they didn't know but what it would take three days to fix it. If I'd 'a' called it a bolt-head it would 'a' done just as well [280–82].

This is the pivotal moment in the novel. Huck has found an identity that he can be comfortable with — as long as Tom Sawyer does not show up — an identity that he can use as a fictive construct, one that will not betray Jim and his plan to free him. As a tourist, Huck does not need to be himself; he can use the facts of Tom's life as his own. He has swapped lives, exchanging his identity with someone who, oddly enough, is more respectable. He can also remove himself as the traveler from the constraints of any presumed ties to society, while fulfilling the role of the traveler who comes back into society with the enlightened outlook of someone knowledgeable about other customs and cultures. As a new member of the Phelps family, he can embellish his observations about the Sawyer family in as many ways as he can invent, because these stories are based on true observations. But he is a new person; he has the mission he started out with, that of freeing Jim, and he needs to continue on that quest with the identity of Tom Sawyer as his baggage. This new and yet acquired knowledge forces Huck into letting Tom run the end game, the final chapters of the novel that some readers find troubling. Huck is still Tom Sawyer in the eyes of the Phelps family; Huck cannot persuade the real Tom Sawyer to let Jim go free, without the usual fictive world that Tom creates at the end; Tom takes charge, and insists on playing the elaborate game of the prisoner and his desperate escape. Jim must pretend that he can write, that he is the natural son of Louis XIV, and that he enjoys the company of snakes and spiders; Tom, after being shot in the leg for his efforts to free Jim by this parody of prison escape, lets Aunt Sally know about his complicated plan:

> "No, I ain't out of my head; I know all what I'm talking about. We did set him free — me and Tom. We laid out to do it, and we done it. And we done it elegant, too." He'd got a start, and she never checked him up, just set and stared and stared, and let him clip along, and I see it warn't no use for me to put in. "Why, Aunty, it costs us a power of work — weeks of it — hours and hours, every night, whilst you was all asleep. And we had to steal candles, and the sheet, and the shirt, and your dress, and spoons, and tin plates, and case-knives, and the warming-pan, and the grindstone, and flour, and just no end of things, and you can't think what work it was to make the saws, and pens, and inscriptions, and one thing or another, and you can't think half the fun it was. And we had to make up the pictures of coffins and things, and nonnamous letters from the robbers, and get up and down the lightning-rod, and dig the hole into the cabin, and make the rope ladder and send it in cooked up in a pie, and send in spoons and things to work with in your apron pocket" [355].

This is a form of knowledge that Twain rejects in *Life on the Mississippi*, a knowledge formed from the world of books, of romance, of the dreaded Sir Walter Scott. By letting Tom Sawyer take over the novel at this point, Twain emphasizes the folly of that knowledge that continues to enslave Jim, and that continues to enslave Tom's narrow world of make believe.

That fictive world that Tom Sawyer creates is a familiar one to Twain's readers. Twain explored earlier in *The Prince and the Pauper* the notions of twins, identities misplaced, and escape from prison, though this escape proves to be an escape from one's own identity. Tom Sawyer exclaims to Aunt Sally, "No, I ain't out of my head; I know all what I'm talking about," when she assumes that he is delirious from his wound (355). This sense of madness when one questions identity is a repeated pattern in Twain's fictive world. In *The Prince and the Pauper*, John Canty finds Edward in the streets, who seeks his help:

> Take me to the king my father, and he will make thee rich beyond thy wildest dreams. Believe me, man, believe me!—I speak no lie, but only the truth!—put forth thy hand and save me! I am indeed the Prince of Wales!"

> The man stared down, stupefied, upon the lad, then shook his head and muttered:
> "Gone stark mad as any Tom o' Bedlam!"—then collared him once more, and said with a coarse laugh and an oath, "But mad or no mad, I and thy Gammer Canty will soon find where the soft places in thy bones lie, or I'm no true man!" [70–71].

St. John in *The Prince and the Pauper* meditates on the boy who does not seem to be the prince any longer, who has forgotten how to be the prince:

> Now were he impostor and called himself prince, look you that would be natural; that would be reasonable. But lived ever an impostor yet, who, being called prince by the king, prince by the court, prince by all, denied his dignity and pleaded against his exaltation? No! By the soul of St. Swithin, no! This is the true prince, gone mad! [96].

Hank Morgan, in *A Connecticut Yankee in King Arthur's Court*, seems equally mad to the inhabitants of sixth-century England, while they first seem to him to be patients at an asylum. Without one's identity in place as a confident mastery of the knowledge of the river — or, here, with Tom Canty, in *The Prince and the Pauper*—the "prince" loses his identity until he can be retrained or educated about the customs of the place, for he does appear to be mentally confused and "mad." The two fictive worlds of Tom Canty and Tom Sawyer are inventions, a kind of madness necessary for their own identities. The "twins" of *The Prince and the Pauper* must adapt to their new identities in order to survive, being reunited and then separated at the end of the novel, with their identities intact. The twins Huck Finn and Tom Sawyer — twins, for they have exchanged identities, and are partners in deception — depart at the end of *The Adventures of Huckleberry Finn* for separate destinations, Huck away from civilization, off to the nostalgic lost world of nature (lost, from Twain's perspective, in the sense of a time and place distant in history), Tom off to the timeless world of his imagination, "most well now, and got his bullet around his neck on a watch-guard for a watch, and is always seeing what time it is" (362). Tom Sawyer's new "watch" reminds him of his glorious adventure, but it is an act of madness that he recalls, the risk and threat of death clearly a memorial object. Huck, with his enlightened experiences of the river of life, needs only his mental agility, the power to lie; his madness only lies in his presumed silence, "so there ain't nothing more to write about, and I am rotten glad of it, because if I'd 'a' knowed what a trouble it was to make a book I wouldn't 'a' tackled it, and ain't a-going to no more" (362). This madness of identity can be explained by writing it out, as Huck Finn and Hank Morgan do in their manuscripts, even if they both must leave, one in death, the other just ahead of civilization. Both Huck and Hank must surely feel, as did Twain in *Roughing It*, as if they are "like the Last Man, neglected of the judgment, and left pinnacled in mid-heaven, a forgotten relic of a vanished world" (550).

Edward, in *The Prince and the Pauper*, must travel through the English landscape, but in a reversal of fortunes, he does not become a Huck Finn who learns the ways of civilization, and who recognizes that he must leave that corrupt and decaying world; Edward, instead, learns the real meaning of civilization, of being human, in order to be a king. He learns compassion:

> Yes, King Edward VI lived only a few years, poor boy, but he lived them worthily. More than once, when some great dignitary, some gilded vassal of the crown, made argument against his leniency, and urged that some law which he was bent upon amending was gentle enough for its purpose, and wrought no suffering or oppression which any one need mightily mind, the young king turned the mournful eloquence of his great compassionate eyes upon him and answered:
> "What dost thou know of suffering and oppression? I and my people know, but not thou" [335].

This is a set of memories that Edward can bring from his journey on the road with Miles Hendon, memories, that, as a tourist, he can explain to his subjects, memories that serve as touchstones to an enlightened mind — and as authentic examples for the community that is also enriched by the traveler's experiences. Miles Hendon is ideal as a mentor, because he has been disavowed by his brother, who also forced Miles's sweetheart, Edith, to marry him after forging a letter that claimed that Miles is dead; he is a man without an identity, someone who is on a parallel journey to reclaim his life and his rightful property. Miles, in fact, questions the sanity and identity of Edward when he claims to be the true king until Edward finally sits on the throne. Edward's journey is similar to Huck Finn's to the degree that he learns hard lessons about the people he wants to rule, becoming more compassionate as a result.

Tom Canty's adjustment to noble life receives scant treatment, perhaps because as a tourist in the palace he is experiencing a less authentic journey. All of the delights of his new life and identity have little substance, but he is adapting well to the pleasures of the palace life. His memory of his original life seems to be dimming:

Did Tom Canty never feel troubled about the poor little rightful prince who had treated him so kindly, and flown out with such hot zeal to avenge him upon the insolent sentinel at the palace-gate? Yes; his first royal days and nights were pretty well sprinkled with painful thoughts about the lost prince, and with sincere longings for his return and happy restoration to his native rights and splendors. But as time wore on, and the prince did not come, Tom's mind became more and more occupied with his new and enchanting experiences, and by little and little the vanished monarch faded almost out of his thoughts; and finally, when he did intrude upon them at intervals, he was become an unwelcome specter, for he made Tom feel guilty and ashamed [297–98].

Tom does feel guilty, but the true king is not much more than a ghost in his memory of him. Twain seems to be thinking of a parallel journey that Tom and Edward are taking, particularly in terms of Tom's diminishing memory of his family, as memory becomes compared to the act of traveling:

Tom's poor mother and sisters traveled the same road out of his mind. At first he pined for them, sorrowed for them, longed to see them; but later, the thought of their coming some day in their rags and dirt, and betraying him with their kisses, and pulling him down from his lofty place, and dragging him back to penury and degradation and the slums, made him shudder. At last they ceased to trouble his thoughts almost wholly. And he was content, even glad; for, whenever their mournful and accusing faces did rise before him now, they made him feel more despicable than the worms that crawl [298].

Tom thinks of the old life that resembles death to him, now that he has experienced the comforts of being a king. Tom's family travels the road of forgetfulness, and he wants to forget them, because his former identity and life are painful memories. That life and that identity led back to the slums, the poverty and death of hope. However, the risk of death is much more apparent to Edward, who has had to deal with it throughout his travels in the countryside:

The miseries of this tramping life, and the weariness and sordidness and meanness and vulgarity of it, became gradually and steadily so intolerable to the captive that he began at last to feel that his release from the hermit's knife must prove only a temporary respite from death, at best [241].

He has had to deal with a gang of thugs, threats from Tom Canty's father; he has observed several women burned at the stake. Even near the end of his return home, when he and Miles Hendon are in London for the coronation of Tom as the king, Edward literally has had to face danger, possibly death, straight on:

The whole journey was made without an adventure of importance. But it ended with one. About ten o'clock on the night of the 19th of February, they stepped upon London Bridge, in the midst of a writhing, struggling jam of howling and hurrahing people, whose beer-jolly faces stood out strongly in the glare from manifold torches — and at that instant the decaying head of some former duke or other grandee tumbled down between them, striking Hendon on the elbow and then bounding off among the hurrying confusion of feet. So evanescent and unstable are men's works in this world! — the late good king is but three weeks dead and three days in his grave, and already the adornments which he took such pains to select from prominent people for his noble bridge are falling. A citizen stumbled over that head, and drove his own head into the back of somebody in front of him, who turned and knocked down the first person that came handy, and was promptly laid out himself by that person's friend. It was the right ripe time for a free fight, for the festivities of the morrow — Coronation Day — were already beginning; everybody was full of strong drink and patriotism; within five minutes the free fight was occupying a good deal of ground; within ten or twelve it covered an acre or so, and was become a riot. By this time Hendon and the king were hopelessly separated from each other and lost in the rush and turmoil of the roaring masses of humanity [293-4].

This is a carnival of life, a fight that proceeds from the Coronation Day festivities. Edward is at serious risk here, having journeyed so far and yet is isolated from his mentor, Miles Hendon. Edward may not quite be ready to face life on his own. He is a tourist still without a plan to recover his own identity as a king. Clearly Edward has acquired memories of death on his journey home, while Tom can barely acknowledge the threat, having had a temporary vacation from his own sordid life.

This historical novel does end happily, with Edward restored to the throne, Tom named chief governor of Christ's Hospital and "King's Ward," and Miles Hendon given back his life, marrying Edith, and given the privilege of being able to sit in the presence of the king. The novel does depend on the unveiling of identities, the search for the missing Great Seal, which Tom has been using to crack nuts, finishing the circle started at the beginning, when the two boys switch clothes and lives, and Edward hides the Great Seal in a suit of armor.

Twain did considerable historical research for this novel, using a style different from much of his writing, imitating the literary style he thought would be appropriate for readers of all ages. It is a remarkable achievement for someone who had genuinely mastered the vernacular language of America and had not written anything quite like this before, except, perhaps, *1601*. Livy adapted the novel into a play that the family would perform at home, Twain usually taking on the role of Miles Hendon and his daughters playing Tom and Edward. Some would suggest that Twain's obsession with identity is linked to his own desire to find respectability as a writer, to be a part of the New England generation of writers. As a way to avoid writing *A Tramp Abroad*, a text giving him fits of frustration, this novel provided Twain a avenue of release. It is a novel that veers away from the parallels to *Tom Sawyer* and *Huckleberry Finn*—the journey that Edward takes being fairly similar to Huck's, the fantasy life that Tom Sawyer imagines and that Tom Canty enjoys, as well as similar characters—in being historical, English, and set in 1547, a time and place antithetical to Twain's best work, *Huckleberry Finn*.

With all three of these works Twain uses the travel experience to show the confusion of identities, to express the usefulness of falsehoods, to reflect on the distortions of memory, and to examine the notion of nostalgia with differing frames of history. Nostalgia for Hannibal governs *Tom Sawyer*, while it denies some of the implications of the diseased society that existed in Twain's childhood, preferring the whitewashing fence episode over the murder in the graveyard, making this novel the stereotypical festival of childhood. Nostalgia in *Huckleberry Finn* is muted, for that nostalgia leads Twain to a kind of denial of that childhood, letting Huck come to terms with grown-up questions. Nostalgia in *Prince and the Pauper* is largely hidden in the plot, where Edward, Miles, and Tom yearn for their former identities, though it can be said that Twain seeks a new identity, that of a writer of literature. Lies in *Tom Sawyer* or in *Prince and the Pauper* are uncovered, while in *Huckleberry Finn* these can lead to a higher appreciation of reality, sometimes supplanting the truth with a better reality. In all three the heroes return home to the joy of their respective communities.

9

Mark Twain's Travel: Looking for Stable Time in His Fiction

> *To succeed in the other trades, capacity must be shown;*
> *in the law, concealment of it will do.*
> — Pudd'nhead Wilson's New Calendar.

The general issues of time, identity, nostalgia, and memory unify both travel works and major fiction. One novel, *A Connecticut Yankee in King Arthur's Court*, has a clear dominant focus on the principle of time. Hank Morgan, in *A Connecticut Yankee in King Arthur's Court*, attempts to defeat time, though he finally is limited by and defeated by death. In that attempt, Hank creates a duplicate universe of nineteenth-century American technology in medieval sixth-century England, and in that political act emphasizes time and history. Critics have long noted that Twain may have tried to show how man's moral progress depends on the ability to adapt to technological change, that science and industry could effect positive enrichment of mankind's moral core. That attempt ends in failure, in part because Twain became disenchanted with technology, thanks to his ill-fated investment in the Paige typesetter, and because Twain could not resist mocking both centuries; the values of superstition and religion of sixth-century England and the values of capitalism of nineteenth-century America are equally suspect. Dan Beard, Twain's approved illustrator, clearly realized this by his depiction of well-known capitalists (such as Jay Gould) in the occasional satirical cartoon on sixth-century religion, politics, or superstition. Letting Hank Morgan blow up his own created technological world in ancient England allows Twain to cast doubt on the whole enterprise of believing that mankind has any chance at any kind of progress, moral or otherwise. This pessimism about mankind's progress thus becomes timeless, suggesting that history does not change.

There is humor in *Connecticut Yankee*, broad, slapstick humor, grim though it may be in the defeat of knights while using a lasso instead of a lance. The humor is a bit awkwardly inhumane when dismissing Sir Dinadan to the hangman's noose, after writing a book on jokes: "If he had left out that old rancid one about the lecturer I wouldn't have said anything; but I couldn't stand that one. I suppressed the book and hanged the author" (443). The humor is farcical when allowing Sandy to talk about anything at length. Physical humor is straightforward when Hank can't reach his handkerchief in order to wipe his brow, clanking along in his armor while on his adventure with Sandy. An occasional witticism emerges: when informed that Clarence is a page Hank says: "Go 'long," I said; "you ain't more than a paragraph" (61). The humor is forced, however, because the novel easily becomes a diatribe against the evils of religion, training or education, politics, and people in general. The challenge for Twain was to write a text that would transcend *Huckleberry Finn* in terms of time, to carry a grown-up version of Huck, someone practical and as Yankee and as northern as he could be, into a different century; *Huckleberry Finn* had moved backwards in time, and *Connecticut Yankee* had to move, it seems, into a far different century in order to distance this text from ordinary humor into broad political satire, so that the nineteenth-century optimism of America's capitalists could be tempered with the reality of the sixth-century English lapse of morality and sense of civilized behavior.

Time, long a theme of discontent in Twain's travel works, challenges Hank Morgan as well. First, he must come to terms with the time travel itself. He has no explanation for it, aside from the crowbar concussion one of his nineteenth-century workers implants on his head, although he alludes to the "transmigration of souls" and the "transposition of epochs — and bodies" early on (48). Sleeping thirteen centuries, after Merlin's magic knocks him out (also unexplained), lacks credibility as well. (How could you have two separate lives, one being born, and the other merely sleeping away for centuries?) It actually doesn't matter; time becomes timeless in this act of accepting the paradoxes by reading the novel. The reader pretends that someone named "M.T." is reading a manuscript prepared by Hank Morgan, with a short postscript added by Clarence, and that "M.T."

merely adds a framework of introduction and conclusion. The pretense is obvious by reading the preface, which clearly provides Twain's presence as a humorist. Time travel is just a given in order to get this work out, and other issues, such as the divine right of kings (not an apparent major theme in this book), can be examined later: "I am not going to have anything particular to do next winter anyway" (45).

What is clear is the ending of the novel in terms of time, for it shapes the rest of the novel; the reader is made aware of the peculiarities of the paradox of time travel, because the magic of Merlin, though a sham in the rest of the text, evidently has worked to keep Hank Morgan in an impossible hibernation for thirteen long centuries. Hank has lived through his own time, while the original Hank was born, grew to manhood, and then disappeared into the mists of time, allowing two Hank Morgans to co-exist, at the very least an improbable scientific condition. Hank is dying, having lost all that he created in sixth-century England; he ought to, in some other parallel universe, be content at being in a century he knows well, as a superintendent at a gun factory in nineteenth-century America. However, he is nostalgic — nostalgia for home the common thread for travel works — for a century long gone, and a home he never really had, since he was always a stranger there. He remains a Connecticut Yankee throughout. In dreams, as Twain begins to recognize late in life, one can create a timeless realm, where the soul can move among histories and locations without regard to time. Hank mutters on his death bed:

> O, Sandy, you are come at last — how I have longed for you! Sit by me — do not leave me — never leave me again, Sandy, never again. Where is your hand — give it me, dear, let me hold it — there — now all is well, all is peace, and I am happy again — we are happy again, isn't it so, Sandy? You are so dim, so vague, you are but a mist, a cloud, but you are here, and that is blessedness sufficient; and I have your hand; don't take it away — it is for only a little while, I shall not require it long.... Was that the child? ... Hello–Central! ... She doesn't answer. Asleep, perhaps? Bring her when she wakes, and let me touch her hands, her face, her hair, and tell her goodbye ... Sandy! ... Yes, you are there. I lost myself a moment, and I thought you were gone.... Have I been sick long? It must be so; it seems months to me. And such dreams! Such strange and awful dreams, Sandy! Dreams that were as real as reality — delirium, of course, but so real! Why, I thought the king was dead, I thought you were in Gaul and couldn't get home, I thought there was a revolution; in the fantastic frenzy of these dreams, I thought that Clarence and I and a handful of my cadets fought and exterminated the whole chivalry of England! But even that was not the strangest. I seemed to be a creature out of a remote unborn age, centuries hence, and even that was as real as the rest! Yes, I seemed to have flown back out of

> that age into this of ours, and then forward to it again, and was set down, a stranger and forlorn in that strange England, with an abyss of thirteen centuries yawning between me and you! between me and my home and my friends! between me and all that is dear to me, all that could make life worth the living! It was awful — awfuler than you can ever imagine, Sandy. Ah, watch by me, Sandy — stay by me every moment — don't let me go out of my mind again; death is nothing, let it come, but not with those dreams, not with the torture of those hideous dreams — I cannot endure that again ... Sandy? [492–93].

Hank confuses time and space; he imagines Sandy, long gone, with him; he imagines the reality of his manuscript becoming dreams, "but so real." The dreams become nightmares of the destruction of England; he collapses time, flying from one era to the other. He becomes nostalgic for nineteenth-century America, a "stranger and forlorn in that strange England," although it is unclear if he is nostalgic for one home "and my friends" in America or the other home in England. He does miss Sandy at the same time he imagines her close at hand. She is absent in time yet close by in his delirium of time. Also, Hank's sleep becomes one long dream, a dream in which the manuscript "M.T." reads contains only the idle thoughts of someone who may not exist; 44, again in *No. 44, The Mysterious Stranger*, claims that "It is true, that which I have revealed to you; there is no God, no universe, no human race, no earthly life, no heaven, no hell. It is all a Dream — a grotesque and foolish dream. Nothing exists but You. And You are but a *Thought* — a vagrant Thought, a useless Thought, a homeless Thought, wandering forlorn among the empty eternities!" (187).

Twain literally wrote Chapter 10 after the bulk of the novel was complete, mostly to explain in a quick descriptive sketch how nineteenth-century civilization suddenly appears — it was a narrative lapse that needed to be covered. It seems clear that the final outcome of the novel was then clear to Twain, that the vast network of technology needed to be destroyed, and that the old familiar volcano from Hawaii could be invoked one more time. Chapter 10 connects metaphorically with the explosion of knights and technology in the final battle, sealing Hank and his followers in their technologically advanced cave, since the metaphor of the volcano proves to be a foreshadowing of the final outcome of Hank's efforts:

> My works showed what a despot could do with the resources of a kingdom at his command. Unsuspected by this dark land, I had the civilization of the nineteenth century booming under its very nose! It was fenced away from the public view, but there it was, a gigantic and unassailable fact — and to be heard from,

yet, if I lived and had luck. There it was, as sure a fact, and as substantial a fact as any serene volcano, standing innocent with its smokeless summit in the blue sky and giving no sign of the rising hell in its bowels [128].

This volcano is described in *Roughing It*, but this volcano has a religious and mythological basis to it:

> A colossal column of cloud towered to a great height in the air immediately above the crater, and the outer swell of every one of its vast folds was dyed with a rich crimson luster, which was subdued to a pale rose tint in the depressions between. It glowed like a muffled torch and stretched upward to a dizzy height toward the zenith. I thought it just possible that its like had not been seen since the children of Israel wandered on their long march through the desert so many centuries ago over a path illuminated by the mysterious "pillar of fire." And I was sure that I now had a vivid conception of what the majestic "pillar of fire" was like, which almost amounted to a revelation [533–34].

God is in every work of nature, even if it portends death and destruction. The volcano, as a capitalized Nature, provides a language that the ordinary mortal can begin to understand, even when Twain does not write of what the "revelation" might mean. The religious image Twain sees in *Roughing It* has now been replaced by the technological horror that Hank creates, which seems apt, since the apparent blame for the demise of Hank's world is religion, also foreshadowed by the same Chapter 10 of *A Connecticut Yankee*:

> I was afraid of a united Church; it makes a mighty power, the mightiest conceivable, and then when it by and by gets into selfish hands, as it is always bound to do, it means death to human liberty, and paralysis to human thought [127].

Thus the volcanic eruption of power, technological and natural, becomes a timeless image, something that Hank cannot defeat, a death of the human spirit as well as the actual — imagined, of course, by the fictive nature of this presumed madman escaped from some asylum — death of the twenty-five thousand knights massed against the fifty-two boys in the cave. This cave proves to be Hank's place of sleep, a kind of stasis of time, the now-quiet volcano. Twain's differing perspectives on nature and religion become combined in this image and description of the volcano. The volcano is a constant theme in Twain's fiction and nonfiction, appearing elsewhere; Twain's view toward nature and religion is a natural process of understanding, one that allows a timeless world in both, and both are equally dangerous and threatening, sometimes occurring in the realm of sleep and dreams. In some ways, Hank's sleep is timeless in itself, just as 44, in *No. 44, The Mysterious Stranger* vanquishes time:

> Look here, August: there are really no divisions of time—none at all. The past is always present when I want it—the *real* past, not an image of it; I can summon it, and there it is. The same with the future: I can summon it out of the unborn ages, and there it is, before my eyes, alive and real, not a fancy, an image, a creation of the imagination [114].

Aside from the timelessness of the entire dream that the manuscript pretends to be, *A Connecticut Yankee* continues the kind of social commentary Twain relished. Hank's physical journey through the English landscape is thrust upon him by the king—he has avoided the search for the Holy Grail successfully—and Hank, dressed in the heavy armor of the time, must ride with Sandy on the grand adventure tour expected of knights of the Round Table. Sandy, delusional with cultural expectations and training that she received, makes Hank save pigs because to her they are noble women. The real satire does not rest with Sandy's delusions—though the humor rescues the text from the satire—but with their visit with Morgan Le Fay, their encounters with a number of peasants and inhabitants of this strange land, and with several presumed magicians. Morgan Le Fay demonstrates her inability to adapt, to change; she murders a page for a minor mistake, paying for his life, a custom that she is unable to explain in Christian terms or any sense of morality. Her treatment of her prisoners is also a monument to her folly, for she cannot remember the crimes of some of these poor souls. This journey leads Hank to remark that the people of sixth-century England are hardly worth saving, because they are ill-equipped to evolve:

> Training—training is everything; training is all there is to a person. We speak of nature; it is folly; there is no such thing as nature; what we call by that misleading name is merely heredity and training. We have no thoughts of our own, no opinions of our own; they are transmitted to us, trained into us. All that is original in us, and therefore fairly creditable or discreditable to us, can be covered up and hidden by the point of a cambric needle, all the rest being atoms contributed by, and inherited from, a procession of ancestors that stretches back a billion years to the Adam-clam or grasshopper or monkey from whom our race has been so tediously and ostentatiously and unprofitably developed. And as for me, all that I think about in this plodding sad pilgrimage, this pathetic drift between the eternities, is to look out and humbly live a pure and high and blameless life, and save that one microscopic atom in me that is truly me: the rest may land in Sheol and welcome for all I care [208].

This is 44's kind of language in *No. 44, The Mysterious Stranger*, and resembles his letters to his fellow angels in *Letters from the Earth*. These are not typical letters that Twain the tourist writes while on some expedition somewhere. But they do follow generally the travel writer's purpose, to describe what one sees on a journey and report back to a community those interesting observations. Satan is visiting the planet Earth and writing back to the angels Michael and Gabriel. As Satan writes of Jesus and God in *Letters from the Earth*, particularly Jesus, "the inventor of hell," "It does not appear that he ever stopped to reflect that *he* was to blame when a man went wrong, inasmuch as the man was merely acting in accordance with the disposition he had afflicted him with" (46).

Hank's adventures with the king reaffirm this belief. Life in this century is miserable; slaves abound; peasants suffer terribly. Though the king does show compassion in the scene at the smallpox hut, when he cares for a dying family, he is difficult to retrain as a peasant. It is difficult to modify his inherited opinions and diseased judgment. A good deal of the novel becomes a satiric review of the society Hank attempts to change. The long discussion of economics in the Marco and Dowley feast that Hank arranges ends poorly, but the ingrained inability to think about wages and the relative cost of living reflects how Marco and Dowley are unable to comprehend the way capitalism might work. Twain's voice comes though in this political satire, and Hank disappears from the text as a narrator. The sketch, "Letter to the Earth," edited (and titled) by Bernard DeVoto, which was originally in the manuscript of *Connecticut Yankee* but discarded by Twain, has much political edginess and sarcasm about the mean-spiritedness of people. And, as with his reflection on Morgan Le Fay, Hank shares Twain's pessimism that "training" or education, particularly from religion, has shackled the minds of men and women so that they are unable to progress morally. With this novel, Twain begins to demonstrate the darker side of his philosophical thinking. He will continue to find people incapable of real progress in *Pudd'nhead Wilson*.

But this is not exactly a glacial shift from his very early regard for people who have been raised in one tradition or culture; in *Innocents Abroad*, Twain writes of the inhabitants of the Azores:

> The good Catholic Portuguese crossed himself and prayed God to shield him from all blasphemous desire to know more than his father did before him. The climate is mild; they never have snow or ice, and I saw no chimneys in the town. The donkeys and the men, women, and children of a family, all eat and sleep in the same room, and are unclean, are ravaged by vermin, and are truly happy. The people lie, and cheat the stranger, and are desperately ignorant and have hardly any reverence for their dead. The latter trait shows how little better they are than the donkeys they eat and sleep with [56].

Surely these inhabitants are also mired in religion and culture, one that they are incapable of changing, or, in the world that Hank would imagine, banding together in an act of revolution. *Innocents Abroad* is also an early text that demonstrates Twain's division of the world's cultures, one that seems criminal and bound by religion, the other, American usually, that seems capable of moral superiority and progress. By equating these peasants with their donkeys, Twain shows an elitism hardly different from Hank's when Hank refers to the knights of the realm as lovable oafs, incapable of real thought and social concern:

> Many a time I had seen a couple of boys, strangers, meet by chance, and say simultaneously, "I can lick you," and go at it on the spot; but I had always imagined until now, that that sort of thing belonged to children only, and was a sign and mark of childhood; but here were these big boobies sticking to it and taking pride in it clear up into full age and beyond. Yet there was something very engaging about these great simplehearted creatures, something attractive and lovable. There did not seem to be brains enough in the entire nursery, so to speak, to bait a fishhook with; but you didn't seem to mind that, after a little, because you soon saw that brains were not needed in a society like that, and, indeed would have marred it, hindered it, spoiled its symmetry — perhaps rendered its existence impossible [68–69].

Within this world where the noble cannot think or understand or evolve, moral progress seems impossible — in short, *Connecticut Yankee* is but part of Twain's considerable efforts to prove that mankind is incapable of moral progress, a theme dominant in late work, and prominent in the anti-war political campaigning that Twain participated in during the last years of the nineteenth century. The venom toward religion, particularly Catholic religion, in both *Connecticut Yankee* and *Innocents Abroad* is a common theme. The venom toward Christianity in general increases in intensity after *Connecticut Yankee* is published. One brief example of this is his short essay, "A Salutation from the 19th to the 20th Century":

> I bring you this stately matron named Christendom, returning bedraggled, besmirched, and dishonored from pirate raids in Kiao-Chow, Manchuria, South Africa, and the Philippines, with her soul full of meanness, her pocket full of boodle, and her mouth full of pious hypocrisies. Give her soap and a towel, but hide the looking-glass.
> New York, Dec. 31, 1900
> [Written For New Year's Eve, 1900, a greeting prepared for a Red Cross Society watch-meeting.][39]

Yet *Connecticut Yankee* does not show that hope is lost for civilization at this stage of Twain's writing. The passage just after writing that "brains were not needed in a society like that" shows Twain veering off to a positive comment on the virtues of the king and his knights:

> There was a fine manliness observable in almost every face; and in some a certain loftiness and sweetness that rebuked your belittling criticisms and stilled them. A most noble benignity and purity reposed in the countenance of him they called Sir Galahad, and likewise in the king's also; and there was majesty and greatness in the giant frame and high bearing of Sir Launcelot of the Lake [69].

This is similar to Twain's respect for Slade in *Roughing It*. Even with the "big boobies" of England's sixth century, there is an admiration of the courage that these knights display. Slade is a murderer yet someone not just feared but admired. Likewise, the knights pick fights with each other as if they were children; they are dangerous to each other because these children have toys or weapons that will kill. Slade is a deadly combination of brains, the brains these knights lack, of courage, the courage the knights seem to have in abundance, and of skill, the skills of hand-to-hand combat that the knights use to vanquish each other. Slade does seem to lack Christian morality, of course. This is an apparent contradiction not easily resolved by Twain. Just as he retained faith in the Paige typesetter long after it should have been apparent that it was a colossal failure, Twain could not quite find a balance between American values of the frontier and the natural progress of mankind. His friendships with capitalists, notably Henry Huttleston Rogers during his final decade, capitalists who were ruthless in reality as much as Slade in *Roughing It*, is a curious thing. Twain, in fact, dedicates *Following the Equator* to Rogers's son, Harry. It is true that Henry Rogers helped save Twain from bankruptcy, but this allegiance and friendship to those who are partially responsible for the wars that Twain hates is a bit of a mystery. Contradictions do abound in Twain's thinking. Twain reports the stereotypical reactions of his generation toward the Mormons, but seems to admire the capitalists who seemingly control the lives of those in that religion and in Utah. Slade, too, is a capitalist, someone who governs with an iron hand and who makes a profit for the company. So, too, Hank Morgan creates an empire with capitalist designs. It is odd that Rogers would still aid someone so vitriolic in his satire in *Connecticut Yankee* toward the robber baron mentality and the world of capitalism; it is also odd that Twain would allow someone like Hank to destroy the civilization that he has created, Twain having so much apparent optimism at the time in the progressive world of the capitalist and the industrialist (though this was somewhat muted later in his career).

Religion, as noted often, hampers the progress of mankind, because religion offers hope and redemption at the same time it offers death and sin. Twain's Satan in *Letters from the Earth* analyzes the contradictory nature of the Old Testament and the New Testament in the Bible, suggesting that much of it was "smouched" from earlier forms of the Bible, from fragments, suggesting that man wrote the word of God. The Old Testament contradicts the New, the Old "is interested mainly in blood and sensuality," the "New one in Salvation. Salvation by fire" (45). The Bible, similarly, is "full of interest. It has noble poetry in it; and some clever fables; and some blood-drenched history; and some good morals; and a wealth of obscenity; and upwards of a thousand lies" (14). Within Hank's world where he has taken advantage of a holy man and his ceaseless bowing motions to make shirts—where he has, in effect, created a machine out of a man—religion can be manipulated. As is clear from the Interdiction at the end of *Connecticut Yankee*, that machine world of men can be brought down by an underlying belief in religion.

Satan in *Letters from the Earth* reveals some of Twain's despair in mankind when mired in principles of technology and genetic inheritance: "The human being is a machine. An automatic machine. It is composed of thousands of complex and delicate mechanisms, which perform their functions harmoniously and perfectly, in accordance with laws devised for their governance, and over which the man himself has no authority, no mastership, no control" (29). In *No. 44, The Mysterious Stranger* 44 affirms that belief: "A man *originates* nothing in his head, he merely observes exterior things, and *combines* them in his head—puts several observed things together and draws a conclusion. His mind is merely a machine, that is all—an *automatic* one, and he has no control over it; it cannot conceive of a *new* thing, an original thing, it can only gather material from the outside and combine it into new *forms* and patterns" (114–15). Hank Morgan actually devises that kind of world, a pseudo God, a Boss, in *Connecticut Yankee*. Satan remarks, however, that "for each one of these thousands of mechanisms the Creator has planned an enemy, whose office is to harass it, pester it, persecute it, damage it, afflict it with pains, and miseries, and ultimate destruction" (29). There are many enemies, "always at work" (29), the main force being the multitude of diseases that afflict mankind. This flaw in mankind to disintegrate because of a necessity in nature's laws to follow the course of inevitable decline into an emptiness of time, which is created by God, is similar to Hank's plea to have just one microscopic atom survive because of some higher purpose or aim, to persevere in the identity "that is truly me." Hank may well wish to defeat the enemies of time, the diseases of mankind, but he cannot defeat religion; Twain's later harsher perspective on religion is blasphemous, Satan's description apt for someone disenchanted with what is left after religion is gone. The individual human being is a fragment, a dream, in *Letters from the Earth*. Twain's hope in a moral being, someone who can "humbly live a pure and high and blameless life," will not rest in Hank Morgan's character, but in Twain's later invention of a dream-self in *No. 44, The Mysterious Stranger* and elsewhere.

The oft-quoted passage on training in Morgan Le Fay's universe does end with that one ray of hope, that the individualist may have some morality left to defend: "And as for me, all that I think about in this plodding sad pilgrimage, this pathetic drift between the eternities, is to look out and humbly live a pure and high and blameless life, and save that one microscopic atom in me that is truly me: the rest may land in Sheol and welcome for all I care" (208). This is a Slade or Huck Finn or Tom Sawyer or Roxy. These are heroes who are occasionally redeemed or lost because of suspect moral codes, but they have a core of identity that makes each someone to admire. The knights in *Connecticut Yankee* demonstrate that sense of identity once in a while, particularly Sir Launcelot when he helps care for an ailing Hello Central.

There are, of course, many instances of Twain finding fault with European culture and systems of education in *Innocents Abroad*; that, and a small measure of admiration for the virtues of American practicality (though not as much for the values represented by Blucher and the Pilgrims), forms the basis for Twain's distrust of the way people are educated. Time travel, as used in *A Connecticut Yankee*, allows Twain to re-examine issues raised in *Huckleberry Finn*, principally questions of nostalgia, the yearning for a golden time (youth and freedom in *Huckleberry Finn*, progress and home in *Connecticut Yankee*), of moral growth (Huck's transformation, his evolved conscience toward slavery, the inability of Hank to manufacture moral change), and of identity, the search for meaning of life (Huck's ability to become Tom Sawyer, Hank's readiness to become The Boss).

Pudd'nhead Wilson is a different book not just because the occasional

Twain arriving in New York 14 April 1910 (courtesy of the Mark Twain Project Bancroft Library University of California, Berkeley).

slapstick humor of earlier fiction and nonfiction seems missing. Here the themes of nostalgia, moral growth, and identity return the reader to the time of *Huckleberry Finn*, but without the sense that freedom will be secured, that mankind will have the potential to progress morally, and that one's identity can be framed positively by society or by genetic inheritance. It may be a different book because the humor has evolved past the point of satire into a realm of cosmic irony, and the outlook for any humor seems grimmer. It is a mad book in the sense that the logic is frightening at the end of the novel, that someone can be property and exempt from the hangman's noose. Identity stands out as a major structural device. David Wilson loses his identity as a lawyer and becomes Pudd'nhead Wilson, the town fool, the fellow obsessed with fingerprints, the marks of one's identity; the Italian twins and their history confuse the inhabitants of Dawson's Landing, both being ciphers to decode, potential assassins yet noble; Tom and Chambers are twins in the cradle, switched in identities by Roxy, and revealed by the now-revered David Wilson, no longer the Pudd'nhead. It is a mad book in that the "The Tragedy of Pudd'nhead Wilson," the real title of the novel, is, in reality, a reversed tragedy where the lowly characters arise, where the comedy genre ought to dominate. Nothing quite makes sense except the lunatic logic of genetics, that perhaps nurture outweighs nature at the same time that nature defeats nurture, an apparent paradox. Not much will change in Twain's mind when he writes in *Letters from the Earth* that "the people are all insane, the other animals are all insane, the earth is insane, Nature itself is insane" (7).

One of the concerns Twain explores in his travel works is the question of identity, as noted before. What makes someone unique? What are the social factors that create an identity? This is one of the constants of Huck Finn's search for meaning, just as it is a constant theme in *Innocents Abroad*, the search for an authentic person in Europe with little success. In *Pudd'nhead Wilson,* the quest for an identity starts with the same kind of sarcasm that Twain had used for both tourists and for local inhabitants. The very first entry from the running jokes of Wilson's calendar, the seeming remnants used in *Following the Equator*, suggests the folly of determining an identity at all:

> There is no character, howsoever good and fine, but it can be destroyed by ridicule, howsoever poor and witless. Observe the ass, for instance: his character is about perfect, he is the choicest spirit among all the humbler animals, yet see what ridicule has brought him to. Instead of feeling complimented when we are called an ass, we are left in doubt [15].

No matter the content of the character, the name given by society governs the stereotype. Wilson, because of his botched joke about the dog, must endure years of his nickname, even if eventually the connotative value dissipates. This ambiguity about identity, one that fades over time, is a parallel plot device to the two children switched after birth, the one raised as a slave, the other as a master. Roxy's attempt to save her own child results in an identity switch that will end in disaster, for neither child will be able to assume the identities they were originally assigned by society. Wilson's fingerprinting skills, which help determine the true identities of these two adults, dooms the one to be sold as an incompetent slave down the river, the other an incompetent master unable to accept his place in society:

> The real heir suddenly found himself rich and free, but in a most embarrassing situation. He could neither read nor write, and his speech was the basest dialect of the negro quarter. His gait, his attitudes, his gestures, his bearing, his laugh — all were vulgar and uncouth; his manners were the manners of a slave. Money and fine clothes could not mend these defects or cover them up; they only made them the more glaring and the more pathetic. The poor fellow could not endure the terrors of the white man's parlor, and felt at home and at peace nowhere but in the kitchen. The family pew was a misery to him, yet he could nevermore enter into the solacing refuge of the "nigger gallery" — that was closed to him for good and all [301–02].

This inverted Greek tragedy creates a confusion of identities. The presumed fool David Wilson becomes mayor of a town of dunces; Tom becomes Chambers, Chambers Tom; Roxy, who had switched the identities successfully, sees her plan fail, her dreams of being supported in old age shattered; the white blood or genetic inheritance becomes black, the black white; Tom dresses in women's clothes to confuse witnesses to his crimes, and Roxy disguises herself as a man. In the traditional tragic mode, the hero or heroine is of noble birth, has a flaw that leads to an arrogance of power or of knowledge, is led astray by that flaw, falls from stature, and is finally exiled from society. Roxy certainly has some of these characteristics, having been in a lineage that includes the first family of Virginia, a noble African, and Pocahontas. Her flaw is that of hubris, a belief that she can switch her child for that of her master's. But this is a tragedy inverted to dark comedy. Identities established at the beginning are reversed; the low character is elevated to a high station in life, the high character to low. The real Chambers is sold down the river, while the real Tom, though now the master, is educationally a slave. Oddly enough, if the real Tom had not been switched, he would have been raised with the same values as the real Chambers — likely becoming a spoiled and shiftless character (similar to the real Chambers), for he has been raised by Roxy as a child.

The nurture vs. nature debate is vital to the text, just as the inexorable logic that leads to an unwholesome conclusion. Roxy believes her child is doomed by the dictates of society, that the one small percentage of slave blood will govern his life and make him a worthless non-entity. She is, herself, a descendant of noble Africans and noble American Indians, and her son a descendant of old Virginia families:

> "Whatever has come o' yo' Essex blood? Dat's what I can't understan'. En it ain't on'y jist Essex blood dat's in you, not by a long sight — 'deed it ain't! My great-great-great-gran'father en yo' great-great-great-great-gran'father was Ole Cap'n John Smith, de highest blood dat Ole Virginny ever turned out, en his great-great-gran'mother or somers along back dah, was Pocahontas de Injun queen, en her husbun' was a nigger king outen Africa — en yit here you is, a slinkin' outen a duel en disgracin' our whole line like a ornery low-down hound! Yes, it's de nigger in you!" [189].

She blames the particle of blood that outweighs the noble lines her son originates from. She does not recognize that her training has had some effect on her son's behavior:

> "Tom" was a bad baby from the very beginning of his usurpation ... Tom got all the petting, Chambers got none. Tom got all the delicacies, Chambers got mush and milk, and clabber without sugar. In consequence, Tom was a sickly child and Chambers wasn't. Tom was "fractious," as Roxy called it, and overbearing; Chambers was meek and docile.
> With all her splendid common sense and practical everyday ability, Roxy was a doting fool of a mother. She was this toward her child — and she was also more than this; by the fiction created by herself, he was become her master; the necessity of recognizing this relation outwardly and of perfecting herself in the forms required to express the recognition, had moved her to such diligence and faithfulness in practicing these forms that this exercise soon concreted itself into habit; it became automatic and unconscious; then a natural result followed; deceptions intended solely for others gradually grew practically into self-deceptions as well; the mock reverence became real reverence, the mock obsequiousness real obsequiousness, the mock homage real homage; the little counterfeit rift of separation between imitation-slave and imitation-master widened and widened, and became an abyss, and a very real one — and on one side of it stood Roxy, the dupe of her own deceptions, and on the other stood her child, no longer a usurper to her, but her accepted and recognized master. He was her darling, her master, and her deity all in one, and in her worship of him she forgot who she was and what he had been [52–56].

Roxy, thus, is partially at fault for her son's poor behavior and poor upbringing, leading to his corruption and decline into gambling, robbery, and murder. Chambers grows up as a survivor, as a slave, but he seems to have an incorruptible nature, though, without the knowledge of how to be anything but a slave, he lacks the ability to adapt to his new identity. The logic of the text dictates that the shallowness of white man's principles as applied to slavery, blood lines or genetic inheritance, and property values will let the murderer go free, straight down the river, into a hell of slavery. This is, of course, a cautionary tale of identities, that society determines an identity. The journeys of these two children differ because the travel guide for both, Roxy, has given them divergent paths to follow. The governing logic lies in the shape of the river, one designed for the Essex line, the other for the Roxy line, both delineated by one of the strongest women in Twain's fiction, but someone flawed with her own criminality and sympathetic virtues or values. She is a mother determined to save her child by any means necessary, but this quickly becomes a morality without rules, a morality that lets her become as culpable (and, to some extent, evil) as her real son.

Roxy is a sympathetic character, for she is seemingly trapped by the blood that determines her as a slave, as property, and her cradle-switching seems an act of defiance against the white society that has made her child another piece of property, the threat of being sold down the river a powerful agent of fear. She is Essex, a product of the white ruling class; she is African, a slave subject to the sexual desires of the Essex white male. She is a powerful figure, arguably the strongest character in Twain's fiction or nonfiction. (One could say that about Joan of Arc, but I won't.) She cannot succeed for any number of reasons, mainly because her own son does not benefit from any morality to be found in white society, becoming corrupted by that culture, but the plot device of David Wilson's fingerprint hobby — this is "The Tragedy of Pudd'nhead Wilson"— brings us back to the inverted tragedy of the novel, that Wilson is the judge-like figure who measures each of the identities in Dawson's Landing, and who solidifies the identity for each person as a stable part of society. If this is a tragedy, it is a tragedy of recognition, *anagnorisis*, the moment Wilson loses his role as "fool" in this town of dunces, the moment the true identities of Tom and Chambers are revealed, and Roxy's plan is upended and unlayered. He alone prevents her plan. He shows how arbitrary racial distinctions are; however, he also makes the community whole again, by reversing the plot to end the racial divide between black and white, thereby making it safe again for the Southern culture to keep that racial distance, while making it still possible to allow the white male to dominate the black female sexually and politically. If this is a tragedy, then Twain has made the novel completely ironic. Wilson is no hero, and Roxy no fool; society suffers the consequence of not learning much from their mistakes of the past.

The Italian twins serve the sub-plot of identity confusion as well. They bring into the text the threat of European mystery, one being as assassin, both suspects in the murder of Judge Driscoll. Tom, disguised as a woman, flees while the twins stand over the victim. Wilson tells Luigi that the "unwritten law of this region requires you to kill Judge Driscoll on sight, and he and the community will expect that attention at your hands" (249), because of the feud between them. These European travelers threaten the fabric of this corrupt American society, and must either be absorbed into this community by following its laws, unwritten or not, or be expelled. They choose exile, even when they become "heroes of romance, now, and with rehabilitated reputations," because they were "weary of Western adventure, and straightway retired to Europe" (301). *Innocents Abroad* allows Americans to plunder Europe; this text attempts to purge Europeans (and their cultures) from America's soil. Twins and their doubled selves alone complicate the identity question, but these two serve as red herrings in the murder sub-plot that allow Wilson to deduce the real murderer at the trial, focusing intensely on the question of what makes a person's character and identity.

In the traditional tragedy, *anagnorisis* leads to an unraveling of the character flaw in the major character and to a temporary dissolution of society's structure, which then must be wrenched back into shape by the death or exile of that figure. *Oedipus Rex* might serve as a classic example of a tragic play. Wilson is elevated, however, into the role of King in Dawson's Landing. In the traditional comedy, *anagnorisis* leads to a festival of life, where the manipulative and deceptive slave (or servant) unites a man and woman, creating harmony in the society. *The Tempest* might serve as a classic play of comedy. Roxy is unable to perform her comedic role, however, and her son becomes the property of this community. Northrop Frye's work on myth comes to mind when relating *Pudd'nhead Wilson* to an analysis of its genre. If so, this novel is an experimental novel, providing a nihilist context for its issues of miscegenation, sexual possession and property, racial inequities, and identity, demonstrating a reversal of expectations, itself a different form of humor, a dark humor, a lapse of faith in mankind's ability to progress beyond its moral compass, mired in a capitalist structure that would make men and women property, to dispense with as necessary. Chambers, the "real heir," becomes feminized, comfortable only in the "kitchen," becoming as powerless and repressed as women in that Southern society. Tom, the impostor who also disguised himself as a woman, is sold down the river. Roxy retreats into "her church and its affairs," her power gone: "The spirit in her eye was quenched, her martial bearing departed with it, and the voice of her laughter ceased in the land" (301). Any joy shuts down, apparently, with religion. But the community, corrupt as it is, goes on.

Both of these major texts demonstrate the dissolution of the hope for stable time to reverse the evils of society that ensnare the inhabitants of these two communities, one mired in the superstition and capitalism of the world created by Hank Morgan, the other bound by laws, unwritten and written, that make slavery a concrete horror. Twain's later works attempt to move outside of these confining mirrors of society by moving into a realm of dreams, where the nihilism becomes even worse, the threats to identity, nostalgia, memory, and time more intensified and problematic. *Following the Equator*, despite its satire and disgust at the human condition, remains one of Twain's last appeals to the healing energies of the mind, to make his memory create a meaningful identity within a timeless world where nostalgia, as an appeal for a home and a family, can make all communities of the world begin to work out the possibilities for tolerance, compassion, and understanding.

Appendix: Travel Works Probably Read and Owned by Mark Twain

This list is lightly annotated to provide basic information about the writer's career. Extracted from Alan Gribben's *Mark Twain's Library: A Reconstruction*, checked against Francis Madigan's "Mark Twain's Passage to India," and Dewey Ganzell's *Mark Twain Abroad*, this selective list of books includes other works, such as history or folklore, used by Twain during the composition of his travel books, and may include works used directly for his novels, such as *The Prince and the Pauper* (a novel underway during the writing of *A Tramp Abroad*).

Presentation copies of travel books given to Twain after 1900 might not appear in this bibliographical appendix simply because he ceased writing travel books after *Following the Equator* and because it is uncertain that Twain read some of the books given to him (hopeful authors would request a "line" of praise or evaluation; one author's work remained unclaimed at the post office), unless Gribben notes that Twain signed or otherwise demonstrated an interest in the presentation copy (marked or annotated in some way).

Twain read widely in newspapers and magazines. These have been generally omitted (Gribben annotates references to journalism that may relate to travel writings, for example, references Twain made to *Punch*, a weekly magazine from London, in *Life on the Mississippi*), unless it is apparent that Twain made use of a specific quotation or lengthy reference in one of his travel books.

Works of literature that relate to travel may be on this list, especially if Twain read these works while on one of his journeys; other works of literature (Shakespeare, for instance) might not appear here, especially if these are used as common sources for quotations. Some works are primarily history texts, and may have been resources for general knowledge contained in Twain's travel works.

Twain may have been aware of or may have read other travel books not included here. For example, he owned a copy of Henry James' *The American Scene*, published in 1907, but it is not known if he read it. If it was clear that Olivia or one of his daughters, Suzy, Clara, or Jane, or his brother Orion, owned or read a travel book in particular, and it is not clear that Twain read or marked the text in some way, then that text does not appear on this list. Editions that appear are the versions that Twain likely read or had in his library.

Bibliography

Abbott, John Stevens Cabot. "Heroic Deeds of Heroic Men." *Harper's Magazine*, 30 (December 1864), 3–20; (January 1865), 150–166; (March 1865), 425–439; andother installments through Vol. 34 (April 1867), 559–571. An American minister, Abbott wrote mainly works on history.

Aberigh-Mackay, George Robert. *Serious Reflections and Other Contributions, Etc.* Bombay: Bombay Gazetteer Press, 1881. An Anglo-Indian writer and educator in India, Aberigh-Mackay is noted for a satire on Anglo-Indian society.

Aflalo, Frederick George. *A Sketch of the Natural History of Australia, with Some Notes on Sport*. Illus. by F. Seth. London: Macmillan and Co., 1896.

Aikin, Lucy. *Memoirs of the Court of King James the First*. 2 vols. Boston: Wells & Lilly, 1822.

_____. *Memoirs of the Court of Queen Elizabeth*. Philadelphia: Abraham Small, 1823. An English writer and historian.

Allen, Elizabeth Ann (Chase) Akers. "Rock Me to Sleep, Mother" (poem, pub. 1860; song, copy. 1860, melody by Ernest Leslie). Allen's authorship of this poem was disputed at first; she was a frequent contributor to periodical literature and published travel letters.

Anderson, Rasmus Bjorn, and Jon Bjarnason, trans. *Viking Tales of the North. The Sagas of Thornstein, Viking's Son, and Fridthjof the Bold. Trans. From the Icelandic by R. B. Anderson and J. Bjarnason. Also Tegner's Fridthjof's Saga, Trans. Into English [in Verse] by G. Stephens*. Chicago: S.C. Griggs & Son, 1877. A Norwegian-American writer, diplomat, and professor, Anderson promoted the theory that the Vikings were the first Europeans in America.

Anderson, Rufus. *The Hawaiian Islands: Their Progress and Condition Under Missionary Labors*. Boston: Gould and Lincoln, 1864. 3rd ed., 1865. An influential evangelist who thought that missionary work should not impose civilization on natives.

Andrews, Lorrin. *A Dictionary of the Hawaiian Language, to Which Is Appended an English-Hawaiian Vocabulary and a Chronological Table of Remarkable Events*. Honolulu: Printed by H. M. Whitney, 1865. Lorrin Andrews was a missionary in Hawaii. His son, Lorrin Andrews Thurston, was responsible for the overthrow of traditional Hawaiian government in 1893.

Appletons' Annual Cyclopaedia and Register of Important Events of the Year. 10 vols. New York: D. Appleton and Co., 1877, 1879, 1880, 1881, 1883, 1884, 1885, 1886.

Arnold, (Sir) Edwin. *India Revisited.* "Author's Edition." Boston: Roberts Brothers, 1886. English journalist and poet who lived in India and Japan.

Atkinson, Edward. Unidentified source. Twain refers to Atkinson in Chapter 28 of *Life on the Mississippi* and Appendix B contains an assessment of the river-control project, dated in Boston on 14 April 1882.

Auerbach, Berthold. *Black Forest Village Stories.* Trans. by Charles Goepp. Illus. New York: Leypolt & Holt, 1869. A German poet and writer who focused on local peasants of the Black Forest.

Bacon, George Washington & Company, Ltd. *Bacon's Midget Map of London.* [London, first edition 1865].

Badlam, Alexander. *The Wonders of Alaska.* Illus., maps. San Francisco: Bancroft Co., 1890.

Baedeker, Karl. *Austria, Including Hungary, Transylvania, Dalmatia, and Bosnia. Handbook for Travellers.*

———. *Italy. Handbook for Travellers.* Part 1, Northern Italy, 4th rev. ed. (1877); Part 2, Central Italy and Rome, 5th rev. ed. (1877); Part 3, Southern Italy and Sicily, 6th rev ed. (1876). 3 vols. Leipzig: Karl Baedeker, 1876–77.

———. *London and Its Environs. Handbook for Travellers.* 10th rev. Ed. Leipzig: Karl Baedeker, 1896.

———. *Paris and Its Environs. Handbook for Travellers.* 6th rev. ed. Leipzig: Karl Baedeker, 1878.

———. *The Rhine from Rotterdam to Constance. Handbook for Travellers.* 6th ed. Leipzig: Karl Baedeker, 1878.

———. *Switzerland and the Adjacent Portions of Italy, Savoy, and the Tyrol. Handbook for Travellers.* 7th ed. Leipzig: Karl Baedeker, 1877.

Baedeker's travel guides were noted for accuracy and detail.

Bagehot, Walter. *Biographical Studies.* London: Longmans, Green and Co., 1895. British journalist and businessman who wrote about government, literature, and economics.

Ballou, Maturin Murray. *Under the Southern Cross; or, Travels in Australia, Tasmania, New Zealand, Samoa, and Other Pacific Islands.* Boston: Ticknor and Co., [1888]. Editor-in-chief of the *Boston Globe* and pioneer in American illustrated journalism.

Bancroft, Hubert Howe. *The Native Races of the Pacific States of North America.* 5 vols. New York: D. Appleton and Co.; San Francisco: A. L. Bancroft & Co., 1874–76. An American historian and ethnologist who accumulated a great library of historical material, and wrote and published history texts. The Bancroft Library at the University of California at Berkeley is named in his honor.

Barclay, James Turner. *The City of the Great King; or, Jerusalem As It Was, As It Is, and As It Is to Be.* Philadelphia: J. Challen and Sons, 1858. Missionary and explorer of Jerusalem.

Barker, Mary Anne (Stewart), afterwards Lady Broome. *Station Amusements in New Zealand, by Lady Barker.* Copyright Edition. British Authors Series. Leipzig: B. Tauchnitz, 1874.

———. *Station Life in New Zealand, by Lady Barker.* Copyright Edition. British Authors Series. Leipzig: B. Tauchnitz, 1874. Journalist educated in England who traveled extensively, writing about South Africa as well as New Zealand.

Barthélemy, Jean-Jacques. *Travels of Anarcharsis the Younger in Greece, During the Middle of the Fourth Century Before the Christian Era. By the Abbé Barthelmi.* Trans. from the French [by William Beaumont]. 4 vols. London: G. G. and J. Robinson, 1796. French writer and numismatist who spent thirty years writing the above text on Greece, providing an account of the customs, government and antiquities of that country.

Bartlett, William Henry. *Walks About the City and Environs of Jerusalem* (London, 1844). A British artist known for steel engravings, Bartlett traveled in the Balkans, the Middle East, and America. He preferred to make impressions of "actual sights."

Beatty, Daniel F. *In Foreign Lands, from Original Notes.* Washington, New Jersey: Daniel F. Beatty, Publisher, 1878.

Becke, Louis. *By Reef and Palm.* Third ed. London: T. Fisher Unwin, 1895. Writer about the South Pacific, raised in Australia.

Beecher, Henry Ward, comp. *Plymouth Collection of Hymns and Tunes; for the Use of Christian Congregations.* New York: A.S. Barnes & Co., 1855. Clergyman, social reformer, abolitionist, and speaker in America, brother of Harriet Beecher Stowe.

Beerbohm, Julius. *Wanderings in Patagonia; or, Life Among the Ostrich-Hunters.* Illus. New York: Henry Holt & Co., 1879.

Bellows, John. *Dictionary for the Pocket: French and English, English and French.* Rev. by Alexandre Beljame. Second ed. London: Trubner & Co., 1877. Printer, lexicographer, and archaeologist.

Benjamin Ben Jonah, of Tudela. *The Itinerary of Rabbi Benjamin of Tudela.* Edition unknown.

Benjamin of Tudela was a traveler who lived in the late twelfth century in medieval Spain, recording life in Jewish communities. As Gribben notes, Twain probably referred to Thomas Wright's version included in *Early Travels in Palestine* (1848).

Benkard, Johann Philipp. *Geschicte der Deutschen Kaiser und Konige. Zu den Bildern des Kaisersaals. 43 aufl.* Illus. Frankfort-a-M: H. Keller, 1869.

Bennett, Emerson. Romance and western writer. Twain referred in Chapter 19 of *Roughing It* to the dime-novel frontier adventure stories that Bennett wrote. No specific source.

Berlichingen, Gotz von. Edition: unknown. Twain referred to Berlichingen's memoirs in Chapter 12 of *A Tramp Abroad.* Sixteenth-century mercenary in Germany.

Bernard, A. Hermann. *Legends of the Rhine.* Trans. by Fr. Arnold. Mayence: Joseph Halenza, n.d. [First English edition pub. 1862.]

Bernard, Frederic. *Wonderful Escapes.* Trans. and ed. by Richard Whiteing. Illus. New York: Scribner, Armstrong & Co., 1872.

Bernard, John. *Retrospections of America, 1797–1811.* Ed. by Mrs. Bernard. Intro., notes, and index by Laurence Hutton and Brander Matthews. New York: Harper & Brothers, 1887.

Bigelow, Poultney. *The German Emperor and His Eastern Neighbors.* New York: Charles L. Webster & Co., 1892.

_____. *Paddles and Politics Down the Danube.* Illus. New York: Charles L. Webster & Co., 1892. American historian and writer.

Birch, Samuel. Twain used quotations about Birch's story from Lady Julia Inglis' *The Siege of Lucknow, A Diary* (see Francis Madigan, 360).

Bliss, William Root. *Paradise in the Pacific; A Book of Travel, Adventure, and Facts in the Sandwich Islands.* New York: Sheldon and Co., 1873.

Bonwick, James, F.R.G.S. *The Lost Tasmanian Race.* London: Sampson Low, Marston, Searle and Rivington, 1884. Born in England and moved to Australia, becoming educator, historian and=writer.

Bothmer, (Countess) Marie von. *German Home Life.* New edition. London: Longmans, Green & Co., 1878.

Boyton, Paul. *The Story of Paul Boyton. Voyages on All the Great Rivers of the World.... A Rare Tale of Travel and Adventure.... A Book for Boys, Old and Young.* Milwaukee: Riverside Printing Co., 1892. American adventurer; innovator of a rubber suit for swimming.

Brassey, (Lady) Anna (Annie) Allnutt. *A Voyage in the Sunbeam, Our Home in the Ocean for Eleven Months.* Copyright Edition. 2 vols. Leipzig: Bernhard Tauchnitz, 1879.

Browne, Charles Farrar, pseud. "Artemus Ward." *Artemus Ward, His Travels.* Illus. New York: Carleton; London: S. Low, Son & Co., 1870. Lecturer, humorist, writer who influenced Twain.

Browne, John Ross. *Crusoe's Island: A Ramble in the Steps of Alexander Selkirk. With Sketches of Adventure in California and Washoe.* New York: Harper & Brothers, 1864.

Browne, Junius Henry. *Sights and Sensations in Europe: Sketches of Travel and Adventure.* Illus. Hartford, Conn.: American Publishing Co., 1871.

Browne, Thomas Alexander, pseud. "Rolf Boldrewood." *Old Melbourne Memories.* London: Macmillan and Co., 1896. Australian author, magistrate, commissioner in the gold fields.

[Buck, Sir Edward.] *Indo-Anglican Literature*. Second Issue. For Private Circulation Only. Calcutta: Thacker, Spink and Co., 1887. Twain refers to this book in Chapter 61 of *Following the Equator*.

Buckingham, James Silk. *America, Historical, Statistic, and Descriptive*. 7 vols. New York, 1841. English writer and traveler.

Buckle, Henry Thomas. *History of Civilization in England*. 2 vols. (First volume pub. 1857; second volume pub 1861.) New York: D. Appleton and Co., 1866. English historian.

Buffum, Edward Gould. *Sights and Sensations in France, Germany, and Switzerland*. New York: Harper & Brothers, 1869. American journalist.

Bullen, Frank Thomas. *The Cruise of the Cachalot Round the World after Sperm Whales*. London, 1898. British adventurer and writer.

Bunyan, John. *The Pilgrim's Progress as Originally Published by John Bunyan, Being a Fac-Simile Reproduction of the First Edition*. London: Elliot Stock, 1875.

Burrows, S. M. *The Buried Cities of Ceylon: A Guide Book to Anuradhapura and Polonnaurua. With Chapters on Dambulla, Lalawewa, Mihintale, and Sigiri*. Second edition. Columbo [Ceylon]: A. M. & J. Ferguson, 1894.

Burton, (Sir) Richard Francis. *Mecca and Medina*. 2 vols. Tauchnitz edition. British writer, soldier, explorer, orientalist, ethnologist, diplomat, linguist, and translator.

Busch, Moritz. *Bismarck in the Franco-German War 1870–1871*. "Authorized Edition." Two vols. in one. New York: Charles Scribner's Sons, n.d. German traveler and writer.

Cameron, Verney Lovett. *Across Africa*. 2 vols. Tauchnitz edition. [Originally pub. 1877.] Famous English traveler in Africa.

Campbell, (Sir) John Logan. *Poenamo; Sketches of the Early Days of New Zealand. Romance and Reality of Antipodean Life in the Infancy of a New Colony*. London: Williams & Norgate, 1881. Born in England, settled in New Zealand, prominent in Auckland.

Cape Town, South Africa. *Photographic Views of Cape Town, South Africa*. Cape Town, 1896.

Carlyle, Thomas. *The French Revolution: A History*. 2 vols. New York: Harper & Brothers, 1856.

_____. *History of Friedrich II of Prussia, Called Frederick the Great*. Illus. 10 vols. London: Chapman & Hall, [1871].

_____. *Sartor Resartus, Heroes and Hero-Worship, and Past and Present ... Complete in One Volume*. London: Ward, Locke, and Co., n.d.

Carnegie, Andrew. *Round the World*. New York: Scribners Sons, 1884. Scottish-American industrialist, philanthropist, businessman, and founder of the Carnegie Steel Company.

Catelin, Camille de (pseud. "Stephen d'Arve"). *Histoire du Mont-Blanc et de la vallée de Chamonix. Ascensions catastrophes célébrés, depuis les premières explorations*. Preface by Francis Wey. 2 vols. in one. Paris: Delagrave, [1878].

Catlin, George. Twain quotes from Catlin's *Indian Tribes* in a discarded chapter of *A Tramp Abroad* (*MELM*; formerly verso of MS p. 70, Box 6, no. 7).

Chaille-Long, Charles. *Central Africa: Naked Truths of Naked People. An Account of Expeditions*. Illus. from sketches by the author. New York: Harper & Brothers, 1877. American soldier, traveler, explorer of Africa, writer.

Chaney, George Leonard. *"Alo'ha": A Hawaiian Salutation*. Boston: Roberts Brothers, 1880.

Cheever, Henry Theodore. *The Island World of the Pacific; Being the Personal Narrative and Results of Travel Through The Sandwich or Hawaiian Island, and Other Parts of Polynesia*. New York: Harper & Brothers, 1851.

Clarke, Marcus Andrew Hislop. *For the Term of His Natural Life*. London: Richard Bentley and Son, 1893. [Australian novel].

_____. "Introduction" in Adam Lindsay Gordon's *Poems*.

_____. *Selected Works, Together with a Biography and Monograph of the Deceased Author, Compiled and Edited by Hamilton Mackinnon*. The Austral Edition. Melbourne: Fergusson & Mitchell, 1890. Australian novelist and poet.

Cobb, August G. "Earth-Burial and Cremation," *North American Review*, 135 (1882), 266–282.

_____. *A Year's Residence in the United States of America ... in Three Parts*. New York, 1819.

Coke, E. T. *A Subaltern's Furlough; Descriptive of Scenes in Various Parts of the United States, Upper and Lower Canada, New-Brunswick, and Nova Scotia, During the Summer and Autumn of 1832*. 2 vols. New York: J & J. Harper, 1833.

Coleman, F. M. *Typical Pictures of Indian Natives, Being Reproductions from ... Photographs*. Illus. Bombay: "Times of India" Office, 1898.

Coleridge, Samuel Taylor. *The Rime of the Ancient Mariner*. Illus. by J. Noel Paton. New York: 1875.

Colombo, Cristoforo. *Writings of Christopher Columbus, Descriptive of the Discovery and Occupation of the New World*. Ed. by Paul Leicester Ford. New York: Charles L. Webster & Co., 1892.

Colvin, Verplanck. *The Adirondack Region*. Illus. Albany, N.Y.: Weed, Parsons & Co., 1880. Lawyer, topographical engineer, and explorer.

Cooper, James Fenimore. *Leather-Stocking Tales: The Pathfinder; The Deerslayer; the Last of the Mohicans*. Unidentified edition.

Combe, George. *Notes on the United States of North America During a Phrenological Visit in 1838-9-40*. 2 vols. Philadelphia: Carey & Hart, 1841. Scottish phrenologist and educator.

Cumming, (Rev.) John. *The Great Consummation. The Millennial Rest; or, the World As It Will Be*. New York: G. W. Carleton, 1863.

Curtis, George William. *The Howadji in Syria*. New York: Harper & Brothers, 1852. American writer, occasional traveler, and lecturer.

Cutter, Bloodgood Haviland. *The Long-Island Farmer's Poems, Lines Written on the "Quaker City" Excursion to Palestine, and Other Poems*. New York: N. Tibbals & Sons, 1886.

Dallas, J. A. "Up the Mississippi," *Emerson's United States Magazine*. [Date and pages unknown. Published in New York between 1854 and 1858.]

Dana, Richard Henry. *To Cuba and Back. A Vacation Voyage*. Boston: James R. Osgood & Company, 1875.

_____. *Two Years Before the Mast: A Personal Narrative. New Edition, with Subsequent Matter by the Author*. Boston: Houghton, Mifflin and Co., 1876.

Darwin, Charles Robert. *Journal of Researches into the Natural History and Geology of the Countries Visited During the Voyage of H. M. S. Beagle Round the World*. New ed. New York: D. Appleton and Co., 1887. [Part of 12-vol. set.] Twain referred to Darwin's other works in *Following the Equator*, *A Tramp Abroad*, and in notebook entries.

Defoe, Daniel. *Life and Strange Surprising Adventures of Robinson Crusoe* [Vol. 1]. *The Further Adventures of Robinson Crusoe, Being the Second and Last Part of His Life* [Vol. 2]. 2 vols. Plates and map. London, 1747.

Dickens, Charles. *American Notes for General Circulation* (pub. 1842).

_____. *Pictures from Italy* (pub. 1846).

Dilke, Charles Wentworth. *Greater Britain: A Record of Travel in English-Speaking Countries During 1866 and 1867* (pub.1868).

Dimsdale, Thomas J. *The Vigilantes of Montana; or, Popular Justice in the Rocky Mountains. Being a Correct and Impartial Narrative of the Chase, Trial, Capture, and Execution of Henry Plummer's Road Agent Band*. Virginia City, Montana Territory: D. W. Tilton & Co., 1866.

Disturnell, John. *Sailing on the Great Lakes and Rivers of America*. Philadelphia: J. Disturnell, 1874.

Dodge, Richard Irving. *Our Wild Indians: Thirty-Three Years' Personal Experience among the Red Men of the Great West ... With Introduction by General Sherman*. Illus. Hartford, Conn.: American Publishing Co., 1883.

_____. *The Plains of the Great West and Their Inhabitants, Being a Description of the Plains,*

Game, Indians &c. of the Great American Desert. Intro. by William Blackmore. Illus. New York: G. P. Putnam's Sons, 1877.
Doré, [Paul] Gustave and Blanchard Jerrold, illus. *London.* French engraver, artist, and illustrator. Twain refers to Doré's illustrations in Chapters 34 and 50 of *A Tramp Abroad.*
Du Chaillu, Paul Belloni. *The Country of the Dwarfs* (pub. 1871).
_____. *Wild Life Under the Equator. Narrated for Young People.* Illus. New York: Harper & Brothers. [cop. 1866]. French-American explorer in Africa.
Dumas, Alexandre, known as Dumas *père. Novels.* Illus. 14 vols. London: Routledge, n.d. [Includes *The Count of Monte Cristo; The Three Musketeers: Twenty Years After; The Viscount of Bragelonne* (2 vols.); *Marguerite de Valois; Chicot the Jester; The Forty-Five Guardsmen; The Conspirators; The Regent's Daughter; Memoirs of a Physician; The Queen's Necklace; The Taking of the Bastille; The Countess de Charny.*]
Dunn, Jacob Piatt. *Massacres of the Mountains: A History of the Indian Wars of the Far West.* Illus. New York: Harper & Brothers, 1886.
Edwards, Amelia Ann Blandford. *Untrodden Peaks and Unfrequented Valleys. A Mid-Summer Ramble in the Dolomites.* Illus. London, 1890. English, novelist, journalist, traveler, and Egyptologist.
Elliott, (Mrs.) Frances Minto (Dickinson). *Diary of an Idle Woman in Italy.* 2 vols. Collection of British Authors Series. Leipzig: Bernhard Tauchnitz, 1872.
Elliott, Charles Wyllys. *Remarkable Characters and Places of the Holy Land.* Hartford, Conn.: J. B. Burr & Co., 1867.
Ellis, William. *Three Visits to Madagascar During the Years 1853–1854–1856.* Illus. New York: Harper & Brothers, 1859. A missionary, Ellis also became a well-known topographical, historical, botanical and ethnographic author about Polynesia.
Evans, (Col.) Albert S. *Our Sister Republic: A Gala Trip Through Tropical Mexico in 1869–70.* Illus. Published by Subscription Only. Hartford, Conn.: Columbian Book Co., 1870.
Eyre, Edward John. *Journals of Expeditions of Discovery into Central Australia, and Overland from Adelaide to King George's Sound, in 1840–1, Including an Account of the Manners and Customs of the Aborigines, and the State of Their Relations with Europeans.* 2 vols. London, 1845. English explorer of Australia, governor of Jamaica.
Fearon, Henry Bradshaw. *Sketches of America. A Narrative of a Journey of Five Thousand Miles Through the Eastern and Western States of America.* Third ed. London: Longman, Hurst, Rees, Orme, and Brown [printed by Straham and Spottiswoode], 1819. English traveler.
Fetridge, William Pembroke. *Harper's Handbook for Travelers in Europe and the East.* New York: Harper and Brothers, 1862. Travelogue writer. *A First German Course, Containing Grammar, Delectus, and Exercise-Book, with Vocabularies, and Materials for German Conversation. On the Plan of Dr. William Smith's [1813–1893] "Principia Latina."* Third ed. Rev. New York: Harper, 1856.
Forbes, Arthur Litton Armitage. *Two Years in Fiji.* London: Longmans, Green and Co., 1875.
Forbes-Mitchell, William. *Reminiscences of the Great Mutiny, 1857–59.* London: Macmillan and Co., 1893.
Galignani's New Paris Guide for 1867. Paris: A. W. Galignani, 1867.
Gane, Douglas M. *New South Wales and Victoria in 1885.* London: Sampson Los, Marston, Searle and Rivington, 1886.
Garrett, [Fydell] Edmund and E. T. Edwards. *The Story of an African Crisis. Being the Truth About the Jameson Raid and Johannesburg Revolt of 1896. Told with the Assistance of the Leading Actors in the Drama.* Westminster: Archibald Constable & Co., 1897. Garrett was a journalist and newspaper editor.
Gibson, William Hamilton. *Highways and By-ways; or Saunterings in New England.* Illus. by the author. New York: Harper & Brothers, 1883. American illustrator, author, and naturalist.
Girdlestone, Arthur Gilbert. *The High Alps Without Guides: Being a Narrative of Adventures in Switzerland.* London: Longmans, Green & Co., 1870.

Goldsmith, Oliver. *The Citizen of the World* (pub. 1762).

_____. *The Deserted Village*. Illus.

Goodrich, C. F. *Report of the British Naval and Military Operations in Egypt, 1882*. Maps and illus. Washington, D.C., 1885.

Gordon, Adam Lindsay. *Poems*. [Preface by Marcus Clarke.] Melbourne, Australia: A.H. Massina & Co., 1894. Australian poet, politician, and jockey.

Gordon, (Gen.) George Henry. *A War Diary of Events in the War of the Great Rebellion*, Boston: J.R. Osgood and Co., 1882. American lawyer and Union general in the Civil War.

Gordon-Cumming, Constance Frederica. *In the Himalayas and on the Indian Plains*. Illus. London: Chatto & Windus, 1886. Prolific travel writer and landscape painter.

Gordon-Cumming, Roualeyn George. *The Lion Hunter in South Africa: Five Years of a Hunter's Life ... with Anecdotes of the Chase and Notices of the Native Tribes*. 2 vols. London, 1850. Madigan, in "Mark Twain's Passage to India," lists *A Hunter's Life among Lions, Elephants and Other Wild Animals of South Africa*, (New York: Derby and Jackson, 1857) and another book *The Africander*.

Gowen, Herbert Henry. *The Paradise of the Pacific. Sketches of Hawaiian Scenery and Life*. London: Skeffington & Son, 1892.

Gray, (Rev.) William. Unidentified source in Chapter 6 of *Following the Equator*; Twain uses this pamphlet with William Wawn's *The South Sea Islanders* to discuss the slave trade in the South Seas.

Greenwood, James. *The Wilds of London*. Illus. London, 1874.

Grey, (Sir) George. *Journals of Two Expeditions of Discovery in North West and Western Australia. During the Years 1837, 38, and 39. With Observations on the Moral and Physical Character of the Aboriginal Inhabitants*. 2 vols. London, 1841. Soldier, explorer, Governor of Cape Colony, Governor of South Australia, twice Governor of New Zealand, Premier of New Zealand, and writer.

Hale, Edward. "The Man Without a Country" (short story, pub. 1863). American author and Unitarian clergyman.

Hall, Basil. *Travels in North America, in the Years 1827 and 1828*. 3 vols. Edinburgh: Cadell and Co., 1829. British naval officer, writer, and traveler.

Hall, Herbert Byng. *The Bric-a-Brac Hunter; or, Chapters on Chinamania*. London, 1875.

Hamerton, Philip Gilbert. *French and English, A Comparison*. Boston: Roberts Brothers, 1889. English artist and author.

Hamilton, Thomas. *Men and Manners in America. By the Author of "Cyril Thornton," &c*. Philadelphia: Carey, Lea & Blanchard, 1833. Scottish writer.

Hammond, Edward Payson. *Sketches of Palestine Descriptive of the Visit of the Rev. Edward Payson Hammond, M.A., to the Holy Land*. Intro. by the Reverend Robert Knox. Boston: Henry Hoyt, n.d. [Introduction dated 8 February 1868.] Evangelist. Twain was particularly derisive of this text.

Hammond, (Mrs.) Natalie (Harris). *A Woman's Part in a Revolution*. New York and Bombay: Longmans, Green, and Co., 1897.

Handbook for Travellers in Ireland. Maps. London, 1871.

Handbook of Florence. Illus. N.p.: M. Contrucci & Co., n.d.

Hare, Augustus John Cuthbert. *Walks in London*. 2 vols. Illus. Daldy, Isbister & Co., [American edition: New York: George Routledge and Sons, 1878.]

_____. *Walks in Rome*. New York, 1874. English writer.

Head, Richard, and Francis Kirkman. *The English Rogue* (pub. 1665–1671).

Headley, Joel Tyler, ed. *Mountain Adventures in Various Parts of the World. Selected from the Narratives of Celebrated Travellers*. Illus. New York: Charles Scribner & Co., 1872.

_____, and Willis Fletcher Johnson. *Stanley's Adventures in the Wilds of Africa*. Illus. [Philadelphia:] Edgewood Publishing Co., [cop. 1889].

Heine, Henrich. "Die Lorelei" (song). Melody by Fridrich Silcher. Twain discusses this song in Chapter 16 of *A Tramp Abroad*.

Hendrik, Hans. *Memoirs of Hans Hendrik, The Arctic Traveller, Serving Under Kane, Hayes, Hall and Nares, 1853–1876. Written by Himself.* Trans. from Eskimo language by Henry Rink. Ed. by George Stephens. London: Trubner & Co., 1878. Arctic traveler and interpreter.

Herndon, William Lewis and Lardner Gibbon. *Exploration of the Valley of the Amazon, Made Under the Direction of the Navy Department.* 2 vols. Washington, D. C.: Robert Armstrong, 1853–1854. American naval officers, and explorers.

Herodotus. *The History of Herodotus. A New English Version.* Trans. by George Rawlinson and others. Maps and illus. 4 vols. New York, 1875.

_____. *The Life and Travels of Herodotus in the Fifth Century Before Christ.* Trans. by J. Talboys Wheeler. 2 vols. New York: Harper & Brothers, 1856.

Hesse-Wartegg, Ernst von. *Mississippi-fahrten: Reisebilder aus dem amerikanischen Suden.* Leipzig: C. Reissner, 1881. Austrian traveler and writer.

Higginson, Thomas Wentworth Storrow. *Travellers and Outlaws, Episodes in American History.* Boston: Lee and Shepard, [cop. 1888]. American author and soldier; mentor to Emily Dickinson.

Hinchliff, Thomas Woodbine. *Summer Months Among the Alps; With the Ascent of Monte Rosa.* London: Longman, Brown, Green, Longmans & Roberts, 1857. Mountaineer and writer.

Historical Records of New South Wales ... 1762–1811. Seven vols. in nine. Vol. 1 edited by A. Britton; Vols. 2–7 ed. by F. M. Bladen. Illus. Sydney: Government Printing, 1892–1901.

Holwell, John Zephaniah. *A Genuine Narrative of the Deplorable Deaths of the English Gentlemen, and Others, Who Were Suffocated in the Black Hole in Fort William, at Calcutta ... in ... June, 1756.* London,1758. Survivor of the Black Hole of Calcutta; surgeon, politician.

Hopkins, Manley. *Hawaii: The Past, Present, and Future of Its Island-Kingdom.* London: Longman, Green, Longman, and Roberts, 1862.

Horner, Susan and Joanne Horner. *Walks in Florence and Its Environs.* 2 vols. London: Smith, Elder & Co., 1884.

Howard, H. R., comp. *The History of Virgil A. Stewart, and His Adventures in Capturing and Exposing the Great 'Western Land Pirate' and His Gang.* New York: Harper & Brothers, 1836.

Howells, William Dean. *Seven English Cities.* New York: Harper & Brothers, 1909.

_____. *Tuscan Cities* (pub. 1886).

_____. *Venetian Life* (pub. 1866).

_____, and Thomas Sergeant Perry, eds. *Library of Universal Adventure by Sea and Land.* New York: Harper & Brothers, 1888.

Huc, Evariste-Régis. *Recollections of a Journey Through Tartary, Thibet, and China, During the Years 1844, 1845, and 1846.* New York: D. Appleton & Co., 1852. French missionary and traveler.

Hugo, Victor-Marie, Comte. *Angelo* (play, prod. 1835).

_____. *The Toilers of the Sea.* New York: Harper & Brothers, 1866.

Hume, David. *The History of England, from the Invasion of Julius Caesar to the Revolution of 1688.* 6 vols. New York: Harper & Brothers, 1854.

Hunt, Leigh. "Abou Ben Adhem" (poem).

_____. *The Town* (pub.1848).

Hunter, William Wilson. *The Indian Empire: Its History, People and Products.* London: Trubner & Co., 1882. Compiler of statistical information and survey on India.

Hurst, John Fletcher. *Indika. The Country and the People of India and Ceylon.* New York: Harper & Brothers, 1891. Bishop in the Methodist Episcopal Church and first chancellor of the American University in Washington, D.C.

Hyde, John, Jr. *Mormonism: Its Leaders and Designs.* New York: W.P. Fetridge & Co., 1857.

Inglis, Julia (Selina). *The Siege of Lucknow. A Diary.* London: Osgood & McIlvaine; Leipzig: Bernhard Tauchnitz, 1892.

Ingraham, Joseph Holt. *The Prince of the House of David* (1855). American writer.
Irving, Washington. *The Adventures of Captain Bonneville*. Lovell's Library Series, No. New York: John W. Lovell Co., n.d.
_____. *The Alhambra: A Series of Tales and Sketches of the Moors and Spaniards* (pub. 1832).
Jackson, Julia Newell. *A Winter Holiday in Summer Lands*. Chicago: A.C. McClurg and Co., 1890.
James, Henry. *A Little Tour in France*. Boston: James R. Osgood and Co., 1885.
Jarves, James Jackson. *History of the Hawaiian or Sandwich Islands*. Second edition. Boston: James Munroe and Co., 1844. American art collector, newspaper editor in Hawaii.
Jericho and the Jordan. Unidentified book that the pilgrims were requested to read for the *Quaker City* voyage. *Daily Alta California*, 5 April 1868.
Jesse, John Heneage. *London: Its Celebrated Characters and Remarkable Places*. 3 vols. London: Richard Bentley, 1871. English historian.
Jeypore Portfolios of Architectural Details. Ed. by Colonel Jacobs. Seven portfolios. No other information available. Clemens discussed these portfolios in a letter to Richard Watson Gilder, written on 12 March 1896; *MEPUL*.
John, Eugenie, pseud. "E. Marlitt." *Das Geheimniss der Alten Mamsell. Roman von E. Marlitt*. Die Deutsche Library. New York: G. Munroe, 1881.
Johnston, Alexander. *Connecticut: A Study of a Commonwealth Democracy*. American Commonwealths Series. Boston: Houghton, Mifflin Co., 1887. American historian.
Jusserand, Jean Adrien Antoine Jules. *English Wayfaring Life in the Middle Ages (XIVth Century)*. Trans. by Lucy T. Smith. Illus. from illuminated manuscripts. New York: G. P. Putnam's Sons, 1889. French author and diplomat.
Kalakaua, David, king of Hawaii. *The Legends and Myths of Hawaii: The Fables and Folk-Lore of a Strange People*. Ed. and with an intro. by Rollin Mallory Daggett. New York: Charles L. Webster & Company, 1888. Daggett was minister resident in Hawaii 1882–85; journalist, editor in California.
Kane, Elisha Kent. *Arctic Explorations: The Second Grinnell Expedition in Search of Sir John Franklin, 1853, '54, '55*. Illus. 2 vols. Philadelphia: Childs & Peterson, 1856. Medical officer in U.S. Navy; Arctic explorer.
Keim, DeBenneville Randolph. *Sheridan's Troopers on the Borders: A Winter Campaign on the Plains*. Philadelphia: Claxton, Remsen & Haffelfinger, 1870.
Kellogg, Robert H. *Life and Death in Rebel Prisons: Giving a Complete History of the Inhuman and Barbarous Treatment ... at Andersonville, Ga., and Florence, S.C., Describing Plans of Escape, Arrival of Prisoners, with.... Anecdotes of Prison Life. By Robert H. Kellogg, Sergeant-Major 16th Regiment Connecticut Volunteers. Prepared from His Daily Journal*. Illus. Sold by Subscription Agents Only. Hartford, Conn.: L. Stebbins, 1865.
Kendall, Henry Clarence. *Leaves from Australian Forests*. Melbourne: George Robertson,1870. Gribben's list includes *Poems of Henry Clarence Kendall*, Ed. by Alexander Sutherland (Melbourne: George Robertson and Co., 1890). Kendall was an Australian poet. The latter book is likely Clara Clemens' copy.
Kennan, George. *Siberia and the Exile System*. 2 vols. New York: The Century Co., 1891. American traveler, writer, and lecturer.
Ker, David. "From the Sea to the Desert," *Cosmopolitan*, 6 (March 1889), 466–470.
Kiefer, F. J. *The Legends of the Rhine from Basle to Rotterdam*. Second Edition. Trans. by L.W. Garnham. Mayence: David Kapp, 1870.
King, Clarence. *Mountaineering in the Sierra Nevada*. Boston: J. R. Osgood, 1872. American geologist and mountaineer.
Kinglake, Alexander William. *Eothen*. Edinburgh: A. W. Blackwood & Sons, 1892. English travel writer and historian.
Kipling, Rudyard. *From Sea to Sea: Letters of Travel*. 2 vols. London: Macmillan and Co., 1900.
Knight, Edward Frederick. *Where Three Empires Meet: A Narrative of Recent Travel in Kashmir, Western Tibet, Gilgit, and the Adjoining Countries*. London: Longmans, Green, and Co., 1893.

Knighton, William. *The Private Life of an Eastern King. By a Member of the Household of His Late Majesty, Mussir-u-Deen, King of Oude*. London: Hope and Co., 1855.
Knox, Thomas Wallace. *Backsheesh! Or, Life and Adventures in the Orient*. Illus. Hartford: A. D. Worthington & Co., 1875.
_____. *The Boy Travelers in Australasia*. Illus. New York: Harper & Brothers, 1899.
_____. *The Boy Travelers in Central Europe*. Illus. New York: Harper & Brothers, [1889].
_____. *The Boy Travelers in Mexico*. Illus. New York: Harper & Brothers, 1905.
_____. *The Boy Travelers in Northern Europe*. Illus. New York: Harper & Brothers, 1905.
_____. *The Boy Travelers in South America*. Illus. New York: Harper & Brothers, [cop. 1885].
_____. *The Boy Travelers in the Far East ... in a Journey to Japan and China*. Illus. New York: Harper & Brothers, [cop. 1879].
_____. *The Boy Travelers in the Far East; Part Second, ... in a Journey to Siam and Java*. Illus. New York: Harper & Brothers, [cop. 1880].
_____. *The Boy Travelers in the Far East; Part Third ... in a Journey to Ceylon and India*. Illus. New York: Harper & Brothers, [cop. 1881].
_____. *The Boy Travelers in the Far East; Part Fourth, ... in a Journey to Egypt and the Holy Land*. Illus. New York: Harper & Brothers, 1905.
_____. *The Boy Travelers in the Far East; Part Fifth ... in a Journey Through Africa*. Illus. New York: Harper & Brothers, 1905.
_____. *The Boy Travelers in the Russian Empire*. Illus. New York: Harper & Brothers, 1905.
_____. *Overland Through Asia; Pictures of Siberian, Chinese, and Tartar Life*. Hartford, Conn.: American Publishing Co., 1871. American travel writer.
Kotzwara, Franz, composer. "The Battle of Prague" (piano solo, 1793?). Twain referred to this musical score in Chapter 32 of *A Tramp Abroad* and Chapter 38 of *Life on the Mississippi*.
Krout, Mary Hannah. According to Francis Madigan's "Mark Twain's Passage to India" (361), Twain consulted Krout's newspaper columns on the Hawaiian political turmoil of the 1890s. Her compiled work, appearing in *Hawaii and a Revolution: The Personal Experiences of a Newspaper Correspondent* (New York: Dodd, Mead, 1898), did not correspond entirely with Twain's quotations in *Following the Equator*.
Lacroix, Paul. *The Arts in the Middle Ages, and at the Period of the Renaissance*. Illus. by F. Kellerhoven. "Fourth Thousand." New York: D. Appleton and Co., 1875.
_____. *Manners, Customs, and Dress During the Middle Ages, and During the Renaissance Period*. Illus. by F. Kellerhoven. London: Chapman and Hall, 1874. French author and journalist.
Lamartine, Alphonse. "Héloise," *Memoirs of Celebrated Characters*. 3 vols. New York: Harper & Brothers, 1854.
_____. *A Pilgrimage to the Holy Land; Comprising Recollections, Sketches, and Reflections Made During a Tour in the East, in 1832–1833* (pub. 1835). Reprinted in New York by Appleton in 1848. French writer, poet, and politician.
Lambert, B. *The History and Survey of London and Its Environs from the Earliest Period to the Present Time*. 4 vols. Plates, portraits, maps. London: Printed for T. Hughes and M. Jones by Dewick and Clarke, 1806.
Landor, Arnold Henry Savage. *The Gems of the East; Sixteen Thousand Miles of Research Travel Among ... Enchanting Islands*. Illus. New York: Harper & Brothers, 1904. Painter, explorer, writer and anthropologist.
Lang, Andrew. *A Monk of Fife: A Romance of the Days of Jeanne d'Arc, Done into English from the Manuscript in the Scots College of Ratisbon*. London: Longmans, Green and Co., 1895. Journalist and writer.
Laurie, James Stuart. *The Story of Australasia: Its Discovery, Colonisation, and Development*. Map. London: Osgood, McIlvaine & Co., 1896.
Lawrence, Henry Montgomery. Francis Madigan suggests that Twain uses a Lawrence quotation from Julia Inglis' *The Siege of Lucknow. A Diary* in *Following the Equator* rather

than from Lawrence's *Adventures of an Officer in the Service of Runjeet Singh* (1845) and *Adventures of an Officer in the Punjaub* (1846). English soldier and administrator in India.

Layard, Austin Henry. *Early Adventures in Persia, Susiana, and Babylonia ... Before the Discovery of Nineveh.* 2 vols. London: John Murray, 1887. British author, diplomat, archaeologist, art historian, and traveler.

Lecky, William Edward. *A History of England in the Eighteenth Century.* 8 vols. New York: D. Appleton and Co., 1887–1890.

_____. *History of European Morals from Augustus to Charlemagne.* 2 vols. New York: D. Appleton and Co., 1874. Irish historian and writer.

Le Row, Caroline Bigelow, comp. *English As She Is Taught. Genuine Answers to Examination Questions in Our Public Schools.* New York: Cassell & Co., 1887.

Lingard, John. *A History of England from the First Invasion by Romans.* Fifth edition. 8 vols. Paris: Baudry's European Library, 1840. Half-title: Collection of Ancient and Modern British Authors. English Roman Catholic priest and historian.

Livingstone, David and Charles Livingstone. *Narrative of an Expedition to the Zambesia and Its Tributaries ... 1858–1864.* Illus. New York: Harper & Brothers, 1886. David Livingstone was the well-known medical missionary in Africa.

Longstreet, (Mrs.) Abby Buchanan. *Social Etiquette of New York.* New York: D. Appleton & Co., 1879.

Loughran, Edward Booth. *'Neath Austral Skies. Poems.* Melbourne: Melville, Mullen & Slade. 1894.

Lubbock, (Sir) John (Baron Avebury). *Ants, Bees, and Wasps: A Record of Observations on the Habits of the Social Hymenoptera.* The International Scientific Series. New York: D. Appleton and Co., 1901. [First pub. in 1882.] English banker, biologist, politician, naturalist and archaeologist.

Luckie, David Mitchell. *The Raid of the Russian Cruiser "Kaskowiski": An Old Story of Auckland. With an Introduction and Appendix on Colonial Defence, Etc.* Well-ington, New Zealand: New Zealand Times Co., 1894. Journalist in New Zealand.

Lyall, (Sir) Alfred Comyn. *Verses Written in India.* London: Kegan Paul, Trench & Co., 1889. British civil servant, poet, and literary historian.

Macaulay, Thomas Babington Macaulay, 1st Baron. *Critical, Historical and Miscellaneous Essays.* 7 vols. New York: D. Appleton and Co., 1859–1861.

_____. "Essay on Lord Clive."

_____. "Essay on Warren Hastings."

_____. *The History of England from the Accession of James II.* Ed. by Hannah More (Macaulay) Trevelyan. 5 vols. Philadelphia: J. B. Lippincott & Co., 1869. English poet, politician, and historian.

MacKay, Alexander. *The Western World; or, Travels in the United States in 1846–47 ... Including a Chapter on California.* 3 vols. London: R. Bentley, 1849.

Malleson, George Bruce. *The Indian Mutiny of 1857.* London: Seely and Co., 1891. English officer and historian in India.

Maning, Frederick Edward, pseud. "A Pakeha Maori." *Old New Zealand, A Tale of the Good Old Times; and a History of the War in the North Against the Chief Heke, in the Year 1845. Told by an Old Chief of the Ngapuhi Tribe.* Intro. by George Robert Charles Herbert, 13th Earl of Pembroke. London: R. Bently and Son, 1887. Irish, settled in New Zealand, lived with native Maori; writer, judge, historian.

Marcy, Randolph Barnes. *Thirty Years of Army Life on the Border, Comprising Descriptions of the Indian Nomads of the Plains, Explorations of New Territory, a Trip Across the Rocky Mountains in the Winter.* Illus. New York: Harper & Brothers, 1866.

Marion, Fulgence. *Wonderful Balloon Ascents; or, the Conquest of the Skies. A History of Balloons and Balloon Voyages. From the French of F. Marion.* Illus. New York: Charles Scribner & Co., 1871.

Marryat, Frederick. *A Diary in America, with Remarks on Its Institutions.* New York: William H. Colyer, 1839.

_____. *The Pacha of Many Tales.* [Author's Edition.] London: George Routledge & Sons, [1874?].

_____. *Second Series of a Diary in America.* Philadelphia, 1840. English novelist, naval officer.

Martineau, Harriet. *Retrospect of Western Travel.* 2 vols. London: Saunders and Otley; New York: Harper & Brothers, 1838.

_____. *Society in America.* 2 vols. Third edition. New York: Saunders and Otley, 1837. English writer, journalist, feminist, and political economist.

Marvin, Charles Thomas. *The Russians at the Gates of Herat.* Maps. Harper's Franklin Square Library, No. 463. New York: Harper & Brothers, [1885]. Writer on Russia.

Michelet, Jules. *Historical View of the French Revolution.* Trans. by Charles Cocks. London: H. G. Bohn, 1848.

Miller, Hugh. *The Cruise of the Betsy; or, A Summer Ramble Among the Fossiliferous Deposits of the Hebrides.* Ed. by W. S. Symonds. Boston: Gould and Lincoln, 1858.

Miller, Joaquin, i.e. Cincinnatus Heine Miller. *Songs of the Sierras.* Boston: Roberts Brothers, 1871.

_____. *Unwritten History: Life Amongst the Modocs.* Hartford: American Publishing Co., 1874.

Mines, John Flavel. *A Tour Around New York.* Illus. New York: Harper & Brothers, 1893.

Modi, (Sir) Jivanji Jamshedji. According to Gribben, "Modi published numerous books in Bombay about the ceremonies and religion of the Parsees" (479).

Monnier, Marc. *The Wonders of Pompeii. Translated from the Original French.* Illus. New York: Scribner, Armstrong & Co., 1872. French writer.

Mookerjee, Mohindonauth. *Onoocool Chunder Mooderjee [1829–1871]; A Memoir. Fifth Edition. Printed Verbatim from the First Edition.* Calcutta: Thacker, Spink and Co., 1895.

Moore, Mrs. Julia A. *Original Poems.* Grand Rapids, Mich.: C.M. Loomis, 1878.

_____. *The Sentimental Song Book.* Grand Rapids, Mich.: C. M. Loomis, 1877.

Morgan, Forrest. According to Gribben, Twain uses a quotation from Morgan in "Stirring Times in Austria" (1898), from Morgan's essay in the *Traveler's Record.*

Morrison, George Ernest. *An Australian in China, Being the Narrative of a Quiet Journey Across China to British Burma.* London: H. Cox, 1895.

Mukerji, Stya Chandra. According to Gribben, Twain "quotes a description of the Taj Mahal" from Mukerji's unidentified guidebook (490), in chapter 59 of *Following the Equator.*

Muller, Friedrich Max. *India: What Can It Teach Us?* New York, London, 1883. German philologist and Orientalist.

Murphy, John Mortimer. *Sporting Adventures in the Far West.* Illus. New York: Harper & Brothers, 1880.

Murray, (Sir) Charles Augustus. *Travels in North America During the Years 1834, 1835 & 1836, Including a Summer Residence with the Pawnee Tribe of Indians, in the Remote Prairies of the Missouri, and a Visit to Cuba and the Azore Islands.* 2 vols. London: R. Bentley, 1839.

Murray, John, publisher in London. *Handbook for North Germany, from the Baltic to the Black Forest, and the Rhine, from Holland to Basle.* Nineteenth edition. Maps. London: John Murray, 1877.

_____. *A Handbook for Travellers in Spain.* Fourth edition. London: John Murray, 1869.

_____. *A Handbook for Travellers in Switzerland, and the Alps of Savoy and Piemont.* Fourteenth edition. London: John Murray, 1871.

_____. *A Handbook for Travellers in Syria and Palestine.* Ed. by Josias Leslie Porter. 2 vols. London: John Murray, 1858.

Nansen, Fridtjof. *Farthest North; Being the Record of a Voyage of Exploration ... 1893–96.* 2 vols. Illus. New York: Harper & Brothers, [copy. 1897].

Neligan, William H. *Rome: Its Churches, Its Charities, and Its Schools.* New York: James B. Kirker, 1858.

New Guinea. According to Gribben, this was an unidentified book that he copied a passage from as he was leaving India in March of 1896, "New Guinea in '77–85 written by a missionary" (NB 36, TS p. 63).

Newson, Thomas McLean. *Indian Legends [of Minnesota Lakes]*. Illus. 2 vols. Minneapolis: [A.S. Dimond], 1881.

New South Wales. *Blue Book for the Year 1894. Compiled from Official Returns in the Registrar General's Office*. Sydney, 1895. [Government publication, issued 1866–1895.]

New Zealand. *Guide to the Collections in the Canterbury Museum, Christchurch, New Zealand*. Illus. Christchurch, New Zealand: Printed for the Board of Governors, 1895.

Nicols, Arthur. *Wild Life and Adventure in the Australian Bush: Four Years' Personal Experience*. Illus. by John Nettleship. 2 vols. London: R. Bentley and Son, 1887.

Ocean Scenes; or, the Perils and Beauties of the Deep; Being Interesting, Instructive, and Graphic Accounts of the Most Popular Voyages on Record, Remarkable Shipwrecks, Hair-Breadth Escapes, Naval Adventures, the Whales Fishery, Etc. Illus. New York: Leavitt & Allen, [1847].

Ollendorff, Heinrich Gottfried. *Ollendorff's New Method of Learning to Read, Write, and Speak the French Language*. New York: D. Appleton, 1864. German language educator.

Omar Khayyam. *Rubaiyat*. Boston, n.d. Twain owned other versions of the Rubaiyat; he referred to Omar Khayyam in Appendix A of *A Tramp Abroad*. Palgrave, (Sir) Francis. *Handbook for Travellers in Northern Italy*. Fourth edition. London: John Murray 1852.

Palmer, John. *Journal of Travels in the United States of North America, and in Lower Canada, ... in 1817*. Map. London: Sherwood, Neely, and Jones, 1818.

Pardon, George Frederick. *Routledge's Guide to London and Its Suburbs: Comprising Descriptions of All Its Points of Interest*. London: George Routledge and Sons, 1866. Journalist and compiler of books on games.

Parker, Arthur. *A Handbook on Benares*. Twain refers to this book in Chapter 50 of *Following the Equator*. See Coleman Parsons, "Mark Twain: Sightseer in India."

Parkin, (Sir) George Robert. *Round the Empire; for the Use of Schools*. Preface by the Earl of Rosebery. Illus. London: Cassell and Co., 1893.

Parkman, Francis. *The Conspiracy of Pontiac and the Indian War After the Conquest of Canada*. Maps. 2 vols. Boston: Little, Brown, and Co., 1880.

_____. *Count Frontenac and New France Under Louis XIV*. Boston: Little, Brown & Co., 1877.

_____. *The Jesuits in North America in the Seventeenth Century*. Fifteenth edition. Boston: Little, Brown, and Co., 1880.

_____. *La Salle and the Discovery of the Great West*. Boston: Little, Brown, and Co., 1879.

_____. *Montcalm and Wolfe*. 2 vols. Sixth edition. Boston: Little, Brown, and Co., 1885.

_____. *The Old Regime in Canada*. Boston: Little, Brown and Co., 1874.

_____. *The Oregon Trail: Sketches of Prairie and Rocky-Mountain Life*. Boston: Little, Brown, and Co., 1880.

_____. *Pioneers of France in the New World*. Boston: Little, Brown, and Co., 1865. Paterson, Andrew Barton. *The Man from Snowy River and Other Verses*. Sydney, Australia, 1895. Australian journalist and writer.

Peck, Wallace. *The Story of a Train of Cars: A Tale of Travel*. Illus. New York: Authors Publishing Association, [cop. 1895].

Perry, Matthew Calbraith. *Narrative of the Expedition of an American Squadron to the China Seas and Japan, Performed in the Years 1852, 1853, and 1854*. Compiled by Francis L. Hawks. Illus. New York: D. Appleton and Co., 1856.

Piatt, Sarah Morgan (Bryan). *A Voyage to the Fortunate Isles*. Boston: J.R. Osgood & Co., 1874. American poet.

Pierson, Hamilton Wilcox. *In the Brush; or, Old-Time Social, Political, and Religious Life in the Southwest*. Illus. by W. L. Sheppard. New York: D. Appleton and Co., 1881.

Plinius Caecilius Secondus, Gaius ("The Younger"). *The Letters of Caius Plinius Caecilius Secundus*. Trans. by William Melmoth. Rev. and corrected, with notes by Frederick Charles Tindal Bosanquet. Bohn's Classical Library Series. London: G. Bell and Sons, 1878.
Poe, Edgar Allan. "The Balloon Hoax" (story). Twain makes a reference to this story in *Roughing It*, Chapter 76.
_____. "The Bells" (poem). Twain refers to this poem in Chapter 36 of *A Tramp Abroad*.
_____. "A Descent into the Maelstrom" (story).
Porter, Josias Leslie. *A Handbook for Travellers in Syria and Palestine*. 2 vols. London: John Murray, 1858.
Praed, Rosa Caroline (Murray-Prior), "Mrs. Campbell Praed." *Australian Life, Black and White*. Illus. London: Chapman & Hall, 1885. Australian novelist.
Prime, William Cowper. *Boat Life in Egypt and Nubia*. New York: Harper & Brothers, 1857.
_____. *Tent Life in the Holy Land*. Illus. New York: Harper & Brothers, 1857.
Pumpelly, Raphael. *Explorations in Turkestan, with an Account of The Basin of Eastern Persia and Sistan. Expedition of 1903*. Publication No. 26. Washington, D. C.: Carnegie Institute of Washington, 1905. It is likely that Twain knew about Pumpelly's *Across America and Asia; Notes of a Five Years' Journey Around the World, and of Residence in Arizona, Japan, and China* (New York: Leypoldt & Holt, 1870). American geologist and explorer who made first survey of the Gobi Desert.
Randall, David Austin. *The Handwriting of God in Egypt, Sinai, and the Holy Land: The Records of a Journey*. 2 vols. in 1. Philadelphia: John E. Potter, 1862.
Richardson, Albert Deane. *Beyond the Mississippi: From the Great River to the Great Ocean. Life and Adventure on the Prairies, Mountains, and Pacific Coast ... 1857–1867*. Illus. Hartford, Conn.: American Publishing Co., [cop. 1867].
Rimmer, Alfred. *Ancient Streets and Homesteads of England*. Intro. by J. S. Howson. 150 engravings by J.D. Cooper, after drawings by the author. London: Macmillan and Co., 1877.
Roberts, William Culver, Jr. *The Boy's Account of It: A Chronicle of Foreign Travel by an Eight-Year-Old. Translated by a Patient Printer from the Manuscript of "Bobs" Roberts*. Illus. with photographs. New York: Waterloo Press, 1909. A presentation copy, this book described the travels of Roberts that were told by Twain in *Innocents Abroad*.
Robinson, Edward. *biblical Researches in Palestine and Adjacent Regions; A Journal of Travels in the Years 1838 & 1852*. By Edward Robinson, Eli Smith [1801–1857, joint author], and Others. Second ed. 3 vols. London: J. Murray, 1856. biblical scholar.
"Roll On, Silver Moon" (anonymous song, pub. 1847). Twain refers to this song in Chapter 38 of *Life on the Mississippi* and in Chapter 3 of *Following the Equator*.
Roosevelt, Theodore. *Good Hunting: In Pursuit of Big Game in the West*. Illus. New York: Harper & Brothers, 1907.
Ross, Malcom. Twain refers to Ross in Chapter 30 of *Following the Equator*, but the source for this reference remains unidentified.
Rouget de Lisle, Claude-Joseph. "La Marseillaise" (French national anthem, pub. 1792). Twain refers to this song in his unfinished play, "The *Quaker City* Holy Land Excursion," in Chapter 11 of *Innocents Abroad*, and in Chapter 38 of *Life on the Mississippi*.
Rousseau, Jean-Jacques. *Les Confessions* (pub. 1781, 1788). Twain makes a reference to Rousseau in Chapter 47 of *A Tramp Abroad*.
_____. "Days of Absence." Twain refers to this song in Chapter 38 of *Life on the Mississippi*.
Rule, William Harris. *History of the Inquisition from Its Establishment in the Twelfth Century to Its Extinction in the Nineteenth*. 2 vols. London, 1874.
Ruskin, John. *Modern Painters* (pub. 1843–1860). Twain refers to Ruskin in Chapter 24 of *A Tramp Abroad*, possibly in Chapter 48 and Chapter 50.
_____. *The Stones of Venice*. 3 vols. Illus. New York: John W. Lovell Co., [cop. 1884].
Russell, Michael (Bishop of Glasgow and Galloway). *Polynesia; or, and Historical Account*

of the Principal Islands of the South Sea including New Zealand; the Introduction of Christianity; and the Actual Conditions of the Inhabitants. New York: Harper & Brothers, 1843.

Russell, Robert. *Natal, the Land and Its Story*. Pietermaritzburg: P. Davis and Sons, 1891.

Sala, George Augustus. *Under the Sun: Essays Mainly Written in Hot Countries*. London: Vizetelly & Co., 1884.

Salvation Through Grace (Salvation by Grace). Unidentified book; Twain uses two different titles without the name of the author. This book was on board the *Quaker City*.

Saraswati, Sri Swami Bhaskaranada (of Benares). Twain claims that he is unable to read Saraswati's book in chapter 53 of *Following the Equator*. Otherwise unidentified.

Schoolcraft, Henry Rowe. *Algic Researches, Comprising Inquiries Respecting the Mental Characteristics of the North American Indians. First Series. Indian Tales and Legends*. 2 vols. New York: Harper & Brothers, 1839.

Schreiner, Olive, and Samuel Cronwright-Schreiner. *The Political Situation [in Cape Colony]*. London: T. Fisher Unwin, 1896. Olive Schreiner was a South African activist and writer.

_____, pseud. "Ralph Iron." *The Story of an African Farm. A Novel*. London, 1883.

Schuyler, Eugene. *Turkistan; Notes of a Journey in Russian Turkistan, Khokand, Bukhara, and Kuldja*. Illus. Maps. 2 vols. New York: Scribner, Armstrong & Co., 1876.

Scollar, Clinton. *On Sunny Shores*. Illus. by Margaret Landers Randolph. New York: Charles L. Webster & Co., 1893.

_____. *Under Summer Skies*. Illus. by Margaret Landers Randolph. New York: Charles L. Webster & Co., 1892.

Seemann, Berthold Carl. *Viti: An Account of a Government Mission to the Vitian or Fijian Islands, in the Years 1860–61*. Cambridge: Macmillan & Co., 1862.

"Sketches on the Upper Mississippi, by the Author of 'Three Weeks in Cuba,'" *Harper's New Monthly Magazine*, 7 (July 1853), 177–190. An anonymous article, this may have been used as a source in Chapter 59 of *Life on the Mississippi*. The writer of the article was probably an artist named A. Hoeffler.

Sleeman, William Henry. *Rambles and Recollections of an Indian Official*. Ed. by Vincent Arthur Smith. New edition. 2 vols. Westminster: Archibald Constable and Co., 1893.

_____. *Report on the Depredations Committed by the Thug Gangs of Upper and Central India*. Calcutta: G.H. Huttmann, Bengal Mily. [Orphan Press], 1840. British soldier and administrator in India, commissioner for the suppression of the Thuggee religion.

Smith, Albert Richard. *The Story of Mont Blanc*. London: D. Bogue, 1853. Twain referred to this book in Chapter 43 of *A Tramp Abroad*.

Smith, Joseph. *The Book of Mormon* (pub. 1833).

Smith, R. A. *Philadelphia As It Is in 1852; Being a Correct Guide to ... Philadelphia and Its Vicinity*. Philadelphia: Lindsay and Blakiston, 1852.

Smyth, Robert Brough. *The Aborigines of Victoria, with Notes Relating to the Habits of the Natives of Other Parts of Australia and Tasmania*. 2 vols. Melbourne, 1878.

Soard's New Orleans Directory for 1882. Twain intended to reproduce four pages from this directory, reduced in size to one page, *in Life on the Mississippi*, but deleted them from the final version.

Somerville, (Mrs.) Mary (Fairfax). *Personal Recollections, from Early Life to Old Age, of Mary Somerville, With Selections from Her Correspondence*. Ed. by Martha Somerville. Boston: Roberts Brothers, 1874.

Sonnichsen, Albert. *Ten Months a Captive among Filipinos; Being a Narrative of ... Imprisonment on the Island of Luzon, P.I.* New York: Charles Scribner's Sons, 1901.

Stanley, Arthur Penrhyn. *Historical Memorials of Westminster Abbey*. Fifth edition. London: John Murray, 1882.

Stanley, (Sir) Henry Morton. *In Darkest Africa; or, the Quest, Rescue, and Retreat of Emin, Governor of Equatoria*. 2 vols. Illus. New York: Charles Scribner's Sons, 1890.

_____. *Slavery and the Slave Trade in Africa*. Illus. New York: Harper & Brothers, 1893.

_____. *Through the Dark Continent; or, The Sources of the Nile.* 2 vols. Illus. New York: Harper & Brothers, 1878.
Statham, Francis Reginald. *South Africa as It Is.* London: T. Fisher Unwin, 1897. Journalist in South Africa.
Steele, Thomas Sedgwick. *Canoe and Camera: A Two Hundred Mile Tour Through the Maine Forests.* Illus. New York: Orange Judd Co., 1880.
_____. *Paddle and Portage, from Moosehead Lake to the Aroostook River, Maine.* Illus. Boston: Estes and Lauriat, 1882.
[Stephens, John Lloyd]. *Incidents of Travel in Greece, Turkey, Russia, and Poland.* 2 vols. New York: Harper & Brothers, 1875.
Sterne, Laurence. *A Sentimental Journey Through France and Italy, by Mr. Yorick* (pub. 1768).
Stevenson, Robert Louis. *An Inland Voyage.* London: Chatto & Windus, 1896.
_____. *Travels with a Donkey in the Cevennes* (pub. 1879).
Stewart, Charles Samuel. *Private Journal of a Voyage to the Pacific Ocean and Residence at the Sandwich Islands, in the Years 1822, 1823, 1824, and 1825.* Intro. by William Ellis. Second edition. New York: John P. Haven, 1828.
Stoddard, Charles Warren. *The Lepers of Molokai.* Notre Dame, Indiana: Ave Maria Press, [cop 1885].
_____. *South-Sea Idyls.* Boston: James R. Osgood and Co., 1873. American traveler and writer.
Stow, John. *A Survey of London* (pub. 1598, 1603; brought down to 1720 by John Strype [1643–1737], who corrected and enlarged the work [1720]).
Sturge, Joseph. *A Visit to the United States in 1841.* Boston: D. S. King, 1842. English radical politician, campaigned against slavery.
Sturt, Charles. *Narrative of an Expedition into Central Australia ... During the Years 1844, 5, and 6.* 2 vols. London: T. and W. Boone, 1849.
Sue, Eugène, actually Marie-Joseph Sue. *The Wandering Jew (Le Juif errant)* (pub. 1844–1845). Mentioned in Chapter 46 and 47 of *Following the Equator.*
A Summer in Africa. Unidentified source. Twain quoted from this book in a discarded chapter of *A Tramp Abroad* (verso of MS p. 75, Box 6, no. 7, *MELM*).
Swift, Jonathan. *Gulliver's Travels.* According to Gribben, "Clemens' copy of this work is not known to exist" (679).
Taine, Hippolyte Adolphe. *The Ancient Regime. Translated.* New York, 1876.
_____. *History of English Literature. A New Edition.* Trans. by Henri Van Laun. 2 vols. London: Chatto & Windus, n.d. [Translator's preface is dated 1871.]
_____. *Notes on England. Translated, with an Introductory Chapter, by W. F. Rae.* New York: Holt & Williams, 1872.
_____. *A Tour Through the Pyrenees.* Trans. by John Safford Fiske. Illus. by Gustave Dore. New York: Henry Holt and Co., 1874.
Tasman, Abel Janszoon. Twain made a reference to Tasman's diary while in Dunedin, New Zealand (*MELM*; formerly Notebook 34, TS p. 30).
Tavernier, Jean Baptiste. *Travels in India.* Ed. and trans. by Valentine Ball. 2 vols. London, New York: Macmillan and Co., 1889.
Taylor, Bayard. *A Visit to India, China, and Japan, in the Year 1853.* New York: G.P. Putnam & Co., 1855. Writer and traveler, known well by Twain.
Taylor, [Philip] Meadows. *Confessions of a Thug.* 3 vols. London: R. Bentley, 1839. English and Indian administrator, novelist.
Temple, (Sir) Richard. Unidentified source cited in chapter 17 of *Following the Equtor.*
Thackeray, William Makepeace. *A Legend of the Rhine.* Twain's "legend of Count Luigi" in Chapter 21 of *Innocents Abroad* probably finds its roots in Thackeray's burlesque. (See Baetzhold, 294).
_____. *Marvels of the New West: A Vivid Portrayal of the Stupendous Marvels in the Vast Wonderland of the Missouri River. Six Books in One Volume, Comprising Marvels of Nature, Marvels of Race, Marvels of Enterprise, Marvels of Mining, Marvels of Stock-Raising, and

Marvels of Agriculture. Sold Only by Subscription. Illus. Norwich, Conn.: Henry Bill Publishing Co., 1888.

Theal, George McCall. *South Africa: The Cape Colony, Natal, Orange Free State, South African Republic, and All Other Territories South of the Zambesi.* The Story of the Nations Series. London: T. Fisher Unwin, 1894. Theal was a prolific and influential South African historian, archivist and genealogist.

Thomas, Charles G. *Johannesburg in Arms 1895–96, Being the Observations of a Casual Spectator.* Illus. London: Smith, Elder & Co., 1896.

Thompson, William Tappan, pseud. "Major Joseph Jones." *Major Jones's Courtship. Detailed, with Humorous Scenes, Incidents, and Adventures.* Rev. and enl. Illus. by Darley and Carey. Philadelphia: T.B. Peterson & Brothers, [cop. 1879].

_____. *Major Jones's Sketches of Travel* (pub. 1847).

Thomson, William McClure. *Central Palestine and Phoenicia.* Illus. New York: Harper & Brothers, 1882.

_____. *The Land and the Book; or, biblical Illustrations Drawn from ... the Holy Land.* Illus. London: T. Nelson and Sons, 1872.

_____. *Lebanon, Damascus and Beyond Jordan.* Illus. New York: Harper & Brothers, 1886.

Timbs, John. *Clubs and Club Life in London, with Anecdotes of Its Famous Coffee Houses, Hostelries, and Taverns, form the Seventeenth Century to the Present Time.* Illus. London, n.d.

_____. *Curiosities of London, Exhibiting the Most Rare and Remarkable Objects of Interest in the Metropolis.* Portrait. London: D. Bogue, n.d.

_____. *Walks and Talks about London.* London, 1865.

Tocqueville, Alexis-Charles-Henri-Maurice Clérel de. *Democracy in America* (pub. 1835).

Townsend, Meredith White. *Asia and Europe: Studies Presenting the Conclusions Formed by the Author in a Long Life Devoted to the Subject of the Relations Between Asia and Europe.* New York: G.P. Putnam's Sons, 1901.

Travels of Two Mohamedans Through India and China in the Ninth Century. Unidentified book. Twain checked this book out from the London Library on 22 October 1896. Call number: I2511R (see *MELM*; formerly Notebook 39, TS, p. 12).

Trenck (Baron) Friedrich von der. *The Life of Baron Frederic Trenck.* Trans. from German (pub. London, 1788–1793). Prussian officer, adventurer, and writer.

Trevelyan, (Sir) George Otto. *Cawnpore.* Fourth edition. London: Macmillan and Co., 1899. English statesman and author.

Trials of Mutinous Convicts. Unidentified book. Twain listed this book among topics about Australia and New Zealand on 1 December 1896 while in Chelsea (*MELM*; formerly Notebook 39, TS p. 28).

Trollope, Anthony. *Australia and New Zealand.* 2 vols. London: Chapman & Hall, 1873.

Trollope, (Mrs.) Frances (Milton). *Domestic Manners of the Americans.* New York, 1832.

Trollope, Thomas Adolphus. *A History of the Commonwealth of Florence, from the Earliest Independence of the Commune to the Fall of the Republic in 1531.* 4 vols. London: Chapman and Hall, 1865.

Tyler, Josiah. *Livingstone Lost and Found; or, Africa and Its Explorers.* Illus. Maps. Hartford, Conn.: Mutual Publishing Co., 1873.

Verne, Jules. *Five Weeks in a Balloon; or, Journeys and Discoveries in Africa, by Three Englishmen. Compiled in French by Jules Verne, from the Original Notes of Dr. Ferguson [pseud.]; and Done into English by William Lackland.* New York: D. Appleton and Co., 1869.

_____. *A Journey to the Centre of the Earth* (pub. 1864; English trans., Boston, 1874).

_____. *The Mysterious Island* (pub. 1870).

_____. *The Tour of the World in Eighty Days.* Trans. George M. Towle. Boston: James R. Osgood and Co., 1874.

_____. *Twenty Thousand Leagues Under the Sea* (pub. 1870).

Versen, Maximilian von. *Reisen in Amerika und der Sudamerikanische krieg.* Breslau: M. Malzer, 1872.
Vincent, Frank. *The Land of the White Elephant: Sights and Scenes in South-eastern Asia. A Personal Narrative of Travel and Adventure in Farther India, Embracing the Countries of Burma, Siam, Cambodia, and Cochin-China.* Illus. New York: Harper & Brothers, 1874.
Waite, (Mrs.) Catherine (Van Valkenburg). *The Mormon Prophet and His Harem; or, an Authentic History of Brigham Young, His Numerous Wives and Children.* Cambridge, Mass.: Riverside Press, 1866.
Wakefield, William. *The Baths, Bathing, and Attractions of Aix-les-Bains, Savoy, Etc.* London: Sampson Low & Co., 1886.
Wallace, Alfred Russel. *Australasia.* Vol. I, *Australia and New Zealand. By Alfred R. Wallace.* New Issue [First pub. 1878.] Maps, illus. Stanford's Compendium of Geography and Travel. London: Edward Stanford, 1893. Vol. II, *Malaysia and the Pacific Archipelagoes. By F.H.H. Guillemard.* London: Edward Stanford, 1894.
———. *Man's Place in the Universe: A Study of the Results of Scientific Research in Relation to the Unity or Plurality of Worlds.* New York: McClure, Phillips & Co., 1903. English explorer, geographer, anthropologist, naturalist and biologist.
Walton, Augustus Q. *A History of the Detection, Conviction, Life and Designs of John A. Murel, the Great Western Land Pirate ... To Which Is Added, a Biographical Sketch of Mr. Virgil A. Stewart.* Athens, Tenn.: G. White, 1835. [Though Twain quoted from John A. Murrell's confession to Virgil A. Stewart in *Life on the Mississippi* (Chapter 29), it is not clear that Twain used this book for his source.]
Warden, William. *Letters Written on Board His Majesty's Ship the Northumberland, and at Saint Helena; in Which the Conduct and Conversations of Napoleon Bonaparte, and His Suite ... Are Faithfully Described. By William Warden, Surgeon on Board the Northumberland.* London, 1816; Philadelphia, New Haven, 1817.
Warner, Charles Dudley. *My Winter on the Nile, Among the Mummies and Moslems.* Hartford: American Publishing Co., 1876.
Wawn, William T. *The South Sea Islanders and the Queensland Labour Trade: A Record of Voyages and Experiences in the Western Pacific, from 1875 to 1891.* Ed. W. D. Hay. Illus. London: Swan Sonnenschein & Co., 1893. Mariner, cartographer, artist and author.
White, Richard Grant. "London Streets," *Atlantic Monthly,* 43 (February 1879), 230–241.
Whitney, Caspar. *On Snow-Shoes to the Barren Ground. Twenty-Eight Hundred Miles After Musk-Oxen and Wood-Bison.* Illus. by Frederic Remington. New York: Harper & Brothers, 1896.
Whymper, Edward. *Scrambles Amongst the Alps in the Years 1860–69.* Illus. London: John Murray, 1871. Mountain climber, explorer, and writer.
Wight, Orland Williams. *Lives and Letters of Abelard and Heloise.* Second edition. New York: M. Doolady, 1861.
Willard, Josiah Flynt, pseud. "Josiah Flynt." *Tramping with Tramps: Studies and Sketches of Vagabond Life.* Preface by Andrew D. White. Illus. New York: Century Co., 1901.
Williams, Thomas and James Calvert. *Fiji and the Fijians.* Vol. I, *The Islands and Their Inhabitants. By Thomas Williams.* Vol. II, *Mission History. By James Calvert.* Ed. by George Stinger Rowe. 2 vols. London: A. Heylin, 1858.
Winterbottom, Thomas Masterman. *An Account of the Native Africans in the Neighbourhood of Sierra Leone.* Illus. 2 vols. London: Printed by C. Whittingham and sold by J. Hatchard, 1803. English physician and philanthropist.
Wise, John. *Through the Air: A Narrative for Forty Years' Experience as an Aeronaut. Comprising a History of the Various Attempts in the Art of Flying by Artificial Means from the Earliest Period Down to the Present Time. With an Account of the Author's Most Important Air-Voyages and His Many Thrilling Adventures and Hairbreadth Escapes.* Illus. Philadelphia: To-Day Printing and Publishing Co., 1873.
Wood, John George. *The Uncivilized Races; or, Natural History of Man; Being a Complete*

Account of the Manners and Customs, and the Physical, Social, and Religious Condition and Characteristics, of the Uncivilized Races of Men, Throughout the Entire World. Illus. 2 vols. Hartford, Conn.: American Publishing Co., 1870.

Wortley, (Lady) Emmeline Charlotte Elizabeth (Manners) Stuart-Wortley. *Travels in the United States, Etc., During 1849 and 1850.* New York: Harper & Brothers, 1851.

Wright, Thomas, ed. *Early Travels in Palestine, Comprising the Narratives of Arculf, Willibald, Bernard, Saewulf, Sigurd, Benjamin of Tudela, Sir John Maundeville, De La Brocquiere, and Maundrell.* Bohn's Antiquarian Library series. London: Henry G. Bohn, 1848.

Wright, William, pseud. "Dan De Quille." *History of the Big Bonanza: An Authentic Account of the Discovery, History, and Working of the World Renowned Comstock Silver Lode of Nevada.* Intro. by Mark Twain. Illus. Hartford, Conn.: American Publishing Co., 1877.

Young, John Russell. *Around the World with General Grant ... in 1877, 1878, 1879.* Illus. Map. 2 vols. New York: American News Co., [1879].

Notes

1. *Postcards from Europe*, a collection of essays on Steves' travels, demonstrates themes of nostalgia within the context of collapsed time. Steves revisits places that he has been before, but with a sense that time has escaped him. With some humor, Steves writes amusingly about the differences between his youthful visits and his mature return to a number of locations, but without the depth that Twain shows concerning his travels. See Rick Steves, *Postcards from Europe: 25 Years of Travel Tales from America's Favorite Guidebook Writer*, Santa Fe: John Muir Publications, 1999. Steves writes about an early tour he had guided in Paris, that, once finished, left him feeling utterly alone: "For three weeks I had been Mr. Travel, showing off Europe to the constant applause of shutter releases. Suddenly, no one in Paris even knew I was alive. Venturing outside the security of friends and the responsibility for followers, I stepped into solitude" (253). He realizes that Europe will not be the same in time: "The culture is changing. As Europe pulls itself into a higher standard of living, slices of its traditional culture slowly drop out of people's lives and into museums.... Prizes I once promoted as cultural treasures have been battered by an onslaught of good living. Many — from beer hall bands to cancan dances — seem to survive only as clichés kept alive for tourism" (259). Steves defends the notion of travel even as he admits nostalgia for home: "Travel broadens my perspective, sharpens my appreciation of things foreign, and adds more ingredients to the create-a-burger line of life. And each of these makes a plane ticket a good value. But above all, travel makes me happier to be home" (260).

2. *Touring Cultures: Transformations of Travel and Theory*, edited by Chris Rojek and John Urry, a collection of sociological essays, considers travel from a modern point of view, but holds a number of interesting insights applicable to the nineteenth century.

3. Jeffrey Alan Melton examines what he terms "touristic" conventions in *Mark Twain, Travel Books, and Tourism: The Tide of a Great Popular Movement*, Tuscaloosa: University of Alabama Press, 2002. This enormously important study focuses on the travel works as central to Twain's output as a writer, not merely, as Melton terms it, as "practice" for his fiction. I am inclined to see the travel writings, however, as occasional practice sessions for his works of fiction. All of his work includes "touristic" conventions, but they also reveal the phenomenological structures that Twain explored throughout his career as a writer. In some ways, all of his writings were practice pieces elaborating on common themes and, as I will argue, all of his writings can be compared to notebooks that trace his observations about the human condition.

See also Hilton Obenzinger, *American Palestine: Melville, Twain, and the Holy Land Mania*, Princeton: Princeton University Press, 1999. Obenzinger's discussion about authenticity have guided my own (see 168–176).

4. Wolfgang Iser, *The Implied Reader: Patterns of Communication in Prose Fiction from Bunyan to Beckett*, Baltimore: The Johns Hopkins University Press, 1974, p. 294.

5. Everett Emerson details Twain's motives for writing travel works, which were mainly to generate income and to establish his reputation. Twain sometimes had a number of ongoing projects, and travel works were generally easier to finish, because they could be viewed as potentially financially rewarding sequels to his very successful *Innocents Abroad*. See Everett Emerson, *Mark Twain: A Literary Life*, Philadelphia: University of Pennsylvania Press, 2000, pp. 70–71. Emerson's excellent biography reminds us that Twain often had no specific goal or even strategy for writing, depending on notes or old ideas that could take years to develop into full drafts. While this seems desultory planning at best, Twain's underlying phenomenological structures helped guide his writing. As I will argue, the plan of reading the river became his plan for writing about life. This plan, if one can call it that, is very flexible, allowing for a good deal of drift. Twain would return time and again to relatively stable issues of identity, nostalgia, and timelessness.

6. See Eliza Lavin, *Good Manners*, New York: The Butterick Company, 1888; and Annie P. White, *Polite Society at Home and Abroad*, Chicago: Monarch Book Company, 1891. Alan Gribben does not list either of these works in his reconstruction of Twain's library.

7. Everett Emerson discusses Olivia Clemens' role as a censor and as an editor. Twain sought her approval in order to fit in with an ideal of an established writer while he also sought to find freedom from that label. See Emerson, pages 178 and following.

8. See Howard G. Baetzhold, *Mark Twain and John Bull: The British Connection*, Bloomington: Indiana University Press, 1970; Everett Emerson, *Mark Twain: A Literary Life*, Philadelphia: University of Pennsylvania Press, 2000; and Robert Rodney, *Mark Twain Overseas: A Biographical Account of His Voyages, Travels, and Reception in Foreign Lands, 1866–1910*, Washington, D.C: Three Continents Press, 1993. These are just representative of a long list of works that deal with Twain's travels abroad and his literary output while outside of the United States.

9. See Jeffrey Alan Melton, "The Wild Teacher of the Pacific Slope: Mark Twain, Travel Books, and Instruction," *Thalia*, 16 (1996), 46–52. Melton's article is useful for reviewing Twain's role as teacher and as a satirist. Melton also refers to another convention of travel writers, that of using "asides," or anecdotal material from the region traveled, "local legends, myths, newspaper extracts, historical accounts," which provide a "pause in the movement of the narrative" (49).

10. See Percy G. Adams, *Travel Literature and the Evolution of the Novel* (Lexington: The University Press of Kentucky, 1983). Adams attempts a thorough classification of the types of travel writings, admitting that the literature of travel "includes countless subtypes that continually approach each other, separate, join, overlap, and consistently defy neat classification" (38). Adams includes notes about one's travel experiences in his analysis of the genre characteristics of travel literature, for example, writing journal entries without the purpose of entertaining or instructing an audience. I use a narrow perspective, one that includes the audience, the text, and the writer as a set of traditions about the act of traveling that inform us about the writer's ideological and phenomenological perspectives.

11. See, for example, Mary Louise Pratt, *Travel Writing and Transculturation* (London: Routledge, 1992).

12. See Dewey Ganzel, *Mark Twain Abroad: The Cruise of the "Quaker City"* (Chicago: The University of Chicago Press, 1968. Ganzel, among other critics, discusses Twain's uneasy relationships with his pious fellow travelers, and with books shelved on board. In particular, Twain found William Prime's *Tent Life in the Holy Land* a partic-

ularly annoying travel guide for its sentimentality (247).

13. See Beverly R. David, "Tragedy and Travesty: Edward Whymper's Scrambles Amongst the Alps and Mark Twain's A Tramp Abroad," *Mark Twain Journal*, 27:1 (Spring 1989), 2–8. David suggests that Whymper embellished his part in the ill-fated expedition up the Matterhorn. Twain, in turn, creates the "Matterhorn chapter" out of a "poor pastiche of borrowed and abridged text, direct and indirect piracy of prints, and alterations of famous illustrations" (8). However, *A Tramp Abroad* is claimed to be a "financial and personal success," which is not the case. Twain's third travel book did not achieve the financial success of his earlier travel works, and the manuscript was an ordeal to him. See Twain's letter to Howells (January 30, 1879); he writes that he has "destroyed such lots of MS written for this book! And I suppose there are such lots left which ought to be destroyed" (*MTHL*). Eventually he did create almost four thousand pages of manuscript, but used only about twenty-six hundred. Early in the composing process, however, Twain assumed that writing the manuscript would not be as taxing as it turned out to be (see his letter to David Gray, Sr., June 2, 1878, *MEPUL*). Still, David's article usefully shows how Twain borrowed material.

14. See Francis Vincent Madigan's 1974 New York University dissertation, "A Genetic Study of *Following the Equator*," 256–57. Madigan lists and describes at least 46 sources/books for *Following the Equator*. Carnegie sent Twain a number of books, one of which, *Triumphant Democracy; or Fifty Years' March of the Republic*, encouraged Twain during the writing of *A Connecticut Yankee*.

15. See the bibliography in this text of travel works that Twain read or possessed in his library. Alan Gribben's *Mark Twain's Library: A Reconstruction*, Boston: G.K. Hall, 1980, is an invaluable tool for research. I am indebted to this essential work.

16. Robert Regan, in "The Reprobate Elect in *The Innocents Abroad, American Literature*, 54: 2 (May 1982), discusses this inversion of the expected distinction made between the "pilgrims" and the "sinners." Pilgrims, the individuals who claim Christian virtues and values, "represent beclouded perception, distorted understanding, and grotesquely inappropriate expression" (250).

17. Richard Bridgman, *Traveling in Mark Twain* (Berkeley: University of California Press, 1987), 12. Further references to Bridgman are indicated by parenthetical page numbers in the text. One could say this about Michael Crichton's *Travels* (New York: Perennial, 2002), though Crichton's book, uneven in terms of organization, contains occasional moments of enlightenment and coherence.

18. Sherwood Cummings, *Mark Twain and Science: Adventures of a Mind* (Baton Rouge, 1988), 93. Cummings notes that the phrase "jubilant delight" can be found in Henry Nash Smith and William M. Gibson (eds.), *Mark Twain-Howells Letters* (2 vols.; Cambridge, Mass., 1960). I, 290. Further references to Cummings are indicated by parenthetical page numbers in the text.

19. Again, see Percy G. Adams, *Travel Literature and the Evolution of the Novel*, (Lexington: The University Press of Kentucky, 1983).

20. See Hippolyte Taine, *The Ancient Regime*, trans. John Durand, Gloucester: Peter Smith, 1962, pp. viii–ix. Taine is viewed as a failure as a historian because of his biased choice of facts and bias toward those in the French Revolution.

21. Samuel Clemens [Mark Twain], *Life on the Mississippi*, Author's National Edition: The Writings of Mark Twain (25 vols.; New York, 1907–18), IX, 86. I will use the first edition; see Mark Twain, *Life on the Mississippi* (Boston: James R. Osgood, 1883), 87. Further references will be to this first edition. I believe that the reader constructs the meaning to the text during the time the edition exists as an entity, so further references to Twain's travel works will be to first editions, rather than to editions that Twain may have revised late in his career. The theory that I am relying on (though a bit old-fashioned) is in Jerome J. McGann's *A Critique of Modern Textual Criticism* (Chicago: University of Chicago Press, 1983). I will rely on scholarly edi-

tions of his fiction because these are generally reconstructions of first editions and because these are more readily available. Scholarly editions for some of the travel works remain to be done.

22. Edgar M. Branch, in "Mark Twain: The Pilot and the Writer," *Mark Twain Journal*, 23:2 (Fall, 1985), 28–43, discusses the instinctual knowledge that a pilot must have. This article suggests that the pilot's knowledge is not unconscious, but depends on empirical facts. Branch also shows how the Darnell-Watson feud in Chapter 26 relates to the Grangerford-Shepherdson feud in *Huckleberry Finn*, not as mere reflections of each other, but as complex differences in narrative technique.

23. In this regard, see Edgar Branch's article, "Mark Twain: The Pilot and the Writer," which defends the Twain's piloting skills.

24. See Ganzel, *Mark Twain Abroad*, 258.

25. See, for example, Carol Crawshaw and John Urry's discussion of the importance of memory, in "Tourism and the Photographic Eye," 179. As Crawshaw and Urry point out, tourists are often "disappointed by their own pictures because their memories of the view were in fact much richer and fuller," 193.

26. See the introduction to Dixon Wecter's edition of Twain's letters, *Mark Twain to Mrs. Fairbanks*, San Marino, California, 1949, especially pages xxiii and following.

27. Robert Hirst details the kinds of revisions that Bliss, Fairbanks, Harte, and Livy may have suggested to Twain. The manuscript, while now lost, seems to have been softened in its criticism toward other passengers. These letters are in *Traveling with the Innocents Abroad: Mark Twain's Original Reports from Europe and the Holy Land*, edited by Daniel Morley McKeithan. Some of the last letters that he also wrote for the *Alta* while traveling from San Francisco to New York and elsewhere (before arranging the *Quaker City* excursion) illustrate his anticipation for the trip (available in *Mark Twain's Travels with Mr. Brown*, edited by Franklin Walker and G. Ezra Dane). Hirst, in particular, discusses Harte's editorial concerns.

28. See Henry Nash Smith, *Mark Twain: The Development of a Writer*, 35–37; John C. Gerber, *Mark Twain*, 31–32. Hirst also discusses the "narrative-plank," 151–52. Hirst, as noted earlier, details the changes which Twain made to the manuscript to make it palatable to his audience, primarily in response to Bret Harte, Mrs. Fairbanks, and Livy. Hirst clearly defines Smith's general comments about the shifts in narrative tone and character of *Innocents Abroad*, showing how the text changes from the hostile letters about his fellow travelers to the extended satire that it becomes in part. The letter to Livy is in *MTL*, Vol. 5, 498.

29. In this regard, I side with Henry Nash Smith's analysis rather than with Forrest G. Robinson's discussion, in "Patterns of Consciousness in *The Innocents Abroad*," *American Literature*, 58 (March 1986), 45–63. Robinson finds a "rapid mental movement between states" (49), which, given Twain's deliberate choice of narrative structure, seems to make sense at first, until Robinson suggests that "the sudden and extreme shifts in tone betray a marked ambivalence about America, and a conspicuous incapacity to sustain a tone of humorous impersonation," which becomes a "failing effort in which good-humored distance is not so much achieved as it is simply received as one phase in the round of extreme, generally unanticipated shifts in point of view" (54). The pattern which Robinson finds, between "generally agreeable states of mind associated with dreaminess and the past, and frequently discordant moods associated with sharply waking perceptions of the present" (58), is, in fact, an anticipated use of narrative structure, one that Twain uses throughout his travel books, as well as his novels. Fred Durden, in "The Aesthetics of Bitterness in *Following the Equator*," *American Literary Realism*, 14 (Autumn, 1981), 277–85, also discusses this narrative pattern, locating it in all the travel books. He describes the device briefly in *The Innocents Abroad* (278) and in *Life on the Mississippi* (285). Smith, in *Mark Twain: The Development of a Writer*, New York: Atheneum Press, 1972, finds that the book contains a number of narrators who coalesce in a "virtual reality," one that allows an "American Adam," an

"innocent" or "hero" to "wear a variety of masks, although this plurality of identities frustrates the writer's effort to subdue him to the uses of art" (50–51). I find, however, the multiplicity of identities quite congruent with Twain's competence as a pilot navigating among different cultures.

30. See George Ritzer and Allan Liska, "'McDisneyization' and 'Post-Tourism,'" in *Touring Cultures: Transformations of Travel and Theory*, edited by Chris Rojek and John Urry, Routledge: New York, 2002. Subsequent parenthetical references are to Ritzer and Liska.

31. Carol Crawshaw and John Urry discuss the historical implications of photography in the changing perspectives of the tourist. Their claim is that the advent of the photograph allowed tourists the ability to fix and to structure their traveling experiences, so that the tourist of the nineteenth century could better understand other cultures and better control a sense of disorientation, while the photograph and the photographer could demonstrate the mastery of humans over nature. See Crawshaw and Urry, "Tourism and the Photographic Eye," in *Touring Cultures: Trans-formations of Travel and Theory*, edited by Chris Rojek and John Urry, Routledge: New York, 2002.

32. Robert Hirst discusses the genesis of *Innocents Abroad*. Hirst suggests that the original manuscript, now lost, conveyed the hostility Twain felt toward his fellow passengers; Twain lowered the level of sarcasm and disgust, creating a text that became more marketable, which Elisha Bliss used to make *Innocents Abroad* a major bestseller. Bliss' son, Frank, published *Following the Equator*, making substantial changes to that travel book. Robert Regan, in "The Reprobate Elect in *The Innocents Abroad*," *American Literature*, 54: 2 (May 1982), 240–57, discusses the evolution of the "pilgrims" and "sinners" division of the travelers, and how Twain uses this division to satirize traveling conventions.

33. Twain is probably referring to Rufus Anderson's *The Hawaiian Islands: Their Progress and Condition Under Missionary Labors*, a text published by Gould and Lincoln in 1864, and Henry Theodore Cheever's *The Island World of the Pacific; Being the Personal Narrative and Results of Travel Through The Sandwich or Hawaiian Island, and Other Parts of Polynesia*, published by Harper & Brothers, 1851.

34. See Lillard, Richard G., and Mary V. Hood. 1973. *Hank Monk and Horace Greeley: An Enduring Episode in Western History*. Georgetown, Calif.: Wilmac Press.

35. James D. Wilson, in "History as Palimpsest: The Layers of Time in *Life on the Mississippi, Journal of the American Studies Association of Texas*, 25: 32–39, offers a full discussion of the attempt by Twain to find "a negation of time, to unify past and present in a single, present, recurring moment" (32).

36. See Dennis Welland, "Mark Twain's Last Travel Book," *Bulletin of the New York Public Library*, 69 (January 1965), 31. Welland's article shows the differences between the English edition, published as *More Tramps Abroad*, and the American edition. He argues persuasively that the English edition ought to be the copy-text for scholars; Andrew Chatto followed Twain's manuscript more faithfully than Frank Bliss, who edited the text on his own. I agree. I have used the American version, which Welland terms "an abridged variant" (48), as the reading version, however, because American response would be to it, not the better English edition.

37. Francis Vincent Madigan offers the best extended analysis of *Following the Equator*, along with astute observations on how Twain probably incorporated Susy's death and his response within the context of India. Madigan discusses the description of the Taj Mahal and a subsequent description of a New England ice storm (which occurred some twenty years earlier) as a moment of imaginative self-realization and acceptance of Susy's life and death. See Madigan's 1974 New York University dissertation "Mark Twain's Passage to India: A Genetic Study of *Following the Equator*," 317–28.

38. Frequently anthologized, this essay appeared in the October 3, 1895 issue of *Youth's Companion*.

39. Published in *Mark Twain, a Biography* by Albert Bigelow Paine, Harper & Brothers: New York, 1912.

Bibliography

Primary Texts

The following list is keyed to the abbreviations used in the text and provides full bibliographic information.

Letters, Manuscripts, Notebooks, and Dictations by Samuel L. Clemens (Mark Twain)

MTHHR. *Mark Twain's Correspondence with Henry Huttleston Rogers, 1893–1909.* Edited by Lewis Leary. Berkeley: University of California Press, 1969.

MTHL. *Mark Twain–Howells Letters: The Correspondence of Samuel L. Clemens and William Dean Howells.* Edited by Henry Nash Smith and William M. Gibson. 2 vols. Cambridge: Harvard University Press, 1960.

MTL. *Mark Twain's Letters.* Vol. 1, 1853–1866, edited by Edgar Marquess Branch, Michael B. Frank, and Kenneth Anderson. Vol. 2, 1867–1868, edited by Harriet Elinor Smith and Richard Bucci. Vol. 3, 1869, edited by Victor Fischer and Michael B. Frank. Vol. 4, 1870–1871, edited by Victor Fischer and Michael B. Frank. Vol. 5, 1872–1873, edited by Lin Salamo and Harriet Elinor Smith. Vol. 6, 1874–1875, edited by Michael B. Frank and Harriet Elinor Smith. Berkeley: University of California Press, 1988–2002.

MPub. *Mark Twain's Letters to His Publishers, 1867–1894.* Edited by Hamlin Hill. Berkeley: University of California Press, 1967.

MTF. *Mark Twain to Mrs. Fairbanks.* Edited by Dixon Wecter. San Marino, Calif.: Huntington Library, 1949.

MTS. *Mark Twain Speaking.* Edited by Paul Fatout. Iowa City: University of Iowa Press, 1976.

MEML. *Microfilm Edition of Mark Twain's Manuscript Letters Now in the Mark Twain Papers.* Prepared by Anh Quynh Bui, Victor Fischer, Michael B. Frank, Robert

H. Hirst, Lin Salamo and Harriet Elinor Smith. 11 vols. Berkeley: The Bancroft Library, 2001. [Letters designated "CU-MARK" in the Mark Twain Project online database.]

MEPUL. *Microfilm Edition of Mark Twain's Previously Unpublished Letters*. Prepared by Anh Quynh Bui, Victor Fischer, Michael B. Frank, Robert H. Hirst, Lin Salamo and Harriet Elinor Smith. 8 vols. Berkeley: The Bancroft Library, 2001. [Letters held by other institutions as found in the Mark Twain Project online database.]

MELM. *Microfilm Edition of Mark Twain's Literary Manuscripts Available in the Mark Twain Papers*. Prepared by Anh Quynh Bui, Victor Fischer, Michael B. Frank, Robert H. Hirst, Lin Salamo and Harriet Elinor Smith. 42 vols. Berkeley: The Bancroft Library, 2001. [Manuscripts, notebooks, and dictations held at the Mark Twain Project.]

Published Travel Works by Samuel L. Clemens (Mark Twain)

Following the Equator: A Journey Around the World. Hartford: American Publishing Co., 1897.
The Innocents Abroad; or, The New Pilgrim's Progress. Hartford: American Publishing Co., 1869.
Life on the Mississippi. Boston: Charles R. Osgood, 1883.
More Tramps Abroad. London: Chatto and Windus, 1897.
Roughing It. Hartford: American Publishing Co., 1872.
A Tramp Abroad. Hartford: American Publishing Co., 1880.

Edited Travel Works by Samuel L. Clemens (Mark Twain)

Mark Twain's Letters from Hawaii. Edited by A. Grove Day. Honolulu: The University Press of Hawaii, 1966.
Mark Twain's Travels with Mr. Brown. Edited by Franklin Walker and G. Ezra Dane. New York: Alfred A. Knopf, 1940.
Traveling with the Innocents Abroad: Mark Twain's Original Reports from Europe and the Holy Land. Edited by Daniel Morley McKeithan. Norman: University of Oklahoma Press, 1958.

Primary Literature Texts by Samuel L. Clemens (Mark Twain)

Adventures of Huckleberry Finn. Edited by Victor Fischer and Lin Salamo. Berkeley: University of California Press, 2001.

The Adventures of Tom Sawyer. The Oxford Mark Twain. Edited by Shelley Fisher Fishkin. New York: Oxford University Press, 1996.
A Connecticut Yankee in King Arthur's Court. Berkeley: University of California Press, 1979.
Letters from the Earth. Edited by Bernard De Voto. New York: Perennial Classics, 2004.
No. 44, The Mysterious Stranger. Edited by John S. Tuckey and William M. Gibson. Berkeley: University of California Press, 1982.
The Prince and the Pauper. Edited by Victor Fisher and Lin Salamo, with the assistance of Mary Jane Jones. Berkeley: University of California Press, 1983.
The Tragedy of Pudd'nhead Wilson and the Comedy Those Extraordinary Twins. The Oxford Mark Twain. Edited by Shelley Fisher Fishkin. New York: Oxford University Press, 1996.

Secondary Works

Adams, Percy G. *Travel Literature and the Evolution of the Novel.* Lexington: The University Press of Kentucky, 1983.
Baetzhold, Howard G. *Mark Twain and John Bull: The British Connection.* Bloomington: Indiana University Press, 1970.
Bassett, John. E. "Life on the Mississippi: Being Shifty in a New Country." *Western American Literature* 21 (1986): 39–45. Beidler, Gretchen. "Huck Finn As Tourist: Mark Twain's Parody Travelogue." *Studies in American Fiction* 20 (Autumn 1992): 155–167.
Beidler, Philip D. "Realistic Style and the Problem of Context in *The Innocents Abroad* and *Roughing It.*" *American Literature* 52 (1980–81): 33–49.
Branch, Edgar M. "Mark Twain: The Pilot and the Writer." *Mark Twain Journal* 23 (Fall 1985): 28–43.
Brazil, John R. "Perception and Structure in Mark Twain's Art and Mind: *Life on the Mississippi.*" *The Mississippi Quarterly* 34 (1981): 91–112.
Briden, Earl F. "Through a Glass Eye, Darkly: The Skeptic Design of *Life on the Mississippi.*" *The Mississippi Quarterly* 48 (1995): 225–37.
Bridgman, Richard. *Traveling in Mark Twain.* Berkeley: University of California Press, 1987.
Caron, James E. "The Comic *Bildungsroman* of Mark Twain." *Modern Language Quarterly* 50 (June 1989): 145–172.
Cox, James M. *Mark Twain: The Fate of Humor.* Princeton: Princeton University Press, 1966.
Cracroft, Richard H. "'Ten Wives Is All You Need': Artemus Twain and the Mormons — Again." *Western Humanities Review* 38 (Fall 1984): 197–211.
Crichton, Michael. *Travels.* New York: Perennial, 2002.
Cummings, Sherwood. *Mark Twain and Science: Adventures of a Mind.* Baton Rouge: Louisiana State University Press, 1988.
David, Beverly R. *Mark Twain and His Illustrators.* 2 Vols. Troy, N.Y.: Whitston Publishing Company, 1986.
_____. "Tragedy and Travesty: Edward Whymper's *Scrambles Amongst the Alps* and Mark Twain's *A Tramp Abroad.*" *Mark Twain Journal* 27, no. 1 (1989): 2–8.
_____. What's in a Name? Twain's Goethe Hero in *A Tramp Abroad.*" *Mark Twain Journal* 26 (Spring 1988): 30–32.
Dolmetsch, Carl. "*Our Famous Guest*": *Mark Twain in Vienna.* Athens: University of Georgia Press, 1992.

Durden, Fred. "The Aesthetics of Bitterness in *Following the Equator.*" *American Literary Realism* 14 (Autumn 1981): 277–85.
Emerson, Everett. *Mark Twain: A Literary Life.* Philadelphia: University of Pennsylvania Press, 2000.
Fishkin, Shelley Fisher. *Lighting Out for the Territory: Reflections on Mark Twain and American Culture.* New York: Oxford University Press, 1997.
Foner, Philip S. *Mark Twain: Social Critic.* New York: International, 1958.
Fussell, Paul. *Abroad: British Literary Traveling Between the Wars.* New York: Oxford University Press, 1980.
Ganzel, Dewey. *Mark Twain Abroad: The Cruise of the "Quaker City."* Chicago and London: University of Chicago Press, 1968.
———. "Twain, Travel Books, and *Life on the Mississippi,*" *American Literature*, 34 (March 1962), 40–55.
Gervais, Ronald J. "What Remains When Everything Is Left Out: The Joke of 'Baker's Blue-Jay Yarn.'" *Mark Twain Journal* 21 (Fall 1983): 12–14.
Gillman, Susan. *Dark Twins: Imposture and Identity in Mark Twain's America.* Chicago: University of Chicago Press, 1989.
Gribben, Alan. *Mark Twain's Library: A Reconstruction.* 2 vols. Boston: G.K. Hall, 1980.
———. "Mark Twain Reads Longstreet's Georgia Scenes." In *Gyascutus: Studies in Antebellum Southern Humorous and Sporting Writing*, ed. James L. W. West, 103–11. Atlantic Highlands, N.J.: Humanities Press, 1978.
Gunn, Drewey Wayne. "The Monomythic Structure of *Roughing It.*" *American Literature* 61 (1989): 563–85.
Hill, Hamlin. *Mark Twain: God's Fool.* New York: Harper and Row, 1973.
Hirst, Robert. "The Making of *The Innocents Abroad: 1867–1872.*" Ph.D. diss., University of California, Berkeley, 1975.
Hirst, Robert H., and Brandt Rowles. "William E. James's Stereoscopic Views of the *Quaker City* Excursion." *Mark Twain Journal* 22 (1984): 15–33.
Hobbs, Michael. "Mark Twain's Infernal Transcendentalism: The Lake Episodes in *Roughing It.*" *American Literary Realism* 26 (Fall 1993): 13–25.
Howe, Lawrence. "Transcending the Limits of Experience: Mark Twain's *Life on the Mississippi.*" *American Literature* 63 (1991): 420–38.
Kaplan, Justin. *Mr. Clemens and Mark Twain.* New York: Simon and Schuster, 1966.
Kemnitz, Charles. "*Roughing It* on the Open Road." *Mark Twain Journal* 21 (Fall 1983): 21–22.
Krause, Sydney J. *Mark Twain As Critic.* Baltimore: Johns Hopkins University Press, 1967.
———. "Olivia Clemens's 'Editing' Reviewed." *American Literature* 39 (1967–68): 325–51.
LeMaster, J. R., and James D. Wilson, eds. *The Mark Twain Encyclopedia.* New York: Garland, 1993.
MacCannell, Dean. *The Tourist: A New Theory of the Leisure Class.* Berkeley: University of California Press, 1999.
Madigan, Francis V. "Mark Twain's Passage to India: A Genetic Study of *Following the Equator.*" Ph.D. diss., New York University 1974.
Melton, Jeffrey Alan. "The Wild Teacher of the Pacific Slope: Mark Twain, Travel Books, and Instruction." *Thalia* 16 (1996): 46–52.
———. *Mark Twain, Travel Books, and Tourism: The Tide of a Great Popular Movement.* Tuscaloosa: The University of Alabama Press, 2002.

Messent, Peter. "Racial and Colonial Discourse in Mark Twain's *Following the Equator*." *Essays in Arts and Sciences* 22 (1993): 67–83.
Michelson, Bruce. "Mark Twain the Tourist: The Form of 'The Innocents Abroad.'" *American Literature* 49 (1977): 385–98.
Obenzinger, Hilton. *American Palestine: Melville, Twain, and the Holy Land Mania.* Princeton: Princeton University Press, 1999.
Parsons, Coleman. "Mark Twain: Sightseer in India." *Mississippi Quarterly*, 16 (1963).
Potts, E. Daniel, and Annette Potts. "The Mark Twain Family in Australia." *Overland* (Melbourne) 70 (1978): 46–50.
Powers, Ron. *Mark Twain: A Life.* New York: Free Press, 2005.
Pratt, Mary L. *Imperial Eyes: Travel Writing and Transculturation.* New York: Routledge, 1992.
Rasmussen, R. Kent. *Mark Twain A to Z: The Essential Reference to His Life and Writings.* New York: Oxford University Press, 1996.
Regan, Robert. "The Reprobate Elect in *The Innocents Abroad*." *American Literature* 54 (1982–83): 240–57.
Robinson, Forrest G. "The Innocent at Large: Mark Twain's Travel Writing." In *The Cambridge Companion to Mark Twain*, ed. Forrest G. Robinson, 27–51. New York: Cambridge University Press, 1995.
_____. Patterns of Consciousness in *The Innocents Abroad*." *American Literature* 58 (1986): 46–63.
_____. "'Seeing the Elephant: Some Perspectives on Mark Twain's *Roughing It*." *American Studies* 21 (1980): 43–64.
Rodney, Robert M. *Mark Twain Overseas: A Biographical Account of His Voyages, Travels, and Reception in Foreign Lands, 1866–1910.* Washington, D.C.: Three Continents Press, 1993.
Skandera-Trombley, Laura. *Mark Twain in the Company of Women.* Philadelphia: University of Pennsylvania Press, 1994.
Smith, Henry Nash. *Mark Twain: The Development of a Writer.* Cambridge: Harvard University Press, 1962.
Steinbrink, Jeffrey. *Getting to Be Mark Twain.* Berkeley: University of California Press, 1991.
_____. "Why the Innocents Went Abroad: Mark Twain and American Tourism in the Late Nineteenth Century." *American Literary Realism* 16 (Autumn 1983): 278-286.
Stowell, Robert F. "River Guide Books and Mark Twain's *Life on the Mississippi*." *Mark Twain Journal* 16 (Summer 1974): 21.
Sumida, Stephen H. "Reevaluating Mark Twain's Novel of Hawaii." *American Literature* 61 (December 1989): 586–609.
Taine, Hippolyte Adolphe. *The Ancient Regime.* Trans. John Durand. New York: Henry Holt, 1876.
Welland, Dennis. "Mark Twain's Last Travel Book." *Bulletin of the New York Public Library* 69 (1965): 31–48.
West, Gary V. "The Development of the Mark Twain Persona in the Early Travel Letters." *Mark Twain Journal* 20 (1980–81): 13–16.
Wilson, James D. "History As Palimpsest: The Layers of Time in *Life on the Mississippi*." *Journal of the American Studies Association of Texas* 25 (1994): 32–39.
Ziff, Larzer. *Return Passages: Great American Travel Writing 1780–1910.* New Haven: Yale University Press, 2000.

Index

Adams, Percy G. 8, 13, 32, 42, 43, 46
The Adventures of Huckleberry Finn 1, 7, 14, 16, 32, 33, 39, 69, 83, 84, 85, 87, 92, 99, 145, 153, 153, 158
The Adventures of Tom Sawyer 1, 14, 21, 92, 115, 144, 162
Alta California 30, 41, 45, 46, 47, 50, 59, 65, 66, 67, 87, 90
American Publishing Company 45, 63
American tourist 23, 27, 86, 89
American values 43, 44, 171
Athens 27, 28
Aunt Sally (character) 152, 157
Australia 19, 25, 31, 122, 133, 136
Authenticity (travel experience) 9, 41, 115
"Autobiographical Dictations" 38, 99, 102
"The Awful German Language" 84, 93, 119
Azores Islands 51, 52, 53, 54, 169

Baetzhold, Howard 17
Baker's blue jay yarn 84, 85, 91
Ballou (character) 74
Beard, Dan 132, 163
Becky Thatcher (character) 144
Bemis (character) 22, 76, 77, 79
Ben Coontz (character) 107, 108
Ben Holliday (character) 68
Bierstadt, Albert 12, 66
Bliss, Elisha 45, 63, 64, 80, 49, 68, 69, 86
Bliss, Frank 80, 81, 117
Blucher (character) 47, 50, 51, 69, 173
Boer (culture) 119, 128, 129, 136
Book of Mormon 72, 73

Bridgman, Richard 4, 5
Brigham Young (character) 22, 72, 73
Buck Fanshaw (character) 19
Buck Grangerford (character) 151

Capitalism 5, 27, 40, 59, 67, 77, 103, 163, 164, 169, 171, 172, 179, 180
Captain Isaiah Sellers (character) 109, 111
Captain Nye (character) 77
Carnegie, Andrew 31
Ceylon 117, 138
Chambers (character) 23, 24, 175, 176, 177, 178, 179
"Charlie Williams" (character) 108
Christianity 2, 14, 21, 23, 30, 31, 32, 49, 50, 54, 64, 65, 66, 108, 129, 137, 168, 170, 171
Civil War 3, 38, 49, 72, 103, 106, 112, 113, 115, 149
Clemens, Clara 23
Clemens, Henry 107, 108, 111, 117
Clemens, Orion 9, 22, 40, 63, 67, 70, 72, 87, 116, 118
Clemens, Livy 21, 23, 46, 57, 63, 81, 95, 127, 161
Clemens, Susy (death of) 20, 23, 116, 118, 133, 140, 141
Cole, Thomas 13
A Connecticut Yankee in King Arthur's Court 1, 9, 14, 21, 24, 33, 39, 72, 84, 103, 104, 132, 158, 163, 164, 167, 168, 169, 170, 171, 172, 173
Constable, John 13
Coon, Ben 107, 109, 114, 116

213

Index

Cowper Prime, William 31
Coyote (character) 40, 70, 71
Craik, Jennifer 13
Crane, Stephen 64, 75
Crane, Susan Langdon 95, 102
Crawshaw, Carol 13, 56
Cub pilot, learning the river 13, 20, 34, 35, 44, 78, 98, 110, 119
Cummings, Sherwood 32, 33, 34

Dane, G. Ezra 65
Darwin, Charles 17
David Wilson (character) 23, 121, 175, 176, 178, 179
Dawson's Landing (as setting) 1, 14, 175, 178, 179
DeVoto, Bernard 169
Dickens, Charles 17
Dimsdale, Thos. J. 69
Dreams, problematic nature of 5, 58, 74, 102, 103, 104, 106, 117, 122, 126, 135, 136, 137, 138, 139, 140, 151, 157, 165, 166, 167, 168, 173, 176, 180
Duke and the King (character) 84, 148, 152, 153, 154, 155
Durand, Asher B. 13

Edward (character) 157, 159, 160, 161, 162
Egypt 20, 23, 41, 49, 57, 58, 59, 60, 145
Elmira 17, 95
Emerson, Everett 17
England 1, 9, 13, 14, 17, 42, 84, 103, 115, 116, 119, 131, 133, 136, 141, 158, 162, 165, 166, 168, 171
Europe 10, 12, 13, 16, 17, 19, 26, 30, 39, 41, 43, 45, 54, 55, 57, 58, 59, 66, 67, 68, 69, 80, 83, 85, 86, 88, 89, 90, 92, 93, 95, 96, 97, 115, 129, 134, 137, 144, 173, 175, 179

Fairbanks, Mary 45, 81
Falsehoods, and truth 15, 22, 79, 84, 92, 108, 109, 115, 152, 153, 162
Flores (island of) 51
Following the Equator 1, 5, 14, 16, 19, 20, 21, 22, 23, 24, 25, 27, 28, 31, 43, 57, 61, 63, 68, 89, 94, 101, 116, 117, 118, 119, 126, 127, 128, 129, 131, 132, 134, 135, 138, 140, 141, 171, 175, 180
France 17, 33, 52, 53, 54, 72, 80, 85, 130, 131
"The French and the Comanches" 96
French civilization 33, 52, 53, 72, 84, 96, 126, 130, 131

Friedrich, Caspar David 13
Fussell, Paul 8, 9, 13, 42

Gadsby's anecdote 84, 90, 91, 93
Gender roles, transformation 16, 19, 24, 93, 94, 134
General Grant (character) 22, 124, 125
General Sherman (character) 49
German (as language) 19, 81, 83, 84, 85, 93, 94, 95, 119
German folktales 22, 83, 85, 92, 95, 97
Germany 13, 80, 81, 85, 93, 95, 131
Gillman, Susan 117, 138
God (character) 23, 57, 59, 64, 76, 136, 144, 150, 166, 167, 169, 172, 173
Gordon-Cumming, Constance Frederica 31
Grand Tour, as concept 13, 30, 39, 49
Grangerford (character of family) 146, 151, 155
Gray, David 80
Greeley, Horace 19, 25, 78, 79, 91, 126

Hank Morgan (character) 9, 23, 24, 71, 103, 104, 158, 159, 163, 164, 165, 166, 167, 168, 169, 170, 171, 172, 173, 180
Hannibal, Missouri 5, 24, 25, 58, 104, 105, 106, 111, 162
Harris (character) 81, 88, 89, 91, 92, 93, 97
Harte, Bret 45, 57
Hawaii 9, 16, 19, 20, 21, 22, 25, 31, 32, 46, 47, 59, 60, 63, 64, 65, 66, 67, 75, 87, 110, 129, 166
Hay, Rosina 95
Heidelberg raft excursion 83, 84, 87
Hero's quest for truth (and meaning) 5, 152
Historical time 2, 14, 55, 101, 141
Horace Bixby 33, 34, 35, 36, 37, 44, 110, 111
Hornet, trial at sea (ship sinks off Hawaii) 63, 64
"How to Tell a Story" 126
Howells, William Dean 10, 81, 83, 98, 118
Huck Finn (character) 1, 5, 14, 16, 18, 19, 21, 22, 23, 24, 33, 71, 75, 84, 89, 92, 111, 115, 124, 145, 146, 147, 148, 149, 150, 151, 152, 153, 154, 155, 156, 157, 158, 159, 162, 164, 173, 175
Hyde vs. Morgan (hoax) 21, 26, 76, 126

Identity, issues of 1, 2, 9, 14, 15, 17, 19, 22, 24, 25, 28, 43, 61, 67, 75, 76, 84,

Index

87, 92, 93, 94, 106, 108, 109, 115, 116, 130, 132, 133, 134, 135, 136, 139, 141, 144, 145, 146, 150, 151, 153, 156, 157, 158, 159, 160, 161, 162, 163, 173, 174, 175, 176, 177, 178, 179, 180
India 18, 20, 23, 24, 31, 39, 41, 70, 78, 118, 119, 124, 130, 134, 135, 136, 138, 139, 140, 177
Injun Joe (character) 144, 145
Innocents Abroad 1, 9, 10, 14, 16, 17, 18, 19, 20, 21, 23, 24, 26, 27, 30, 32, 41, 43, 45, 46, 47, 49, 57, 59, 60, 63, 64, 65, 66, 67, 68, 69, 79, 81, 85, 96, 97, 101, 102, 117, 118, 130, 131, 144, 145, 169, 170, 173, 175, 179
Iser, Wolfgang 13
Italian twins (character) 1, 14, 175, 179

"Jack Hunt" (character) 108
Jack Slade (character) 22, 23, 24, 40, 67, 69, 70, 71, 171, 173
James Barry (character) 24, 134, 135
Jameson Raid (South Africa) 119, 127
Jim (character) 21, 23, 24, 84, 145, 146, 148, 149, 150, 151, 152, 154, 155, 156, 157
Jim Blaine (character) 19, 20, 79, 99
Jimmy Finn (character) 107
Joanna Wilks (character) 155
John Brown (character) 22, 125, 126
John Canty (character) 157
Judge Driscoll (character) 179
Judge Thatcher (character) 144, 147

Kamehameha 129
Kaplan, Justin 138
Kilauea 25, 59, 64, 65
"Knave of Bergen" story 85, 92
Kruger, President 127, 128

Lady Gertrude (character) 87
Lake Tahoe 19, 75, 87
Langdon, Jervis 63
Last Man (self-portrayal) 69, 159
Lavin, Eliza 17
Legends of the Rhine from Basle to Rotterdam (F. J. Kiefer, trans. L. W. Garnham 92
Letters from Hawaii (and references to) 31, 32, 47, 63, 64, 65, 87, 110
Letters from the Earth 81, 96, 168, 169, 172, 173, 175
Life on the Mississippi 1, 14, 19, 20, 22, 23, 24, 30, 57, 66, 81, 85, 87, 93, 95,

98, 99, 101, 103, 108, 109, 110, 110, 115, 119, 122, 132, 145, 157
Liska, Allan 13, 50, 51
Loftus, Judith (character) 24, 153
London 27, 94, 113, 116, 160, 161
Lorelei (reference) 97

MacCannell, Dean 9, 10, 13
Madigan, Francis 140
Mark Twain Club 19, 25
Marseilles 53, 54
Mary Jane Wilks (character) 152, 155
McDonaldization (as theoretical phrase) 13
McDonaldized lifeworld (as theoretical concept) 50, 51
McFarland, James 58
Melton, Jeffrey Alan 3, 4, 5
Memory 19, 20, 21, 22, 34, 35, 37, 38, 39, 40, 41, 55, 56, 57, 59, 60, 67, 69, 86, 91, 92, 96, 99, 101, 102, 104, 106, 107, 110, 111, 114, 117, 118, 124, 125, 126, 127, 136, 137, 138, 139, 140, 141, 143, 144, 145, 150, 159, 160, 162, 163, 180
Milan 58
Miles Hendon (character) 159, 160, 161, 162
Missouri 5, 18, 20, 56, 58, 65, 105, 138, 141
Mr. B., Mr. Brown (person in South Africa) 128
Mr. Blank (character) 25
Mr. Brown (character) 31, 46, 47, 63, 64, 65, 87, 99, 105, 110
Mitchell, Captain Josiah (of Hornet fame) 64
Mono Lake 19
Moore, Julia 122
Morgan Le Fay (character) 168, 169, 173
Mormon 21, 22, 67, 70, 71, 72, 73, 78, 171
"Mysterious Avenger" (as Hannibal character) 106
The Mysterious Stranger 1, 14, 23, 24, 117, 166, 167, 168, 172, 173

Nature, as compelling force 1, 2, 13, 14, 25, 29, 30, 34, 59, 60, 61, 65, 68, 71, 74, 75, 76, 87, 94, 95, 105, 122, 139, 140, 158, 167, 172, 175, 176
New Orleans 56, 98, 113
New Orleans *Picayune* 109
New Orleans *True Delta* 109
New Testament 72, 172

216 Index

New York *Herald* 45, 67
New York *Tribune* 45, 66, 67
New Zealand 31, 136
Nostalgia 2, 14, 19, 20, 28, 36, 43, 44, 49, 50, 52, 53, 54, 57, 61, 64, 79, 87, 103, 104, 106, 116, 139, 144, 145, 155, 162, 163, 165, 173, 174, 180
Nye, Emma 63

Old Blue China (reference) 97
Old Testament 72, 172
"Old Times on the Mississippi" 34, 98, 111
Ollendorff (character) 74
Osgood, James R. 98, 99

Pap Finn (character) 23, 24, 146, 147, 148, 149, 150, 151, 153
Parkman, Francis 31
Parody 5, 15, 30, 41, 42, 45, 58, 84, 94, 97, 109, 148, 157
Phelps (character of family) 22, 24, 92, 124, 155, 156, 157
Phelps, Roswell H. 98
Phenomenology 2, 3, 5, 7, 8, 13, 28, 39
Pilgrims (as characters) 21, 30, 47, 50, 51, 52, 54, 55, 96, 173
Pilots' Benevolent Association 103
"Plank" narrative system 26, 46, 47, 54, 112
Polyphemous (character) 3
The Prince and the Pauper 1, 14, 32, 33, 83, 84, 115, 145, 157, 158, 159, 162
"The Professor's Yarn" 93, 108
Providence (as concept) 21, 22, 150, 155, 156
Pudd'nhead Wilson 1, 7, 14, 16, 29, 84, 121, 124, 134, 169, 173, 175, 179
"Pudd'nhead Wilson's Calendar" 1, 7, 121, 124
"Pudd'nhead Wilson's New Calendar" 29, 45, 61, 80, 98, 116, 119, 134, 144, 163

Quaker City (ship excursion) 12, 27, 45, 46, 55, 65, 66
Quarry Farm 95

Rainbow Falls 19, 60
Read(ing) the river 13, 36
"Recent Carnival of Crime in Connecticut" 137
Religion 19, 20, 21, 22, 23, 42, 43, 49, 52, 65, 71, 72, 73, 119, 131, 134, 135, 153, 163, 164, 167, 169, 170, 171, 172, 173, 180
Rev. Henry Ward Beecher (character) 49
Rhodes, Cecil 119, 136, 137
Riffelberg (fictitious ascent) 30, 84, 88, 89, 97
Riley, James Whitcomb 118
Riley, John Henry 90
Ritzer, George 13, 50, 51
River boat pilot (skills of) 20, 24, 40, 66, 67, 78, 88, 110, 114
River, facts about 38, 111
River, shape of 34, 35, 39, 40, 46, 56, 88, 99, 111, 178
Rodney, Robert 4, 5, 17
Rogers, Henry Huttleston 117, 121, 127, 171
Roughing It 1, 3, 9, 14, 15, 16, 18, 19, 20, 21, 22, 23, 24, 25, 26, 28, 30, 40, 43, 59, 60, 61, 63, 64, 66, 67, 68, 69, 70, 71, 73, 77, 78, 79, 80, 87, 89, 91, 97, 99, 101, 118, 126, 159, 167, 171
Roxy (character) 16, 24, 121, 134, 173, 175, 176, 177, 178, 179, 180

Sacramento Union 63
St. Louis 56, 98, 105
San Francisco 45, 65, 67, 90
Sandy (character) 84, 164, 165, 166, 168
Satan (character) 5, 23, 24, 169, 172, 173
"Satan" (as Indian servant) 23, 135
Scotty Briggs (character) 19
Scrambles Amongst the Alps (Edward Whymper) 30
Shepherdson (character of family) 146, 151
Simons, Michael Laird 46
Sinners (as characters) 50, 54, 55
Sir Walter Scott (character) 24, 112, 115, 153, 157
Sir Wendel Lobenfeld (character) 87
"Skeleton for Black Forest Novel," (chapter title in *A Tramp Abroad*) 97
Slavery 5, 20, 117, 128, 136, 137, 138, 149, 150, 152, 173, 177, 178, 180
Smith, Henry Nash 19, 46
South Africa 16, 20, 24, 31, 119, 127, 128, 131, 134, 136, 137, 138, 170
Spaulding, Clara 81, 95
Sphinx (character) 20, 23, 24, 40, 41, 55, 57, 58, 59, 60, 69, 101, 102, 103, 145
Stable moment in time 102
Stevenson, Robert Louis 137
Steves, Rick 7, 29
Stolen White Elephant, Etc. 81

Susan Wilks (character) 155

Taine, Hippolyte 33, 34, 95
Taj Mahal 20, 118, 139, 140, 141
Taylor, Bayard 31, 79, 90
Thuggee 21, 119, 130, 135, 140
Tichborne Claimant case 25
Timeless moment 43, 102, 103, 106, 117, 125, 138, 143, 152
Timeless state 2, 14, 54, 56, 57, 59, 60, 87, 91, 102, 103, 104, 118, 125, 137, 139, 140, 141, 144, 145, 158, 164, 165, 167, 168, 180
Timeless traveler, ship, or journey 54, 55, 103, 145, 163, 165
Tom Canty (character) 158, 159, 160, 162
Tom Sawyer (character) 18, 22, 24, 92, 144, 153, 156, 157, 158, 162, 173
Tourist 3, 9, 10, 13, 18, 19, 20, 21, 23, 25, 27, 41, 45, 50, 51, 54, 56, 59, 60, 85, 86, 89, 90, 96, 97, 109, 113, 114, 144, 145, 146, 152, 156, 159, 161, 168, 175
A Tramp Abroad 1, 12, 14, 19, 20, 22, 23, 24, 26, 27, 28, 30, 32, 33, 72, 80, 83, 84, 85, 86, 87, 91, 92, 93, 95, 99, 108, 115, 119, 122, 130, 131, 145, 162
Travel literature 1, 7, 8, 14, 15, 29, 30, 31, 42, 43, 46, 55, 64, 85, 99, 116, 152

Travel writer 8, 16, 25, 30, 31, 32, 40, 65, 96, 99, 122, 169
Travel writing, genre of 5, 7, 8, 18, 26, 31, 32, 42, 66, 92, 97, 179
Traveling 4, 5, 7, 8, 9, 15, 16, 17, 29, 32, 34, 43, 49, 50, 54, 56, 81, 89, 95, 97, 110, 126, 144, 160
Twichell, Joseph 80, 81, 89, 92, 95, 98, 118

Uncle Mumford's monologue 110
United States 1, 3, 9, 12, 17, 18, 19, 20, 23, 27, 41, 42, 43, 46, 49, 50, 52. 53, 59, 60, 61, 66, 68, 69, 86, 87, 89, 93, 115, 116, 119, 125, 131, 133, 134, 137, 138, 161, 163, 164, 165, 166, 179
Urry, John 13, 56

Vicksburg 113, 114, 115
Volcanoes, general importance 20, 25, 59, 64, 65, 68, 75, 166, 167

Walker, Franklin 65
Wandering Jew 54
Warner, Charles Dudley 108
Watkins Glen 19, 60
White, Annie P. 17
Whymper, Edward 30, 90
Widow Douglas (character) 21, 147, 151
Wilks (character of family) 152, 153, 155

www.ingramcontent.com/pod-product-compliance
Lightning Source LLC
Chambersburg PA
CBHW032053300426
44116CB00007B/725